MW00808249

Praise for *Regicide in the Family*

Sarah Dixwell Brown's *Regicide in the Family* delivers a warm and wonderful meditation on the constant interplay of history and memory; on fact, fiction, and historical imagination; and on librarians, archivists, and the delights of collegialities formed in the hunt. Most of all, Brown's lively and thoughtful narrative celebrates the ways in which long and multilayered family histories across generations shape how we understand ourselves today; the book is a testament to the power of family, friendship, memory, and place, and the many ways that the past—near and far, distant and recent—reaches out to forge and sustain the connections that give meaning to our lives in the present.
—Marla Miller, Department of History, University of Massachusetts, Amherst

Imagine discovering in your family tree a man who sentenced a king to death—a regicide. With humor and not a little chagrin, Sarah Dixwell Brown uncovers layer by layer two interwoven stories. The first is her discovery, breaking through her father's reticence on the topic, of John Dixwell, her seventeenth-century ancestor who hightailed it to the New World to escape the henchmen of British King Charles II, himself bent on avenging his father's beheading. She reconstructs Dixwell's life, starting with one lone clue, a large seventeenth-century key. Along the way a second story shines through—of Brown's own family and a meditation on her own life midst generations of New England Puritan heritage. *Regicide in the Family* is a fine mosaic of autobiography, family lore, and the social history of seventeenth-century England seen through the magnifying glass of this historical detective.
—Edith Clowes, Brown-Forman Professor, Department of Slavic Languages
    and Literatures, University of Virginia

An ancient key passed down from John Dixwell in the seventeenth century to his descendants over the following three centuries comes into the possession of his namesake, Sarah Dixwell Brown, his "seven greats granddaughter." Reputed to be the key to Dover Castle, a military fortification on the southeast coast of England, it impels Sarah to begin a journey of discovery that will eventually reveal the truth of the key's provenance and at the same time unravel the complex and controversial reputation of a man directly involved in the trial and execution of Charles I, England's martyred king. The result is a compelling narrative of that journey, part history, part memoir, and a testament to the rewards of tireless research.
—Howard Nenner, Roe/Straut Professor Emeritus in the Humanities,
    Smith College

Sarah Dixwell Brown takes her distinctive voice on an ancestral quest that begins with an ancient iron key and ends with the skull of her namesake, who launched her genealogical line by killing a king. It's a riveting read.
—Joseph J. Ellis, Author of *The Cause: The American Revolution and Its Discontents*

Sarah Dixwell Brown could have borrowed a title from John Dixwell's near-contemporary John Bunyan: *The Pilgrim's Progress from This World, to That Which Is to Come*. Dixwell literally journeyed to a new world, but he also sought a better one in which tyranny would give way to liberty, as it did, to some extent, in England and America, after his death. But the author is also a pilgrim, whose view of her forebear progresses from dishonor to dignity. Initially almost ashamed to bear the name of a "king-killer," she ultimately reclaims him as a patriot and a profile in courage.
—Bruce M. Penniman, Ed.D., Graduate Certificate in the Teaching of Writing Coordinator, Western Massachusetts Writing Project, University of Massachusetts Amherst, author of *Building the English Classroom: Foundations, Support, Success*

The beginning chapters of *Regicide in the Family* are more personal and compelling than the opening of the *DaVinci Code*, and its unfolding story is just as richly imbued with the sense of mystery and code-cracking. It is an irresistible invitation to join the author's journey back in time and to share both the search and a story of regicide that is also part of our national legacy as a fragile democracy.
—Thomas N. Gardner, MPA, PhD Chair, Department of Communication, Westfield State University

Ever been tempted to write a family history but weren't sure how? Here is a brilliant model, engagingly told not just as history and biography, but as an account of the author's investigation of how her family made, kept, neglected, and then recovered its past. The story is built around the saga of John Dixwell who, as a member of the British Parliament, signed the death warrant of King Charles I in 1649, helped introduce republican government to England and, after that experiment failed in 1660, spent the rest of his life hiding from royal agents in the wilds of colonial New England.
—Chris Pyle, Professor of Law and Politics, Emeritus, Mount Holyoke College

Regicide in the Family

Regicide in the Family

Finding John Dixwell

Sarah Dixwell Brown

Levellers Press
AMHERST, MASSACHUSETTS

Levellers Press
71 South Pleasant Street
Amherst, Massachusetts 01002
www.levellerspress.com

Copyright © 2022 by Sarah Dixwell Brown

All rights reserved. No part of this book may be reproduced in any
form or by any electronic or mechanical means, including information
storage and retrieval systems, without permission in writing from the
publisher, except by a reviewer who may quote brief passages in a review.

Library of Congress Control Number: 2022908103
ISBN: 978-1-951928-46-9

First Edition
Printed in Amherst, Massachusetts, U.S.A.

Interior design: Greta D. Sibley
Unless otherwise noted, photographs by Sarah Dixwell Brown
Pages x, xi, maps: Joe LeMonnier
Page 87, photo by author: Reproduced by permission of the
    Provost and Fellows of Eton College, Audit Book ECR 62 06.
Page 120, photo by author: Reproduced with the permission of
    the Honourable Society of Lincoln's Inn.
Pages 233, 234, 235, photos by author: Included with permission
    of the New Haven Museum.
Page 269, family tree drawing: Dennis Nolan
Page 291, author photo: Michael Zide
Afterword: Excerpts from the Wigglesworth Family Papers,
    used with permission of the Massachusetts Historical Society.
Color insert, page 3, Anthony Van Dyck's portrait of Sir Basil Dixwell:
    Courtesy of Canterbury Museums and Galleries, U.K.

To Heidi, Rob, and Emma,

my dearest of Dixwell's descendants

CONTENTS

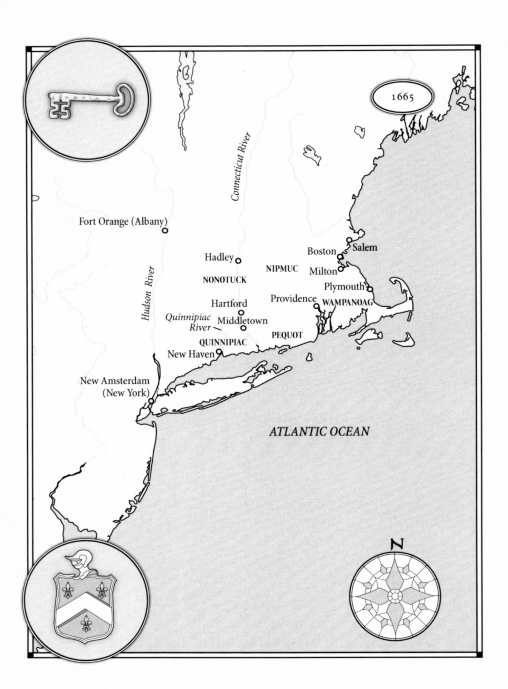

1665

Connecticut River

Hudson River

Fort Orange (Albany)

Hadley

NONOTUCK

NIPMUC

Boston Salem

Milton

Providence Plymouth

Hartford

WAMPANOAG

Quinnipiac River

Middletown

PEQUOT

QUINNIPIAC

New Haven

New Amsterdam (New York)

ATLANTIC OCEAN

N

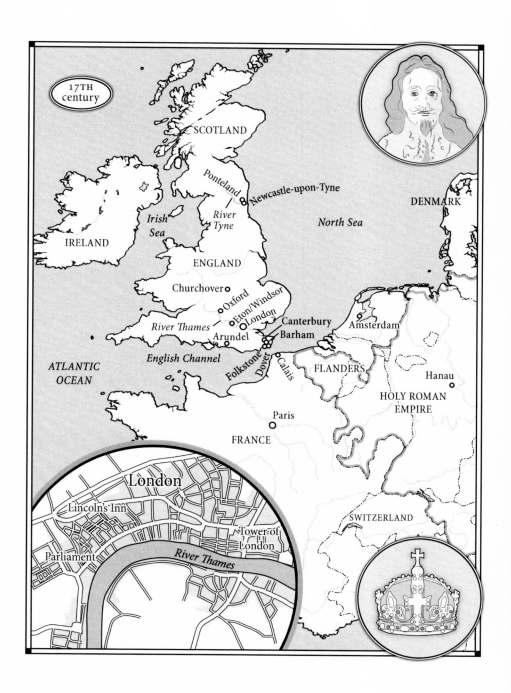

Part One

As a writing man, or secretary, I have always felt charged with the safekeeping of all unexpected items of worldly or unworldly enchantment, as though I might be held responsible if even a small one were to be lost.

E. B. White, "The Ring of Time"

John Dixwell's 1659 key to Dover Castle with my great great grandfather Epes Sargent Dixwell's nineteenth-century broken and yellowed labels.

1

A Key and a Quest

THE LAST TIME the big iron key in my desk drawer was turned in a lock was late spring of 1660. John Dixwell locked the door of the governor's quarters at Dover Castle, the military fortification overlooking the English Channel, and then he fled for his life.

Everything Dixwell had fought for was in tatters. He had wanted England to be a republic governed by the consent of its people, not a monarchy subject to the whims of a king or queen. John Dixwell had wanted this so badly that he agreed to be one of the fifty-nine men who served as judges of King Charles the First. In 1649, after they found Charles guilty of tyranny and treason, they had him beheaded in a public execution attended by a vast crowd of his subjects.

For the next eleven years John Dixwell was part of the complicated machinery of a new form of government being invented and reinvented. It ended badly and now Charles the Second, the dead king's son, was returning triumphantly from France to be crowned. Soon John Dixwell and the other judges were ordered to appear in court for their role in the killing of their king.

It was time to leave, quickly and quietly. Dixwell arranged for passage across the channel then got himself safely to Hanau, Germany where he was able to live openly with several other judges, called regicides now that the monarchy had been re-established. But then the noose tightened. Several of them were caught, taken back to London and drawn and quartered. John Dixwell fled again. He wound up living under an assumed name in New Haven, Connecticut, and had children for the first time late in his life, which is why he has untold numbers of descendants in the United States. I wonder how many of them know what he did in 1649.

ALTHOUGH JOHN DIXWELL is my seven greats grandfather and my parents named me Sarah Dixwell Brown, I didn't know he existed until I found him in an old book in the British Museum when I was twenty-eight. His story, in my branch of his descendants, had all but disappeared.

John Dixwell's key to Dover Castle was another thing I knew nothing about until my father gave it to me unceremoniously one day when I was in my early forties. He'd bundled it in a plastic produce bag from the local supermarket. "You should have this," he said, "Your name is Dixwell. Besides, you're the only one who's taken the time to find out about him."

The strangeness of that moment has stayed with me all the decades since. Why wasn't my father excited to be in the eighth generation to own that key? If anything, he seemed a bit embarrassed to be burdening me, the ninth, with the unusual responsibility of owning the key of a king killer.

Wrapped around the rough, rusty shaft of the key was a small label covered with the handwriting of my great great grandfather Epes Sargent Dixwell (1807-1899). "John Dixwell, regicide, in Command," he'd written on one side, and on the other, switching to capital letters in what looks like enthusiasm, "Dover CASTLE," and his initials, "E.S.D."

It shocked me to hold that key in my hands and stare mutely at the word "regicide." Epes had attached his label so long ago, some later descendant had fortified it with cracked and yellowing cellotape. I did not yet know a whole lot about John Dixwell, but right then I realized that owning his key obliged me to find out everything I could about the man who turned it in the lock the day he fled.

. . .

HUMAN HISTORY is full of times when people resorted to violence in their desperation to effect political and social change. In the United States we have had our own revolutionary war and then civil war, the first to throw off British rule and the second to end slavery. Gradual, diplomatic means had not worked. In seventeenth-century England, the people who felt it imperative to end Charles's despotic rule decided slowly, and reluctantly, that the only way to stop him was to kill him. It wasn't their first choice, or even their fourth. For years, Parliament had tried to come to agreements with the King. By the time they brought him to trial the country had been through two civil wars and considerable chaos and suffering.

In a way, the regicide was but one storm in a sea of dramatic changes. It was a time of fascinating ferment. In the wake of the Protestant Reformation a century earlier, new religions sprang up, and people questioned having a state-sponsored church. In the decade before the king was killed there was an explosion of uncensored publishing of opinionated pamphlets. It was inexpensive and easy to spread new ideas. A young generation of lawyers brought their skills to contemplating not only how to limit or abolish the monarchy but to restrict the powers of the State over the liberty of individuals.

Ideas of religious tolerance and checks and balances on the powers of the king, parliament and the army were ahead of their time, but a century later, they would inform the American Revolution. The framers of our own constitution benefited from looking back at both what had and had not worked.

On the day I encountered John Dixwell for the first time, I did not understand how world-shifting his beliefs were. But as the years went by and I delved deeper into finding everything I could about his life and his era, I felt so lucky to have him as a lens for seeing how an individual played a vital role in the forcing of changes that helped later generations hammer out the democracy I live in now. What were the particular circumstances of his journey, from birth to death, that shaped him into a person who acted so boldly? I wanted to know.

2

Surprise in the British Museum

I ONLY REQUESTED the book because it had the name Dixwell in its title. I was supposed to be researching a paper for a master's degree I was earning back in California, but in an idle moment I decided to look up old family names in the card catalogue. Yes, card catalogue. I was in the Reading Room of the British Museum, in London, that spring day in 1980, and the card catalogue with its countless narrow wooden drawers was the most beautifully extensive one I'd ever seen.

The library's collection was astonishing. It was a massive task, in that pre-digital world of 1980, to get your hands on obscure documents, but the Reading Room seemed to have anything and everything that had ever been published. Sure enough, there were two books about someone named John Dixwell. I copied their titles carefully into the red notebook I'd bought at a quaint stationer's across the street from the museum.

The first book's title began with a word new to me: *The Regicides in Connecticut*, Welles, Lemuel A., 1935. What was a regicide, and why Connecticut? Then high school Latin came back to me. Regicide must mean "king killer." My scalp prickled.

The other book was *A History of Three of the Judges of Charles I. Major-General Whalley, Major-General Goffe, and Colonel Dixwell*, Stiles, Ezra, 1794.

The way you got books in the British Museum was to fill out a little paper request, whereupon gentle Reading Room employees would pad silently into the stacks to fetch whatever you wanted. I requested the Stiles book first, attracted by its antiquity. While I waited I gazed up at the robin's egg blue dome high above long tables where silent patrons sat immovably, their work lit by brass lamps with green opaque glass shades. Everyone seemed so British and proper, and suddenly I felt awkward and American and even a little nervous. Dixwell was an uncommon name. Might I be related in some way to this John Dixwell?

I still have the red notebook with my careful notes from Stiles's book, a first edition in excellent condition that probably hadn't been requested for a hundred years. Its title went on and on:

"who, at the Restoration, 1660, fled to America; and were secreted and concealed . . . for near thirty years."

Then Ezra Stiles, in 1794 the president of Yale and no doubt in a ferment of patriotism in the wake of the American Revolution, dedicated his book to "All the patrons of real, perfect and unpolluted liberty, civil and religious, throughout the world; this history of three of its most illustrious and heroic, but unfortunate defenders, is humbly submitted, and dedicated, by a hitherto uncorrupted friend to universal liberty."[1]

Stiles seemed awestruck; I was shocked. Someone sharing my unusual name was one of fifty-nine judges who signed the death warrant for Charles I. It was the first and only time in England that ordinary persons, instead of resorting to assassination, had the conviction and boldness to bring their king to trial, find him guilty of treason and execute him in as nearly a legal fashion as they could muster. It alarmed royal families throughout Europe. Many of Charles's subjects, horrified by the execution, concluded he was a Christian martyr, a title he holds to this day. The Society of King Charles the Martyr was formed in 1894. Its American Region currently has more than 400 members.

He was no martyr to Ezra Stiles, who might have been talking about the future impeachment of Donald Trump right there on the second page of his narrative: "The era is now arrived, when the tribunal for the trial of delinquent Majesty, of Kings and Sovereign Rulers will be provided for, in the future policies and constitutions of Sovereignties, Empires and Republics: when this heroic and high example of doing justice to criminal Royalty . . . will be contemplated with justice and impartiality."[2]

Stiles said twenty-four of the original fifty-nine judges were dead by 1660 when, after eleven years of England having no king, the monarchy was restored and Charles II embarked on avenging his father. Some regicides fled to Switzerland, Holland and Germany. Quite a few were put to death. Three of them, Major-General Edward Whalley, Major-General William Goffe and Colonel John Dixwell crossed the Atlantic to the New World, where they "found a friendly asylum and concealment in Massachusetts and Connecticut."[3]

This caught my attention. If John Dixwell wound up in New England, I might be descended from him. The possibility both electrified and upset me. In the hushed, deeply British decorum of the Reading Room my heart began to race. I'd always known I was descended on both sides from English ancestors, but not from someone who'd done something like this. If I were related to the regicide sharing my name, would I even now be an enemy of England? Queen Elizabeth would not have me to tea, though I had secretly and atavistically hoped she would, my being so very English in my roots. Perhaps I should turn up my collar, sink down in my chair and make sure none of the mesmerized readers under the timeless blue dome realized a Dixwell from the wrong side might be in their midst.

I began leafing through Ezra Stiles's book. Could this John Dixwell have had kids in the New World?

"He came to New England a bachelor," I read, relieved.

It sounded as if he was rich. "The Colonel was a gentleman in good and easy circumstances, being possessed of a manor and sundry other estates in England."[4] Still, I thought to myself, he couldn't have been too rich after becoming a fugitive from justice. A grudging concern for the man came unbidden. What did he live on after he fled?

Stiles had the answer. When Dixwell got to New Haven, he moved in with an elderly childless couple, Benjamin and Joanna Ling. He had changed his name to James Davids to avoid capture. Just before Mr. Ling died, "Mr. Davids" helped him settle his estate and agreed to take care of his wife. Oh good, I thought to myself, he may have killed a king, but he was kind to the Lings. Then, on the very next page, Stiles listed worrisome information he got from "New-Haven records."

"Mr. James Davids and Mrs. Joanna Ling were married by Mr. James Bishop the 3d of Nov. 1673."

"Mrs. Joanna Davids, wife of Mr. James Davids, died (between 15th and 26th in the entries) Nov. 1673."

My eyes widened. Joanna died not only in the same year as their marriage but in the *same month*. Had this man not only signed the death warrant for a king but also speedily dispatched his first wife in order to get a house and money?

The next entry, from four years later, was even worse:

"Mr. James Davids and Bathsheba How were married the 23rd of October, before James Bishop, assistant, 1677."[5]

I felt sick. It looked as if this Dixwell person, who had lots of money and land and prestige in England, but had to flee for his life to New England, lacked a moral compass. He had gotten back on his feet by marrying an aged widow, perhaps hastening her death by who knows what means. Because the Lings had had no children, Dixwell inherited everything. He got not only their house, where he lived for the rest of his life, but, Stiles wrote, eight or nine hundred pounds. Then, four years later, he married *another* woman and had children with her. I was transfixed. I would have been even more amazed had Stiles included the year of Dixwell's birth, which he did not. Later I read in various publications that John Dixwell was born about 1607, making him seventy when he married Bathsheba. Even later I would find out she was, at thirty-one, about forty years his junior, having been born in 1648.

The next three entries in my red notebook list the three children born to them: Mary, about eighteen months after their marriage, on June 9, 1679, John on March 6, 1681 and Elizabeth on July 14, 1682.

I continued to put things together in unsettling ways. He had children in the New World after maybe murdering his first wife, so I *might* be descended from this shady character. "John Dixwell," I read of his son, "settled in Boston around 1707 as a goldsmith."[6] Boston, city of my birth. Oh no.

3

Was I Named After a King Killer?

THAT EVENING, in the flat my then husband and I had rented in Wimbledon, I said nothing about the regicide and was awake most of the night. John Dixwell couldn't be a member of my family. We weren't lawbreakers. Why Fanny Dixwell, my great great aunt, had married the Supreme Court Justice Oliver Wendell Holmes. We didn't go around killing kings and running from the law. I didn't know then that Holmes was an influential supporter of eugenics.

The next morning I was back beneath the blue dome, digging deeper. Soon I began wondering if John Dixwell's decision to judge his king had made him the black sheep of the family. Black sheep was my term, and it came to me as I perused quintessentially British tomes like the 1841 edition of John Burke's *Extinct Baronetcies*, because it had Dixwells in it. I almost laughed aloud at the title. How bizarre that a baronetcy, in England's intricate, male chauvinist class system, becomes extinct in the absence of a male heir, girls being less satisfactory, though there's such a thing as a baronetess. How unreal to devote an entire book to listing baronets who had become extinct. But the part that was upsetting as opposed to funny was that in the entry about the Dixwells, a number of whom had been made baronets by one king or another, John Dixwell was not mentioned. Had he been omitted?

I reread the entry. One Dixwell, who was created a baronet in 1627, was a man named Basil, an unmarried man whose various estates, after his 1641 death, went to his nephew Mark. The baronetcy became extinct. Both names caught my attention, for Stiles wrote that John had an older brother named Mark, who died, whereupon John became responsible for his young children. Mark's oldest son's name was Basil. Two Basils and a Mark? This might well be John Dixwell's family, but where was John?

My old notes document my increasing dismay. I wrote, "Mark an older brother of John the Judge?" and bracketed it to remind myself that this was my conjecture, not Burke's text. Clearly I was intent on establishing John's place in the family. If I was descended from the man, I wanted to know where he fit in.

It's interesting that I used the term "judge" back then, as opposed to "regicide." I was influenced by Ezra Stiles, who titled his book about the three men who fled to New England, "A history of three of the judges" and not "A history of three of the regicides." It was a most American choice of terms. In England the fifty-nine men who signed the death warrant are called regicides.

Ezra Stiles also used the adjectives "illustrious and heroic," but he was so enthusiastic in his praise of the three men who'd fled to his corner of the world that I felt suspicious. What if Ezra Stiles were wrong and John Dixwell and the other fifty-eight cosigners had done something terrible?

Meanwhile, though, something else was happening. Burke's book about extinct baronetcies, each with its own coat of arms, was giving me delusions of grandeur. Laboriously, I sketched every detail of the Dixwell one. It had three fleurs de lis. How elegant. Maybe I was connected to a really fancy family.

Burke wrote, "This family was originally of Dixwell Hall, and lords of the manor Dixwell."[1] Lords of the manor! I thought, forgetting for the moment about the decapitation of King Charles I.

Burke described a large Dixwell monument made of alabaster on the south interior wall of a church in Churchover, in county Warwick, that had been erected in 1641. It commemorated Charles and Abigail Dixwell, parents of the aforementioned uncle Basil.

I dragged my husband, just in case I was related, all the way from London to Churchover, where we found an ancient church, located its interior south wall, and gaped at the magnificent Dixwell monument. It was 340 years old but looked almost new, protected as it was from the acid rain gently dissolving the inscriptions on the gravestones of the less wealthy or perhaps less pretentious people buried in the churchyard. I asked my husband if he didn't think my nose was the same shape as the noses of the four sons (William, Edward, Humphrey and Basil) and one daughter (Barbara) carved in bas-relief, hands piously folded. Above them, Charles and Abigail faced each other, hands also folded in prayer, kneeling on puffy stone cushions.

After photographing the monument, and my nose, we ran into the minister, the Reverend Edwin Morris, who lived with his wife Pauline in the nearby rectory. He was intrigued to meet a possible descendant of the notorious John Dixwell, because he had just returned from New Haven, where he'd been invited to share what he knew of the regicide's English past.

It was affirming and alarming, talking to the Reverend Morris. There really had been someone named John Dixwell in the very family that was missing his name in Burke's book. His father had grown up right here, where we stood, though Morris wasn't sure whether he was William or Edward. He said the fourth son, Basil, had probably raised John and Mark after their father died. It would be years before I learned why Basil, despite being the youngest of the four brothers, was the one with the fanciest title in the inscription above his parents' heads. "Sir Basil Dixwell, Knight and Baronet."

It was helpful to pin down one of the Basil Dixwells in Burke's *Extinct Baronetcies*, as there were several. All the titles had eventually petered out for lack of male heirs. I had copied most of the Dixwell entry into my red notebook, and had tried to guess where John would have fit in, had he been included. Now, thanks to Reverend Morris, I was sure.

I asked him if this Sir Basil was the same one who, Burke said, had moved to Broome in the county of Kent, and "erected a handsome mansion house." It was. Basil had been extremely rich. Morris told us the mansion was still standing. There wouldn't be enough time for us to go there while we were in England, but I hoped to visit it one day.

From Ezra Stiles's book I knew that John's brother Mark died in 1644, only three years after the death of their Uncle Basil, leaving future regicide John not only the guardian of Mark's children but responsible for a large estate. It would be years before it occurred to me to wonder what it was like for him, an unmarried man still in his thirties, to be managing everyone else's affairs in the wake of so much death.

Today, when I look at those notes, it's evident I already cared about John Dixwell, months before I learned I was his direct descendant. I seem to have been indignant that his family had erased him for I wrote, underlining it twice, "So!" and then "John must have been the grandson of Charles and Abigail!" I had, in fact, solved the riddle of John's place in the family tree before we met the Reverend Morris.

I must have been hoping I was descended from a less violent Dixwell, for my notes from Burke go on to catalog another Dixwell baronet descended from Charles and Abigail. But he "died without issue 14 Jan 1757. Baronetcy extinct."[2] It looked as if Dixwells had a perennial problem with producing sons to carry on the family name.

What I mostly recall from the months I spent in England after I discovered the existence of John Dixwell was how stirred up I felt. I'd been groomed by my father to be a law-abiding citizen. This John Dixwell had so flouted the law of the land that his family had removed him from the record altogether. If he turned out to be mine, how was I to feel about him? Further research added to my dismay. Ezra Stiles described the ways American Dixwells tried to get in on British Dixwells' land and money in the early 1700s, and I wondered if they had the right to do so, given John Dixwell's condemning of a king. Stiles had devoted pages to the intricacies of the efforts of the regicide's only son, the John Dixwell who'd "settled in Boston around 1707 as a goldsmith." He went to England in 1710 "to recover his father's estate and was kindly received by Sir Basil Dixwell."[3] He got nothing for his trouble but the tantalizing tease that if he named one of his sons Basil that child might inherit the estate if there were no Dixwell heirs in England. John Dixwell did just that. He named his first child, born in 1711, Basil. But Basil inherited nothing.

I remember feeling embarrassed by the younger John Dixwell's temerity. Why would his English relatives be willing to hand over an inheritance to the child of a regicide? Then my mind took a U-turn. Might he have had a legitimate claim? Despite my having dismissed the British class system with its landed gentry as unfair and absurd, the truth is I felt tempted, especially because Stiles said the case was "open to this day, it not being confiscated."[4] Might I, Sarah Dixwell Brown, be entitled to a little something, say a few hundred acres of land down in Kent, or a generous bedroom in Basil's big mansion? I did not, however, admit any of this to my husband.

4

My Father Tells the Truth

ON OUR WAY HOME from London we stopped in Massachusetts to visit my parents before continuing to California. I waited until my husband went off to take a nap before broaching the topic of the regicide. I was on edge. I had not written them about my discovery.

"I found a book in the British Museum about someone named John Dixwell," I said. "He was a king killer. We're not . . . are we?"

My father hung his head. "Yuh," he said under his breath. There was a weird pause, then he mumbled, "Actually, we're direct descendants."

An electrical sensation went through my nervous system, followed immediately by bafflement. If Dad was this uncomfortable with the guy why did he and my mother name me, the youngest of their four children, Sarah Dixwell Brown, linking me for life to John Dixwell?

But I couldn't bring myself to ask and now, so many years after his death, I can't. The reason could be trivial. It may not have crossed his mind, when I joined the family, that he was naming me after a man still considered a traitor and a murderer by staunch royalists in England. He was probably too busy thinking about bones (he was an orthopedic surgeon) to even remember that the original Dixwell to arrive on North American shores was a wanted man.

Still, it was clear he was caught off guard and bothered. Was it shame he was experiencing in that first admission of our direct descent, or guilt, as if we were still responsible for the decapitation of a king? I had felt both in my first encounter with John Dixwell in the Reading Room. I wish I knew what Dad thought about Dixwell's actions, but how strange that on the day he acknowledged our descent, he said nothing to suggest Dixwell might have done something important, even exceedingly brave, on the world stage.

It wasn't until I got back to California that a childhood memory surfaced that suggests my father preferred John Dixwell to remain a blank in the family tree. Our family was driving through New Haven, Connecticut when an exit for Dixwell Avenue caught my attention. I may have been ten. It was the first time I'd seen my middle name out in the world. Who knew that the street was named in honor of the fugitive himself?

"Dixwell Avenue!" I exclaimed, and asked if there was a family connection.

"Hmm," said Dad. There was a short pause. My father was generally not a talker. Then he murmured that he thought there was a connection, but either he couldn't remember what it was, or he wasn't willing to tell the story, so he lapsed back into his customary silence. The moment passed.

Maybe he thought I was too little and it would upset me to learn where my name came from. Now, though, there was no getting out of it. He knew very well who John Dixwell was. His eyes met mine, then dropped. He gazed at the floor and shrugged his shoulders.

Mum, on the other hand, was amazed and thrilled. Clearly, Dad hadn't told her about the regicide either. Easy for her to be delighted, I thought irritably, she doesn't carry any of John Dixwell's genes. Irrationally, I felt as though I, of their four children, was more implicated in the beheading, or at least more identifiable, and now I was mad at Mum. She was my mother. I needed her, out of solidarity, to be a bit horrified. But she wasn't. Where Dad seemed gloomy about our Dixwell connection, Mum, who loved history and read voraciously, was fascinated.

That summer of 1980 they were still living in the great big brick house

I'd grown up in, the house where Dad and his three siblings had grown up as well. My brother Eddy lived in it until recently, so his two daughters were the fourth generation to grow up there. How ironic that I'd coveted a room in Basil Dixwell's "handsome mansion house" down in Kent, the one we hadn't had time to visit, when the house I grew up in has eight fireplaces and seven bathrooms if you count the half ones.

From my puritanical father I had learned that money is a corrupting thing, which made me increasingly self-conscious as I grew up in the American equivalent of a manor house. Dad communicated silently that you should be ashamed of inherited wealth, even as we enjoyed its privileges. You weren't supposed to talk about it; you lived and dressed modestly. The same rules applied to your activities. It was Dad's policy to deprecate himself all the time. It confused his kids that he described himself as a failure even though he was the editor of the *Journal of Bone and Joint Surgery*, taught at Harvard Medical School and was acting chief of orthopedics at Massachusetts General Hospital. If this was failure, what was success?

Dad never stopped striving for a second. The minute he got home from work he'd change into what Mum called his "play clothes," which were full of holes and stained with tar and creosote, and dive into maintaining his giant house in a seat-of-the-pants fashion. We tried not to look when he was up on the slate roof of our three-story brick house, painting tar here and there to stop leaks. He felt responsible for other buildings as well. Even on Sundays, well into his seventies, he might be on a tall ladder at the Unitarian church, repairing the gutters, or on the ground digging ditches. Ever since a very rainy, very hard sojourn on several South Pacific islands during World War Two, my father had been a self-appointed authority on drainage.

But to return to the scene at hand my father now said, offhandedly, "There's some Dixwell paraphernalia around here somewhere." What? Clearly, he'd known about the man all along.

"Oh?" I said, trying not to sound excited. Dad headed upstairs, not inviting me to come. I wish I could remember if he'd gone all the way up to the attic. Meanwhile, Mum went off to get her family tree. I waited, trying to digest the fact that I was descended not from some Mayflower type but a wanted man.

My eyes wandered to a pedestalled silver pitcher on the sill of the dining room's picture window.

Didn't that pitcher have the name Dixwell on it? I went over and picked it up. "E.S. Dixwell Esq From his Pupils," it said. The date 1839 was cut faintly into the underside of its base. I knew that Epes Sargent Dixwell was my great great grandfather. I didn't yet know that Epes had once owned all the letters John Dixwell had received in exile, and had given them to a museum in New Haven for safekeeping.

No, Dad had never told any stories about Dixwells, but that pitcher brought me back to my childhood. For years, Dad had used it to pour fresh water into the tank he'd fashioned out of sheet aluminum for our green slider turtles.

Now he came back with two documents. One was a copy of Charles the First's death warrant. Although it was likely a nineteenth-century fake made to sell to London tourists, it had the signatures of all fifty-nine regicides. There was Dixwell's, number thirty-eight. His tidy handwriting made me wince. The warrant was printed on heavy paper and had a pen and ink sketch of the king at the top, looking dapper. The real warrant, which you can view online, has no sketch of Charles. It's austere, save for the bright blobs of sealing wax beside each signature. John Dixwell's name is perfectly legible, and really is the thirty-eighth.

The other was a facsimile of a handwritten legal document dated 1682. It stated the regicide's true name as well as his alias of James Davids, and laid out reasons why his young American children were entitled to money and property in England. I already knew they never got much of anything.

Dad made no mention of another thing he had stashed away, the key to Dover Castle John Dixwell brought with him when he fled that had been passed down through eight generations. Maybe it's just as well. A few days later we flew back to California, and entered the blur of finishing our respective degrees, having two children, and moving across the country three times in less than four years before we settled in Massachusetts.

John Dixwell became an anecdote I could trot out to amuse people, but I didn't think about him too often.

There was, though, one odd occurrence. In late September of 1983, when we were living in Santa Clara, California, I received a handwritten letter from Hawaii, from a man I'd never heard of, who said he was "functioning as de facto President of the U of Hawaii, a very complicated operation."

"Dear Sarah, I am writing to you mainly because of your middle name. In the history of mid 19th century Boston there was an excellent schoolmaster who prepared the Brahmin kids for Harvard, Epes Dixwell. His daughter Fanny married Oliver Wendell Holmes Jr 1840-1935. He and Fanny had, I think, no children, but you could anyhow descend from the famous Epes Dixwell or his ancestors." The letter went on to encourage John to come be a doctor and me a teacher in Hawaii. "We need teachers and writers like you here, and competent physicians and/or surgeons. The two major organized crime families of Hawaii are expected soon to move elsewhere; and so Hilo is going to be an excellent place to raise kids."

I was so puzzled by the letter I put it aside for a long time. When I finally answered, the writer never responded.

5

Why Did John Dixwell Do It?

DURING THE SIX YEARS we lived on the west coast I taught freshman English at two different universities and changed a lot of diapers. John Dixwell entered my mind only occasionally, but when he did, I dabbled in research. I found an entry on Dixwell in the fifth volume of the *Dictionary of National Biography*, a 1908 British publication that had been edited by Virginia Woolf's father, Leslie Stephen.

The entry did nothing to alleviate the dismay I'd felt in the British Museum's Reading Room. Its author clearly assumed his audience, in the first decade of the twentieth century, would be as disapproving as he of the actions of the men who'd agreed to judge a king. Right after "Dixwell, John" came the damning word "regicide." Next was confirmation of his removal from the family tree: "In pedigrees of the family he is usually ignored, as, for instance, in those contained in 'Burke's Extinct Baronetage,' and he is also passed over in the account of the Dixwell family given in Halsted's 'Kent.'"[1]

I felt both insulted (how dare he describe my ancestor that way?) and guilty (was he an especially bad man?). I also experienced what was becoming a familiar confusion. How was I to think about John Dixwell and what he had chosen to do? This task was complicated by the fact that I had always struggled with history. In truth, even trying to learn it made me anxious. Nevertheless, I studied that faded 1908 volume doggedly, slogging ahead to a detailed account of the seminal event in John Dixwell's life: "He was appointed one of the commissioners for the trial of Charles I, attended the court with great regularity, was present when sentence was pronounced, and signed the death-warrant."[2]

The writer of the entry, Charles Harding Firth, seemed intent on building a case that proved Dixwell was not only a black sheep in the Dixwell family, but wasn't the least ambivalent about his decision to do away with Charles I. Dixwell didn't just attend the 1649 trial "with great regularity," but was there when the king was found guilty and subsequently signed the death warrant. Was it subjective of me to feel Mr. Firth's prose dripped contempt?

"In 1650 Dixwell was a colonel of militia in Kent, commanding a regiment of foot." It sounded as if Dixwell had a lot of responsibility. "On 25 Nov. 1651 he was elected a member of the council of state."[3]

"When the Dutch war broke out, Dixwell was sent into Kent with powers to raise the county to guard the coast." I had no idea what the "Dutch war" was. The next sentence had some vaguely familiar terms that I suspected I should have learned in high school, but had not retained. "During the Protectorate he disappeared from public life; but when the Rump was recalled to power he again joined the council of state 19 May 1659."[4]

It would be decades of several more major moves, a divorce, and many years of difficult single parenting before I had time to learn enough history to understand nearly everything in that Dixwell entry. Now I was struck by the date: "19 May 1659." Almost exactly a year later Charles the Second, joyfully welcomed home from his exile in France, would take on the task of punishing those who had meted out the death penalty to his father. John Dixwell, along with everyone else who had signed the death warrant or been involved in any way with the trial and execution, was in the crosshairs.

Mr. Firth explains how Dixwell was duplicitous to save his skin. "On 17 May an order was issued to seize him [Dixwell] and sequester his estates. On 20 June 1660 the speaker informed the House of Commons that he had received a petition from a relative of Colonel Dixwell, stating that Dixwell was ill, and begging that he might not lose the benefit of the king's proclamation by his inability to surrender himself within the time fixed. The request was granted, but Dixwell, instead of surrendering, fled to the continent."[5]

Well really, if he hadn't been clever, would I be here now, bearing his name? Several men who didn't make themselves scarce were hanged, drawn and quartered as crowds of jeering subjects watched the show. Dixwell, the entry continues, "resided some time in Hanau [Germany] and even became a burgess [Burghers were urban citizens at the top of the social order] of that city. In 1664 or 1665 he took refuge in America, joining his fellow regicides, Goffe and Whalley, at Hadley, in New England."[6]

The rest of the entry I was familiar with, for it had been taken from Ezra Stiles's book, duly cited in the endnotes. John Dixwell's decision to judge a king led the British Dixwells to erase him from the family tree. Did none of them go on caring about him? I did not yet know that if they'd been caught helping him they would have been killed.

Were any of them secretly proud of him or was it so dangerous to be related to such a man that they never spoke of him? Perhaps they managed, over time, to pretend that he had never existed, as if the beheading of Charles I, and the eleven years in which John Dixwell held prestigious positions, were illusions.

My father's grandmother, Mary Catherine, the Dixwell who married George Wigglesworth on the twentieth of June 1878 and died the year of my birth in 1951, was fond of saying, "Least said, soonest mended." This meant, "If you don't talk about it, it'll go away." I've always hated that maxim, but it worked just fine for the British Dixwells. They said nothing about John Dixwell, and he went away, never to return.

Things mended for them at once. For two more generations Basils went on being appointed baronets by one king or another. It upset me that they had figuratively rubbed John out.

My upset probably sprang from the fact that one of my most vivid childhood experiences involved having my own name expunged. I was in the sixth grade. We had a tiny teacher who terrified me. His name was

Roy Patterson, and he told us on the first day of class that we were to address him as Sir. "Yes *Sir*, no *Sir*, anything you want to say—*Sir*," he said, as he strode over to close the classroom door at the front of the room. He didn't grab the knob. He slipped his hand between the hinges and the doorframe, then applied pressure. As the heavy door began to swing shut, he withdrew his hand just before his fingers were amputated. The sixth graders watched wide-eyed as Sir walked in silence to his desk. Nothing would be explained; obedience was assumed.

I was tiny myself, so to me, Sir was enormous. He liked to give his pupils new vocabulary words to read aloud that captured some aspect of their beings. Once, mine was "puny," a word I had never seen before and which I promptly mispronounced "punny."

I was so scared of Sir that I went blank whenever he called on me.

It was worst in history. The endless dates and facts refused to stick in my head. In another family I might have asked for help from my parents, but asking for help wasn't part of our family's culture. My three older siblings had sailed through Sir's class. My mother and her twin Mary had skipped a grade in elementary school. It wasn't possible that I would have trouble in school, so my struggles in history became a secret even from myself.

I didn't know, after our first history exam, about Sir's tradition of posting everyone's scores on the blackboard at the front of the classroom. When I came in after lunch everyone was crowded around the board, announcing each other's scores and then trying to figure out the especially interesting aspect of the list. Whose names had been omitted?

"Dixie!" someone said. "And Teddy!" someone else exclaimed. It took a few moments for me to grasp that the omission of our names meant we had failed.

As the realization dawned, a congealed feeling went down my body, as if ice were forming not just inside my lungs and heart, but over every inch of my skin. Brown children did not flunk exams. There was no place in my world for this new nightmare.

I had been expunged, but my parents, as I recall, said and did nothing in response. Did they apply the "least said, soonest mended" maxim?

Perhaps this trouble Dixie was having in history would go away if no one said a word.

My parents were kind and well intentioned, but distant. In the absence of support, let alone acknowledgement of my difficulties, I arrived at adulthood with an outsized fear that I was no good at history. How ironic that the middle name they chose for their youngest led me into the most complex history assignment of my life.

6

How Charles the First Lost His Head

I MIGHT HAVE LET MY HISTORY INSECURITIES carry the day and relegated John Dixwell to the back of my mind, if my father hadn't eventually trotted out the key to Dover Castle. He hadn't produced it, back in 1980 when I came back from London and asked him if we were related to John Dixwell. Maybe he didn't remember he had it.

When I recall the day I got it, I realize they were no longer living in the huge house where I'd grown up, for I can picture us in the energy-efficient solar house they'd built, thanks to my mother's passionate commitment to the environment. Prying my father from the ancestral mansion had been wrenching for both of them. My father had trouble throwing anything out, even his desiccated frog from fifth grade, and the big house was full of stuff from at least five generations. Luckily for him the new house, though small, had tons of storage space, which meant he'd brought everything he couldn't part with, including the big iron key last turned in its lock in 1660. It's possible he happened on it for the first time in the process of going through some of the endless boxes. Then what? Where did he choose to stash it? Was it hidden in a box under the roof that sported photovoltaic panels? Was it in the loft over the garage that you got to after passing the composting toilet? That toilet developed the most amazing cloud of fruit flies, and the sod roof over the living room began to leak within the first few years and had to be removed. Nevertheless, it pleased me that they had moved away from Dad's childhood home and were trying something new and idealistic. They were so excited.

But Dad did not seem excited when he gave me John Dixwell's key. There was nothing ceremonial about the moment I became the ninth generation to receive it. Dad appeared in the kitchen, where I was helping Mum peel potatoes, and he had something in one fist. "You might as well have this. Your name is Dixwell," he said, his tone apologetic, as if he was about to burden me.

He handed me something surprisingly dense bundled up in a plastic produce bag from the local supermarket. It was recycled, of course. My parents, who'd lived through the Great Depression, reused aluminum foil and string. I put down my potato peeler and took it. Who knows if I even washed my hands?

"You should have it," he went on wearily. "You're the one who's found out the most about John Dixwell." I could see he felt guilty that he didn't know more himself, as if his twelve-hour-a-day schedule as an editor and an orthopedist should have left him time to do genealogy.

"What is it?" I asked. He didn't answer, just waited as I opened the bag, on which was printed, in orange and brown, "The Fruit Center Mar-ket-place, A Shopping Adventure," and pulled out the big, rough iron key.

"Good heavens," said my mother.

It isn't every day that your father gives you a seventeenth-century key to a castle in England. Several moments went by before I remembered to breathe. Here's an odd thing, though. You might think that it's being a key to a castle would have aroused my curiosity. I might have wondered why John Dixwell had the key to a particular castle, and what he did there, but it didn't occur to me to wonder, nor did Dad say anything about it. Instead, my eyes were fixed on the word on its yellowed label, the word I'd learned for the first time in the Reading Room of the British Museum.

"Regicide," I said aloud. "King-killer," I added, as if we needed the definition in order the grasp the severity of what our forebear had done. Dad shook his head ruefully, and I felt a mix of awe and horror. Something about holding the key in my hand and reading Epes's notes brought the execution of Charles I right into the room with us. John Dixwell really had done that. I really was his descendant, for here was his key, passed down through three hundred years to me, his namesake.

"Dad's right," Mum said. "You should have it." She took it from me, studied the label, then handed it back to me. As carefully as if it were fine china, I rolled it back up in the produce bag. If Mum thought Dad's wrapping job was a bit casual for something with this much historical significance, she didn't say so, and neither did I. I put it in my pocketbook.

As I drove to my home in Western Massachusetts later that day, I couldn't stop thinking about axes. My father was skillful with an axe, splitting all the wood we burned for heat in the winter. His chopping block was a big stump he'd placed in the circle in front of our big house. The circle also had a massive ash tree from which he'd hung an odd red metal disk of a swing for me, the littlest child. It wasn't a good swing for pumping yourself higher and higher. You needed two ropes for that, and this had only one, right in the center. But it was good for quietly dangling near my father. He never had time to play with me, but I loved being close to him, adoring him as he worked himself into a sweat. I swung lazily in desultory circles, watching his axe swoop down on each chunk of wood, splitting it so forcefully the halves flew apart. Dad was tall, and had broad shoulders. Up went the axe over his head then down with deadly accuracy. He never missed his mark.

He disliked another use of his axe—the beheading of our chickens when they got too old to lay eggs—and so did we. My next-up sister Nina and I would peer miserably through the upstairs bannisters as Dad came in the front door, holding a chicken or two by the legs, blood dripping from the stumps where their heads used to be. Our mother waited in the kitchen with a vat of boiling water into which she plunged each chicken until its feathers were loose enough to pluck.

No wonder the removal of a king's head was so vivid for me. I knew exactly how that executioner raised his axe, and the noise it made as it tore through Charles's neck. Thwack. Had John Dixwell attended the execution? Was he close enough to hear that sound? Was it such an appalling moment that he wondered if he'd done the right thing by signing that warrant?

When I got home I hid the key in my desk drawer, irrationally afraid someone might recognize its historical value and try to steal it. But even from its drawer, muffled in its plastic produce bag, it was working on me, prodding me to learn how it came to pass that Charles I wound up with the dubious distinction of being the only ruling British monarch ever to be formally executed by his own people.

My task was easier than I expected, for so many years had passed since I first encountered Dixwell in the British Museum that the internet was in full swing. I no longer had to visit a library to get the broad outlines. I found much disagreement. An American website places the blame squarely on the King's shoulders: "King Charles I was his own worst enemy. Self-righteous, arrogant, and unscrupulous, he had a penchant for making bad decisions. His troubles began the moment he ascended the throne in 1625 upon the death of his father James I. Charles simultaneously alienated both his subjects and his Parliament, prompting a series of events that ultimately led to civil war, his own death and the abolition of the English monarchy."[1]

On the other hand, a British academic describes the execution as "This supreme act of stupidity." And he says of Charles: "Graceful in his movements, measured in his speech, handsome and elegant, he had to an eminent degree that 'style' which James [his father] could never aspire to."[2]

In England, Charles continues to be mourned to this day: "Charles's statue stands at the spot of his execution in London. Flowers of remembrance are still laid at its base by his supporters on the anniversary of his death."[3]

Americans, if they know of the regicides, which they often don't, tend to see them as brave men who held a tyrant to account for his actions and sought to establish a country ruled by its citizens, but a British historian, well versed in the events of the seventeenth century in her country, takes a more nuanced view:

For many historians, the regicides were 'rogues and knaves', or self-righteous fanatics driven to an Old Testament-inspired vengeance against an ungodly king who wantonly reopened the civil war in 1648 and could never be trusted to make a settled peace. No one would claim that the trial and execution of Charles I was widely supported by political elites, or met with popular acclaim . . . [but] it is misleading to present the regicide only as a monstrous aberration; it is part of the comforting, moderate mythology of English history that the English do not do this sort of thing, and when it somehow happens, it is an unnatural mistake, the product of extreme short-term crisis.

The regicide "was not simply a result of the impasse of 1648, but a solution made thinkable by longer-term aspects of English political culture and history."[4]

Many of the "aspects" that led to Charles's execution sprang from passionate disagreements about religion. In 1517, the German monk and Catholic priest Martin Luther, less than a century before John Dixwell's birth, had launched the Protestant Reformation with his ninety-five theses criticizing the current practice of Catholicism. Not much later England's Henry VIII, seeking a divorce, would find the questioning of Rome's authority convenient in a country that had been more or less contentedly Catholic for centuries.

After Charles I became king in 1625, his largely Protestant subjects began to worry about his French Catholic wife Henrietta Maria and the royal couple's love of fun. Puritans wrote pamphlets denouncing the lavish musical theatricals staged for the king, his queen and nobles. They were appalled when he reissued, in 1633, the Book of Sports, which authorized various forms of recreation on Sundays. A Protestant lawyer, William Prynne, published a criticism of the queen dancing and called female actors whores. He was sentenced to life in prison and had his ears cut off. Nevertheless, numerous sects of Protestantism proliferated. The more radical of their members, determined to root out what they saw as idolatry verging on Catholicism, smashed stained glass windows and destroyed priceless art in cathedrals and in the homes of royalists.

The turbulence did not shake Charles's belief that he ruled by divine rights. As king, he was second only to God in the Great Chain of Being ordained by God since time immemorial, with everything from angels to earthworms to minerals in appointed places. Charles thought absolute power over his subjects was not only his right, but also his duty. To subdue resistance to his increasingly tyrannical policies, he instigated not one but two civil wars against his own people. To fund the wars, he levied various capricious taxes that drained the country's resources. The loss of life was probably higher than that of the First World War. Unpaid troops plundered freely. Impoverished citizens were required to house soldiers from both sides of the conflict. Wounded war veterans begged in the streets. The weather was terrible. Crops failed.

When Parliament sought to curb him, Charles dismissed it and sent its members home. Perhaps he didn't understand to what extent his belief system was becoming obsolete. Classical learning for students in grammar schools and universities "familiarized them with a broadly republican understanding of political structures as mutable human contrivances, subject to corruption and decay, unless a system of checks and balances with regular public participation counteracted this."[5] Although submitting to God remained the ideal, submitting to a human king was debatable. Shouldn't a good government involve cooperation between kings and parliaments? But Charles was incapable of imagining shared power.

My favorite description of the last weeks of Charles's life is in a book by C. V. Wedgwood entitled *A Coffin for King Charles*. When he was brought to trial, after spending two and a half years on the Isle of Wight as a prisoner of Parliament, his emotional suffering was evident. "He was by this time inured to misfortune. In the last years he had grown to look old and strained; his cheeks sagged, he had deep pouches under his eyes, his hair and beard were very grey. He had been gradually deprived of everything that he most valued and of the people on whom he most depended." He hadn't seen his wife for four years, nor had he seen any of his children for the past year.[6]

Even while under house arrest, however, Charles still managed to stir up Royalist risings. "His plots were unceasing and often of a self-contradictory complexity. He became used to writing a feigned hand, to sending and receiving coded letters which were hidden in a laundry basket, or slipped into the finger of a glove."[7] It was this behavior, over the nearly quarter century of Charles's reign, that drove quite a few men in power, most of whom had no desire to actually kill him, to realize he'd never stop sabotaging their efforts at compromise. They were going to have to take extreme measures.

As I learned more I began to see what an intensely confusing and painful time it was for everyone. The British, then as now, had a habit of adoring their monarch. Even when Charles was being brought to London for his trial, "local gentry gathered to kiss his hand," dressed in their finest, and "country-folk crowded to see him and some brought sick children to receive the healing royal touch."[8]

There were likable things about him. He had behaved badly as a ruler, but was also deeply intelligent and sensitive—a man whose certainty about his divine position gave him the strength to face his accusers, and then his own execution, with calm dignity. His judges were in the wrong, he was sure, and had no legal grounds to bring him to trial and punishment. He was so convinced of his divine rights and God's favor that he spoke eloquently at his trial, without the stutter that usually troubled him, arguing, with good reason, that the hastily assembled court of judges was not legitimate. His judges were men who'd seized power and created the legal basis for his trial on the spot. They were able to carry off the execution without a hitch, for the truth is that no one, in his own kingdom or in Europe, made more than half-hearted attempts to save him. But what they couldn't do was control the reaction of the populace. To add to the difficulties of the about-to-be born republic, Charles behaved so regally in the last weeks of his life and on the scaffold itself, many of his subjects decided he was a Christian martyr.

Many sources describe how on the day of his execution Charles, that lover of theater, played his part to the hilt. He wore two thick shirts because he didn't want to shiver in the bitter January chill. He would go to his death with no show of fear. He would be England's king to the very end. Once he stood on the scaffold erected in front of Whitehall Palace, he spoke of things ecclesiastical and governmental, while clerks took notes, right up to the moment he knelt down before the block.

He asked the executioner, who surely was in agony over the part he had to play in the drama, if his hair was arranged so as to make it easy for the single stroke of the axe to find its mark. He had chosen William Juxon, bishop of London, to accompany him to his death, and it was Juxon who helped him push his long hair under his cap.

An immense crowd filled the streets. The scene on the scaffold and the conversation between Charles, his bishop and the executioner are described in detail in a 1687 British book entitled *The Works of King Charles the Martyr.*[9] Charles turned to the bishop and said, "I have a good cause, and a gracious God on my side."

His bishop offered words of comfort:

"There is but one stage more, which, though turbulent and troublesome, yet is a very short one. You may consider it will soon carry you a very great way; it will carry you from earth to heaven; and there you shall find to your great joy the prize you hasten to, a crown of glory."

Charles replied, "I go from a corruptible to an incorruptible crown; where no disturbance can be, no disturbance in the world."

Next, the king removed his jeweled pendant and made a few more inquiries about his hair and the height of the block. He told the executioner to wait until he gave him a sign with his hands. The seventeenth century account continues:

> Then having said a few words to himself, as he stood, with hands and eyes lift up, immediately stooping down he laid his neck upon the block; and the executioner, again putting his hair under his cap, his Majesty, thinking he had been going to strike, bade him, 'Stay for the sign.'
>
> Executioner: 'Yes, I will, and it please your Majesty.'" [Note that the executioner's humble words show that he still saw the king as his ruler, to whom he owed obedience and respect even as he raised the axe.]
>
> After a very short pause, his Majesty stretching forth his hands, the executioner at one blow severed his head from body; which, being held

up and showed to the people, was with his body put into a coffin covered with black velvet and carried into his lodging.

His blood was taken up by divers persons for different ends: by some as trophies of their villainy; by others as relics of a martyr; and in some hath had the same effect, by the blessing of God, which was often found in his sacred touch when living.[10]

There is a poignant description of the moment of Charles's death in a journal entry by a member of the crowd: "A boy of seventeen, standing a long way off in the throng, saw the axe fall. He would remember as long as he lived the sound that broke out from the crowd, 'such a groan as I never heard before, and desire that I may never hear again.'"[11]

Charles was forty-eight years old. England would now spend eleven years being governed not by a monarch but by the men who'd seized and wielded the power to eliminate the king. John Dixwell was one of them. But in the end, the experiment crumbled. Meanwhile, across the Channel in France, the king's son was waiting for his moment. Only eighteen when his father was beheaded, Charles the Second was turning thirty when he was crowned. At first, there was talk of leniency towards those who had served as judges, but it wasn't long before young Charles sent out commissioners to hunt down the men who had signed his father's death warrant. They were not judges in his mind. They were regicides breaking the law. They deserved to die.

7

Conscience and Consequences

TECHNICALLY, of course, John Dixwell did deserve to die. He, among his fifty-eight fellow judges, must have been especially cognizant of that fact because he'd become a barrister a decade before he served at the king's trial. There was no English law that sanctioned what the regicides did, though they brought in a Dutch lawyer to establish precedent. They were on thin ice, but what about the king's repeated violations of his subjects' human rights? In my early years as a teacher, I loved getting my tenth graders all stirred up by Sophocles's story of Antigone. She breaks the rules of the state by burying her brother's dead body. Under what circumstances, I asked my students, would they break the law in order to be true to their consciences? Would they, like Antigone, be willing to die for their principles?

In John Dixwell's case, his finding King Charles guilty of treason was such a radical act he essentially put a bounty on his own head for the rest of his life. In full knowledge of the consequences, should their fledgling republic fail (and surely he knew it might), he put his life in permanent jeopardy with a signature and a stamp of his family's coat of arms on a hot blob of red wax.

King Creon punished Antigone by sealing her in a cave. His plan was for a slow death, but Antigone hastened the process by hanging herself.

John Dixwell was never caught and brought to justice. Instead, he lived another forty years after signing Charles's death warrant. He had the strange luxury of being granted four decades to reflect on his choice to condemn a king. Did a day go by in which he didn't think about it?

My father died, at the age of eighty-six, on the Fourth of July 2000. How fitting that one person in the centuries-long chain of John Dixwell's keepers of the key died on the very day that England's North American colonies declared their independence from the Kingdom of Great Britain.

I like to think Dixwell's actions had something to do with our nation's founders coming to the conclusion that they could and should govern themselves. They made that declaration in 1776, less than a century (eighty-seven years, to be precise) after Dixwell had been laid to rest in New Haven, Connecticut under a simple stone bearing only the initials J.D.

The year of his death was 1689. He knew he was still so hated by the Crown that he wanted only his initials on his grave, for he knew in frightening detail the dismemberment that would be his corpse's due should the King's officers figure out who lay beneath his unobtrusive grave marker. His small sandstone tombstone is a far cry from the alabaster family monument I'd seen on the south wall of that English church in the spring of 1980.

A few years after my father died I drove to New Haven to see for myself John Dixwell's grave behind the Center Church on New Haven's Green. Ezra Stiles had included a detailed sketch of it in his 1794 book, so I knew what it said, but even in the twenty-first century it was still legible:

"J.D. ESQ. Deceased March ye 18th in ye 82nd year of his age 1688-9." His grave, however, is no longer a modest affair. Behind it rises a nineteenth-century marble obelisk that must have cost a lot of money. I soon learned it had been funded by three Dixwell brothers, one of whom was my great great grandfather Epes Sargent Dixwell, the man whose handwriting is on the label around the key to Dover Castle. A sturdy iron fence encloses both markers.

It was instructive to realize, when I thought back to my father's sheepish admission that we were direct descendants of a regicide and my own first reaction of deep dismay, that those three Dixwell brothers had been fiercely proud. On one side of the obelisk was the family coat of arms, with its three fleurs de lis, that I'd copied into my red notebook back in 1980, and the inscription "Esse quam videri" which means "To be, rather than to seem."

On the second side were carved the words on the original gravestone, and on the third and fourth were lengthy passages, fascinating to me because they showed not only what was known about John Dixwell in the nineteenth century, but what was important to the Dixwell brothers:

> Here rest the remains of John DIXWELL, Esq., of the Priory of Kent, in the county of Kent, England, of a family long prominent in Kent and Warwickshire, and himself possessing large estates, and much influence in his country; he espoused the popular cause in the revolution of 1640. Between 1640 and 1660, he was colonel in the army, an active member of four parliaments, thrice in the council of state, and one of the high court which tried and condemned *King Charles the First*. At the restoration of the monarchy, he was compelled to leave his country; and, after a brief residence in Germany, came to New Haven, and here lived in seclusion, but enjoying the esteem and friendship of its most worthy citizens, till his death, in 1688-9. (West side of monument.)

> John DIXWELL, a zealous patriot, a sincere Christian, an honest man; he was faithful to duty through good and through evil report; and, having lost fortune, position, and home in the cause of his country, and of human rights, found shelter and sympathy here, among the fathers of New England. His descendants have erected this monument as a tribute of respect to his memory, and as a grateful record of the generous protection extended to him by the early inhabitants of *New Haven*. Erected A.D. 1849. (East side of monument.)

I WALKED AROUND IT, photographing all four sides and then, the original small stone. Because it was behind the church and quite a few people without homes spend their days on the Green, there was a pretty strong smell of urine. Wow, I thought, well over 300 years after his death he's getting the same treatment I'd read about in Ezra Stiles, so many years ago:

"So late as the last French war, 1760, some British officers passing through New-Haven, and hearing of Dixwell's grave, visited it, and declared with rancorous and malicious vengeance, that if the British ministry knew it, they would even then cause their bodies [sic] to be dug up and vilified. Often have we heard the Crown Officers aspersing and vilifying them; and some so late as 1775 visited and treated the grave with marks of indignity too indecent to be mentioned."[1]

I remember feeling frightened, when I first read that passage in the British Museum, at how hated John Dixwell was, how hated all the men who'd been part of the regicide were. Later, I'd be horrified by what was done posthumously to Oliver Cromwell. Cromwell was such a key figure in not only the civil wars of the 1640s but of the interregnum government, that he is the subject of the next chapter. But what happened to him after he died belongs here, because it captures the loathing royalists felt for the regicides. The fact that Cromwell had been moldering in his grave since 1658 did nothing to deter Charles II from having the body dug up, hanged, then decapitated. His head was displayed on a twenty-foot pole above Westminster Hall for the next twenty-five years, until a storm broke the pole and the head went into the hands of various private collectors and a few museums until it was buried at Sidney Sussex College in Cambridge, in 1960.

John Dixwell surely knew of Cromwell's head's ignominy, despite his being, at that point, across the English Channel in Hanau, Germany. Years later, when he was in his late 70s, thousands of miles across the Atlantic, and living in Benjamin and Joanna Ling's modest house with Bathsheba and small children, he must also have heard of the 1685 beheading of Lady Alice Lisle, back in England.

Her crime? She had sheltered, for one night, a nonconformist minister named John Hickes who'd been part of a plan to overthrow James II, Charles the Second's despotic brother who'd become king upon Charles's death earlier that year. They were going to burn her to death, but because she was a member of the peerage, they dignified her with decapitation instead.

Plotting to overthrow kings, let alone signing their death warrants, guaranteed a gruesomely punishing death in seventeenth-century England. Every one of the signers of Charles I's death warrant must have been well aware of what lay in the future should the monarchy be restored. How inconceivably brave they were. As it turns out, the unfortunate Lady Lisle was connected to John Dixwell by more than her actions in 1685. She was the widow of a judge of Charles I. Her husband, John Lisle, was one of nineteen judges who did not sign the warrant, perhaps because the court only needed fifty-nine for the document to be quasi-legal. In the end, though, it was just as dangerous for the nineteen, after the restoration of Charles II, as for the fifty-nine. Lisle, who was a member of the House of Lords, escaped to Lausanne, Switzerland, where he was killed by an Irish Royalist in 1664.

John Lisle's role in Charles I's trial didn't help his widow plead her own case, thirty-six years after Charles's beheading. Lady Lisle wasn't allowed to speak on her own behalf during the trial, though she wanted to. The judge told her that her husband had once condemned a man to death without letting him speak (an oversimplification). She was beheaded to keep the fear of God and king alive and well in the citizenry.

These sobering stories, for quite a while, led me to assume that John Dixwell spent the twenty-nine years of his exile in constant fear, but what if that wasn't true? May his key remind me of the complexities of unlocking people's stories. Maybe he was so convinced he had done the right thing in judging Charles I that it gave him strength for the rest of his long life. Evidence for that possibility is the fact that Dixwell, safe under his assumed name in New Haven, started a family for the first time in his seventies. And the Dixwell Papers housed in the New Haven Museum, which I saw the same day I visited his grave, include his strenuous efforts, in his last years, to get a large sum of money he felt was owed him, back in England. He never lost hope that he could reclaim it and pass it on to his young wife and children.

That didn't happen. On the other hand, here I am, and thousands of his other descendants, spread out across North America. He lives on in us.

8

Tyrant Number Two: Oliver Cromwell

JOHN DIXWELL probably didn't like Oliver Cromwell very much, especially after Cromwell became, almost against his will, every bit as tyrannical as Charles the First. How bitter for Dixwell, who had staked his life on ridding England of a tyrant. But the civil wars couldn't have been won against the royalists without Cromwell's brilliant skills as a general. Nor could the government—carved out of thin air after the king was executed—have succeeded as long as it did without his firm leadership.

There's a lot to hate about Cromwell. He was a religious fanatic who considered the Pope the Anti-Christ. This thinking led to the atrocities that went on in Ireland under his watch. In 1649, when he took the town of Drogheda, his men killed almost 3,500 people. Warring led to famine, followed by an outbreak of bubonic plague. More than half the land (11 million acres) was confiscated and divided among English settlers, which meant thousands of original landowners lost everything. 30,000 Irishmen went into exile; thousands were transported to Barbados.[1] The suffering was terrible, but Cromwell operated from a certainty that he had God's favor.

Earlier, during the civil wars of the mid-1640s, it was this same certainty that made it possible for him to overcome seemingly insuperable obstacles on various battlefields. The Calvinist idea of predestination convinced him he was saved not by faith, or works, but by grace. Therefore, whenever he succeeded in battle or later, in governance, it proved he was doing God's will.

The "Protectorate" was put in place after the first few years of the newly kingless government's attempt to be a republic. Headed by Cromwell, the "Lord Protector," it devolved into a military dictatorship in which individual freedom was at a low ebb, spies were everywhere, and taxes were high to fund the military control of the country.

By dividing England into districts and putting each under the charge of a Major-general, Cromwell further strengthened the army's power. This interested me because the other two regicides who fled to New England, Edward Whalley and William Goffe, were Major-generals. Each had charge of a district. John Dixwell was only a colonel. I was glad he had not been one of Cromwell's strongmen under whom England had a miserable time. Everything was done according to Cromwell's rigidly Puritanical idea of God's will. This mixing of church and state affairs made for a murkiness that was difficult to endure. The Major-generals: "were to see to the execution of Government ordinances, to keep a record of the inhabitants of their districts and to record their comings and goings, and, strange confusion of police and moral measures, were to 'promote godliness and virtue' by all the means in their power. They had authority to break up public meetings, to close ale-houses and to search dwellings."[2]

People disliked Cromwell's policies so much that powerful judges resigned in protest. In time, I would discover that Dixwell's actions during the Protectorate show he shared their sentiments. Meanwhile Cromwell, more and more disliked at home, was successful abroad, and although in his head it was all about God, in reality it was often about money as he grabbed for England in the West Indies, the Mediterranean, and Dunkirk in the Spanish Netherlands. "The guns were not to defend Zion. They were to blast the rival trader."[3]

Likewise blasted, under Cromwell, were the hopes of the radical sects of Protestantism. Levellers, Quakers, Anabaptists, and many other sectaries had pushed for bigger changes such as wider voting rights, even votes for women, and for a sharing of wealth and of land so the propertied landed gentry who had monopolized England's wealth and political power for generations might make room for others. But in the end Cromwell was conservative. He protected the "haves" as opposed to the "have-nots," and so it continued until his death in office, as well as during the short and failed tenure of his son Richard and finally on into the restored monarchy under Charles the Second.

Back in the twenty-first century, where my understanding of England's seventeenth-century cast of characters and political upheavals was deepening, I went on wondering about John Dixwell. It was important to learn about Charles the First and about Oliver Cromwell, but my real interest was my ancestor. John Dixwell, more and more, was a growing preoccupation.

What could I learn about his early life and young adulthood to help me imagine how he became willing to serve as the judge of his king? What were the eleven years of the interregnum like for him, both when England was a republic and then when it was under the iron control of Oliver Cromwell? How did he get safely to Germany, then across the wide Atlantic to Whalley and Goffe's hideout in Hadley, which by the way is the next town over from where I live in Western Massachusetts? And finally, what was his life like in exile? What gave him the chutzpah, after seventeen years of hiding from the law, to marry young Bathsheba Howe and have three children in his seventies?

9

Enter: Mijung Kim

I FOUND TANTALIZING TIDBITS, some in books, some online, but not enough to satisfy my curiosity. Meanwhile, the key to Dover Castle lay in its plastic produce bag in my desk drawer, silently reminding me of the man who'd brought it with him when he fled. People reminded me too, loudly. My writer friends thought I should take the key back to the castle and try it in the lock. While I was there, I could find out more about Dixwell's life. There might be original materials. No way, I said. I couldn't imagine an undertaking of that magnitude. Besides, my parents were dying; my children needed me; the dog herniated two disks in her neck.

Then fate intervened. Mijung Kim, a Korean woman I've taught privately for years, asked me about my Dixwell research. She loves history. It was her undergraduate major.

I groaned aloud. "It's taking forever and all my writer friends say I have to go to England and take the key back to Dover Castle."

Her eyes lit up. "Will you do it?" she asked eagerly.

"I doubt it," I said. "I can't imagine doing such a big trip by myself."

She sat in silence, seemingly lost in thought, then said quietly, "Why don't I go with you?"

In some ways that moment was as intense for me as being given the key by Dad. I smiled politely and said, "Wow! Really? Maybe we could!" but in truth I was horrified. Now I was in for it. I might actually have to go. I might have to give my project the serious attention it deserved. That's what scared me the most.

Maybe she'd think better of it.

She didn't. Mijung, I should explain, for all the years I'd been working with her, had been busy raising her three boys alone except when her husband, a professor at a university in Seoul, flew to the U.S. for his time off. Now, though, two sons were in college, and her husband was about to have a sabbatical. Before a week went by, during which I rehearsed my exit speech, he volunteered to care for their youngest so Mijung could accompany me. I couldn't get out of it now. I couldn't do that to Mijung, who had never been to England. She had never traveled much at all. She wanted to go. For years there had been compelling reasons not to give all my attention to my Dixwell project. How very strange that one of my students was now making it possible for me to jump in with both feet. The trouble was, I had no training in historical research, I wasn't currently affiliated with a university, nor had I a book contract with a nice advance. Never mind. We were going.

I went into a frenzy of emailing complete strangers, from archivists at Dover Castle to Jason Peacey, the professor at University College London who'd written the entry on John Dixwell for the 2004 *Oxford Dictionary of National Biography*. Would they be able to meet with me in May? Mijung and I hoped we could go then, but it made no sense to make plane reservations until I had lined up enough interviewees to make my trip worthwhile.

Peacey answered at once. He was intrigued to meet a descendant of John Dixwell, and yes, he had time in May. His email was charming: "I must confess that I found it hard not to empathise with Dixwell. I'm sure historians are supposed to be a bit more detached!" And indeed, the tone of his entry in the ODNB had pleased me. It was so much less disapproving than the entry I had photocopied years ago from the 1908 edition of the same publication. That one makes no bones about Dixwell's bad repu-

Enter: Mijung Kim   45

tation, leading off with: "Dixwell, John (d. 1689), regicide, was a member of the family of that name settled in Warwickshire and Kent. In pedigrees of the family he is usually ignored,"[1] whereas Peacey's entry begins not with the word regicide, but "politician" and doesn't even mention his family expunging him.[2] In short, he treats John Dixwell with respect. In Peacey's next email, he asked politely if I could send him a photo of my key, which I did.

But weeks went by while I waited for a response from Dover Castle. I resorted to a handwritten letter on nice stationery. This yielded nothing. At long last a Dover Castle curator emailed me about a senior curator with the wonderful name Rowena Willard-Wright who had "recently carried out some work on the keys of Dover Castle." Delighted, I fired off an exuberant email to Ms. Willard-Wright. Silence.

Gradually, it dawned on me that if someone is studying "the keys" there must be lots of them, Dover Castle being a fortification whose various incarnations date back to the Iron Age when it was a hill fort atop the white cliffs of Dover overlooking the shortest crossing to Europe. About a century after the Romans arrived in 55 BC, they built a stone lighthouse, which is still part of the place today. King Henry II began building the castle in the 1160s, and it was garrisoned continuously from then until 1958.

More time passed. No email from Rowena. I began to worry that I wouldn't, after all, get to show anyone my key or try it in an ancient door somewhere on the premises. I worried too that Mijung might not get her trip to England. As another week went by, I started to get paranoid. Had I struck the wrong tone in my enthusiasm? Should I have apologized for being related to a regicide and having the temerity to set foot on English soil with the key to Dover Castle in my pocket? I went back to the first curator's email and scrolled down to something I hadn't noticed before and she perhaps hadn't realized was still attached at the bottom:

Hello ladies,
Would one of you ladies like to deal with Dixie! Or is there somebody else you would prefer I send it to . . .

I winced, then a sane part of me took over and I burst out laughing. "Deal with Dixie!" I'm not special to these people, I thought to myself. I am probably one of scores of excited people who arrive hyperventilating at Dover Castle, each with a key handed down for generations. Perhaps they take turns, those curators, dealing with us. Then the paranoia crept in. Are we all annoying or is it just me? What if these loyal British curators think executing Charles was such a violent, crazy thing to do, that they still think of it with horror? After all, people put flowers at the feet of Charles I's statue in London every January 30. That's approaching 400 years of continuous grieving.

I sent curator number one a second, slightly whiny email about my limited time in England and my need to know if Rowena or anyone would be willing to meet me. Eight days went by before Rowena herself, perhaps nudged by curator number one, emailed me. She didn't sound at all excited. On the contrary she was brief, to the point and not to be rushed.

> Dear Dixie, I apologise for not replying earlier, this is the busiest part of our year with a major project at Osbourne house underway. I will be around then so I look forward to hearing rom [sic] you closer to the time. Kind regards, Rowena

I felt a bit chilled. She'd dashed off that email without even noticing her typo in the second sentence. Either she disapproves of my ancestor, I thought to myself, or this key of mine is no big deal to her, or it's a bit of both. Clearly, she's not planning to roll out the red carpet for me. She better not be nicer to other, non-regicidal key-holders. Should I bring her a present, to sweeten her up? I drove over to a sugarhouse in Hadley, only a few miles from my house, and bought five expensive, toothsome, individually wrapped maple sugar confections in the shape of thick maple leaves. Hadley is where the regicides Edward Whalley and William Goffe were sheltered, so I liked that each package was printed with the town's name. Jason Peacey definitely deserved one, but I remained undecided about Rowena.

Still, having two meetings set up emboldened me. What if, after England, I went to Germany, the first place Dixwell went after he fled? Many sources say Dixwell spent several years in Hanau. I asked one of my former ESL students, who lives hear Hanau, for help. She put me in contact with Professor Annegret Wenz-Haubfleisch. Just as I had with Rowena Willard-Wright, I worried about her reaction to Dixwell's deeds. The German professor did seem to disapprove. Although she was entirely kind, she referred to John Dixwell and his fellow judges as "the murderers." She found a 1662 Hanau file (fond 86, No. 31128) which mentioned regicides who had fled to Germany after the Restoration of Charles II. She emailed me: "John Okey, John Barkstead and Miles Corbet were suspected of having fled to Hanau by King Charles [Charles II]. Therefore, he wrote a letter to the count of Hanau in order to prove this suspicion. The count informed him that there were indeed four Englishmen living as 'Buerger' [citizens] in Hanau but none of them identical with one of the murderers. John Dixwell is not mentioned in this file, and I could not identify any other records relating to him."

This was so fascinating that it inspired me to rise above the word "murderer." I wrote her right back, asking if she could look again under the name James Davids, the pseudonym Dixwell used in New Haven until his death. Alas, she found nothing. "Unfortunately our archives cannot supply any evidence that John Dixwell really fled to Hanau." It sounded as if she thought I should give up.

I decided not to add Germany to my itinerary, but I remained convinced he did go there. The three she mentioned all were caught in 1662, taken back to England and drawn and quartered. Surely the fourth one was Dixwell. Somehow, he gave them the slip. But where was he for the next three years? So far, I knew nothing more about him until he showed up in the aforementioned Hadley, in the winter of 1665 and stayed for at least six weeks with Whalley and Goffe, safely hidden in the Reverend John Russell's house.

It's serendipitous that Hadley is next door to Amherst, where I came to live in 1987. For many years I wasn't aware that I was so close to the place my ancestor had been. I didn't yet have his key. I was too busy with my young children to recall what I'd learned from Ezra Stiles in the British Museum: Hadley was the first place John Dixwell showed up in the New World. How curious that I, the descendant who was given his key, can drive in ten minutes to the graveyard where Russell's and his wife's table-top graves stand close to the banks of the Connecticut River. It's almost as if the key contrived to wind up near its first New England home.

10

Jumping Off the Deep End

MEANWHILE, Mijung was calmly and carefully thinking about our trip. Once I had some meetings lined up she embarked on getting her plane ticket in a way so different from my own. Suffice it to say, she let things evolve. She didn't rush to finalize plans. If it were an essay we were writing together, we would not have stated the thesis until the last sentence of the concluding paragraph. It was not clear for the longest time whether Mijung would actually get a ticket. She researched it, and thought about it. Researched it some more. I was waiting for Rowena; I was waiting for Mijung. I so wanted closure, and I wasn't going to get it until it happened. It was like a spiritual practice.

But then, lo, she bought her plane ticket; she was actually coming. I bought mine. Thereafter, trip planning with her proved to be the most relaxed and sane I've ever done in my life. She took me to Marshall's for the tiniest and most fashionable umbrella, then to Macy's for the latest and lightest suitcases. I needed two, she said, one medium size and one small. She helped me find the best raincoat, online, and choose which of my scarves to wear with it. She figured out, in Korean, all the city buses and rural trains from the comfort of her home in Amherst.

Packing was the last thing on my mind. I had just discovered on the web what looked like John Dixwell's true birthdate: March 21, 1613, not 1607, which I had believed for decades and had used to calculate all the ages he was when the momentous events of his life took place. It's true that all the sources that say 1607 preface it with a "c." for "circa," i.e., approximately. But a six-year difference? That's a lot! It meant what I'd already written about John and his second wife Bathsheba was untrue. If my new information was correct, John didn't have children for the first time in his seventies, but in his sixties. He wasn't forty-one years Bathsheba's senior, but thirty-five. He wasn't eighty-two when he died, as it says on his grave in New Haven, but seventy-six.

Could this be true? In Ezra Stiles's history of the regicides, my first, my favorite, and my most lushly detailed account of John Dixwell, Stiles includes his careful sketch of the modest grave I'd visited in New Haven and its inscription, including that he was eighty-two and he died in "1688-9." The hyphenated year is a tombstone's nod to that era's evolving ideas about whether New Year's Day should be in January or March, but that was minor compared to the new question: Did John Dixwell make himself six years older than he actually was? Surely he could not have been that confused about the year of his birth. Or was it part of concealing his identity?

After a few days, I began coming up with new scenarios. I went back to my red notebook, to what I'd written about the Dixwell monument on the interior south wall of the church in Churchover. You may recall I decided, in 1980, that I had the same nose as the Dixwells carved on it. The monument displays John's grandparents Charles and Abigail Dixwell kneeling in prayer with their five children (William, Edward, Humphrey, Basil, and Barbara), also praying, arranged in a line below them. Charles died in 1591, Abigail in 1635, forty-four years later. Even if John's new birth year turned out to be accurate, he was eighteen when she died, plenty old enough to have known her.

Many sources I'd consulted over the years say William was John's father, but Jason Peacey's *Dictionary of National Biography* entry says it was Edward. I asked Google. Instantly, a long thread from GEN-MEDIEVAL-L Archives in Rootsweb.com appeared on my screen naming Edward as the actual dad and the birthdates of each of his six children. John was the fifth.[1] Oh no! It said Edward died a few months before John turned three. How sad. That must be why John and his older brother Mark wound up being raised by their Uncle Basil.

Many people, from archivists at Oxford University to staff at the Los Angeles Public Library had contributed to the thread, which ended up shaping my itinerary. It said Edward Dixwell, second son of Charles and Abigail, is named in the Eton College Register 1441-1698 as having attended that school, starting in 1588. I wanted to see that entry for myself. Could I visit Eton? It is a private school for boys age thirteen to eighteen (though you could start at age nine in Edward's time), founded by King Henry VI in 1440, and a stone's throw from Windsor Castle where Queen Elizabeth still spends much of her time. When Prince William was an Eton student he often had tea with his grandmother at Windsor, who still wasn't going to include me. But I soon got an invitation to the college. An Eton archivist would show me Edward Dixwell's entry.

It boggled my mind that John's father went to Eton, prep school of princes, but that was just the beginning of his impressive education. In 1593, the thread said, Edward went to Oxford University, where he earned a bachelor's degree and then a master's degree, in 1600. I emailed an archivist there who kindly agreed to meet with me. Now I had lots of interviewees lined up, each with a name as quirkily English as Rowena Williard-Wright's. Eleanor Cracknell, the archivist at Eton College, would show me Edward Dixwell's bills from the 1580s. At Merton College at Oxford University, Julian Reid would show me the records of Edward's 1590s studies there. Librarian Guy Holborn offered to help me with archival material at Lincoln's Inn in London, where John Dixwell spent seven years studying law.

It was exciting, even before I left for England, to learn enough about his family to imagine what influenced him and what hurt him. Though he was fortunate to have a father who had been educated at excellent schools, Edward's early death has to have been traumatic for three-year-old John, and what a change to wind up in the care of Edward's wildly rich but uneducated younger brother Basil.

Then I discovered someone else who had been imagining John Dix-well's inner life. An Englishman named Roger Hailwood, a retired math teacher, became so interested in genealogy and local history that he wrote a little book about Broome Park, the house down in County Kent built by John's Uncle Basil Dixwell. When I contacted him he suggested we meet at Churchover, in County Warwick and visit the church I'd last seen in 1980. This worked for both of us. It's not far from where he lives, and I wanted very much to study the Dixwell monument. As for Broome Park, the place is now a golf resort and timeshare where I could reserve a room. I decided to stay there at the end of my trip, after Mijung went home, the night before the climax of my trip, my visit to Dover Castle, key in hand.

Roger's book is titled *Looking Back at Broome Park, the story of England's Finest Carolean Mansion.*[2] "Carolean" means it was built during the reign of Charles I. He covers the history of Broome Park right up to the present, but what interested me most was Hailwood's imaginative rendering of John Dixwell's flight from England and his years in Germany. It describes John's thoughts and emotions as he fled and his life in Germany. I wanted to ask Roger which parts are fact and which fancy, and what evidence he was able to find in his research. He would get a leaf no matter the ratio.

I was amazed at how many places and people I would get to see in the short space of two weeks. Could I stuff in anything else? At the last minute I decided to travel three hours north from London to Ponteland, near Newcastle upon Tyne, to witness for myself the record of John's birth in a parish register in the Northumberland Archives. All I knew about the woman appointed as my mentor was her first name: June. At first, I thought they had mixed up the months. "May, not June," I emailed, and had to be set straight.

Part Two

The individual—stupendous and beautiful paradox—is at once infinitesimal dust and the cause of all things.

C. V. Wedgwood, *The Thirty Years War*

11

London 365 Years Later

MIJUNG AND I FLEW OUT OF BOSTON at 10:45 p.m. I went through airport security with the key inside its plastic bag, inside a small blue backpack. I had called airport security beforehand to make sure they'd let my
key through. I was told a key, even a big antique key, would be fine.

The entire flight I was awash in a stew of fear, excitement and awestruck gratitude at how many people in England had agreed to help me.
It felt so self-indulgent to be doing this, and so compelling. For years, I
had joked about taking my key to Dover Castle and trying it in the lock.
Perhaps, now that Rowena was on board, I would get to do just that. But
the key, I thought to myself as we hurtled through the darkness, was only
the impetus, the thing that got me going. The real purpose of my trip was
to honor the increasingly passionate connection I felt with John Dixwell.
How magical that well over three centuries after his death in New Haven,
Connecticut, so far from everything he knew and did in England, a small
female descendant, child of his child of his child down through the ages
would decide to go to the places he never got to see again and take his key
back to the castle.

How strange and wonderful that I was ignorant of his existence despite his historical importance, until I happened to be studying in the British Museum's Reading Room in 1980. And how equally strange that Dad, who I think knew only the bare outlines of Dixwell's life, was the one who got the key and therefore ended up giving it to me because my name was Dixwell and because, as he said on that long-ago day, I was the only one in the family who'd learned anything about him.

I confess that another thing I felt as we flew above the Atlantic was guilt about Dixwell's role in the beheading of a king. I realize this was absurd. My connection to him is as slender as a spider's filament. John Dixwell is only one of 512 seven greats grandparents who have contributed to my genome. And I, in turn, am only one of thousands of people descended from him. Nonetheless, I felt weird about showing all those academic Brits my key and asking them about John Dixwell's times. Would they think of him with contempt? And what would they think of me and my historical quest when I wasn't even a history professor?

We flew all night, eating first dinner, then breakfast. We were given tiny toothbrushes and even tinier tubes of toothpaste. Once we landed, my anxiety evaporated, replaced by delight. A van arranged for by Mijung drove us into London to our Quaker accommodations. The Penn Club has a bright red door and sits on a short street called Bedford Place that runs from Bloomsbury Square to Russell Square. Both squares were full of May flowers, lovely old trees, and grass still the bright green of spring.

The rooms in the Penn Club were small and simple. Mine had a twin bed, a little sink, and a combination desk and set of drawers. Mijung's was next door and almost identical. No phone, no television. A shared bathroom was down a corridor then another corridor. A giant English breakfast was included in the price. I loved everything but staggering with my suitcases up two long flights of stairs. I unpacked some clothes into the drawers, hung others on the six hangers in the closet, put my books on the tiny shelf over the bed, and we headed out to explore.

Jet lag, friends had told me, is best dealt with by staying up all your first day, even if you don't, and I didn't, sleep a wink on the flight. Therefore, Mijung and I walked for miles, studying my accordioned cardboard map of

London every block or so. I wanted to find University College London so I would be all set to meet and interview Jason Peacey in a few days. Then I wanted to find Lincoln's Inn, where I would meet Guy Holborn on Tuesday.

I felt giddy when we found the university, for one thing because the building displaying its name was so beautiful. Across the street was a quadrangle with a porter at the gate. He didn't try to stop me as I wandered by, attracted by a magnificent building fronted with Corinthian columns. I did not yet know I would have tea with Jason Peacey in a faculty common room just to the left of the columns.

The walk from there to Lincoln's Inn was a lot longer, my spacey fatigue was increasing, and the street that my map showed running along one side of it was so tiny it didn't have a name. I suggested returning to the Penn Club and collapsing but Mijung, being only in her forties, was up for more exploring. We trudged down a wide street named High Holborn, in what felt like the heart of the business district. I laughed because at Lincoln's Inn I would meet with Guy Holborn. Soon we walked past the massive Holborn Town Hall.

An astonishing number of London's buildings were architectural stunners in perfect repair, decorated with a great deal of gold leaf. "Who pays for all the maintenance?" I asked Mijung, small town American that I am, disapproval trumping my awe. I couldn't tell what she thought. Then a tiny alley caught my eye, we turned down it and there, immediately, was a sign: "Lincoln's Inn Fields," and a large open green, almost empty of people in the dusk. The field was on our right, to the left was a long brick wall, higher than our heads, and way down at the end of the lane an elegant edifice which turned out to be the Royal Courts of Justice. It had outsized wooden doors with curlicues of iron, each ending in a hinge, and lanterns (already lit) straight out of Dickens. Speaking of Dickens, had we gone left, and then left again, we would have come upon Chancery Lane.

Instead, we walked back up the alley to the main entrance of Lincoln's Inn. It had elaborate twin towers, an electric barrier that would have had to be raised if we were in a car, and a porter's house, complete with porter. He came out as I sidled through and inquired about my business.

"I'm meeting Guy Holborn here in a few days," I said hesitantly.

Miraculously, as if the name itself served as a key to the inner sanctum, the porter's demeanor changed from official, keep-out-the-riffraff severity to friendliness. "Oh, the librarian," he said. "He's a very busy man." Then he not only ushered us in, but insisted on walking us to the building where I was to conduct my interview.

Best of all, he went back to his post and left us alone to explore. Excitement gave me a second wind. Because it was Saturday, and almost dark, no one was around to be offended if I snooped, so I did. If Mijung disapproved, she didn't admit it. There was a big quadrangle of grass surrounded by buildings where barristers have their chambers and conduct their legal work. To the side of a little green door on one building, a simple wooden sign between two skinny espaliered fig trees listed the barristers within. The first six names were followed with the letters "QC," meaning Queen's Council, i.e., very important, top-of-the-heap practitioners of the law.

We crept back out, I smiling and nodding my thanks to the porter, and walked down to the Royal Courts of Justice. There we turned left and left again to come up Chancery Lane to High Holborn, marveling at how unobtrusive Lincoln's Inn is. You would not know it was there, this center of power. The only clue along Chancery was a tiny alley through the brick wall with a padlocked iron gate to keep out intruders and a small sign that read:

HIGHWAYS ACT 1959 – SECTION 34
THIS IS A PRIVATE PATH.
MEMBERS OF THE PUBLIC USE IT
ONLY WITH THE CONSENT OF
THE HONOURABLE SOCIETY
OF LINCOLN'S INN.

It felt so British, that understated yet commanding sign. With the prestige that comes with being a member of the Honourable Society of Lincoln's Inn, there is no need to raise your voice. I had to resist a sudden urge to break a few rules.

12

Finding the Scene of the Crime

THE NEXT DAY WAS SUNDAY, which was lucky because I needed another day to get used to the five-hour time difference. Down in the Penn Club's dining room, various Brits were eating black sausage, bacon, eggs, and innumerable triangles of slightly burnt toast brought to their tables in metal racks. In the proper order, they poured milk from tiny white pitchers into their teacups before adding the tea. The atmosphere was hushed. The talk, which I strained to overhear, was of social justice. The staff, padding quietly to and fro, was young and entirely Eastern European.

I felt too shy to sit with anyone and pick his or her brains about British history and John Dixwell's role in it, but I wanted to. They looked so coolly competent, all those inhabitants of the Old Country softly pouring their tea in their lovely Quaker club just around the corner from the British Museum. Then I decided it was just as well they knew nothing about me. Mightn't these peace-loving English guests think that killing a king, albeit in a quasi-legal way, was a terrible thing to do? I ordered not one but two poached eggs, and bacon, but couldn't bring myself to try the black sausage. I knew it was dark-colored because blood was a primary ingredient and bloodshed was very much on my mind.

Sunday's goal was to locate the place where Charles was beheaded, but first I needed a functional phone. A Czech Penn Club employee told me to walk to Tottenham Court Road if I wanted to buy a cheap cell phone, since mine wouldn't work in England. I bought an inexpensive one with many minutes from a young man who told me he was from Turkey. Only one day into my two weeks in England I was fascinated by how international London's young workforce is.

In the afternoon, after a bit of a struggle with pounds and pence, Mijung and I managed to take a bus down to the City of Westminster. Westminster is the London borough containing the Houses of Parliament, and the place where all the action took place in late 1648 and early 1649, when a select group of fifty-nine men tried King Charles in Westminster Hall, found him guilty of "High Treason and other high Crymes" against his own people and voted to execute him by "the severinge of his head from his body."[1] Perhaps as part of looking at my own complicated feelings about being descended from a regicide, I needed to locate the spot where the beheading was carried out. The hooded executioner who wielded the axe must have been awash in complicated feelings, fear perhaps foremost. To this day, his identity has never been definitively established.

First, though, we decided we had to hear the choirboys at Westminster Abbey. Down the endless aisle they processed in bright red robes, stiff frilly white ruffs around their necks. They looked so angelic I found myself hoping they had contraband in their pockets.

There were so many congregants we had to be herded like sheep into various transepts. Underfoot were famous graves. I walked over D.H. Lawrence, George Eliot, and Dylan Thomas, to name a few. It was all so important and moneyed and hierarchical I couldn't wait to get out of there, though the singing was sublime. I even disliked the leather pouch, thrust down the pews on a long wooden pole, into which we were supposed to put our donations. When we came out into the sunshine I had to get an ice cream cone to recover my equilibrium.

Mijung was finding British accents incomprehensible so I promised her I would do all the talking if we had trouble locating the places where everything happened in 1649. Parliament is extensive and grand, with Big Ben rising majestically above. It takes a lot of time just to walk its length, and there are statues all over the place. First we found Oliver Cromwell. His head, as I said earlier, was severed from his exhumed corpse after the restoration, displayed on a spike above Westminster Hall for many years, then disappeared for centuries. But at the end of the nineteenth century, after much dispute, a statue of him was commissioned and placed in front of the House of Commons. He stands tall, prepared for battle with a sword in one hand and a Bible in the other.

I asked a police officer to point us toward the spot where Charles the First was beheaded. I could tell she was irked that she didn't know, but then her face brightened as she told me, in gleeful tones, that a tiny bust of Charles is situated on the side of the church directly across the street from Cromwell so that the two ancient enemies have no choice but to stare at one another.

We went on walking. I wanted to find the Whitehall Palace Banqueting House, somewhere back up the street towards Trafalgar Square, because that is where the execution took place before throngs of horrified people. A whole series of persons I asked didn't know where to send us, but eventually we found the palace ourselves. On its leftmost corner is an unobtrusive bust of Charles quite high above the ground, this one in an

Charles at the site of his execution.

oval niche above a plaque. Hooray for optical zoom! On the little screen of my new camera I was able to read, after snapping the picture: "His Majesty King Charles I passed through this hall and out of a window nearly over this tablet to the scaffold in Whitehall where he was beheaded on 30th January 1649."

Those words shifted my mood abruptly. I stood perfectly still, as everyone must have stood perfectly still on that day as they waited for the axe to fall. I wondered if John Dixwell had witnessed "justice," as determined by fifty-nine surely anxious men, being done. Would he have been required to?

In a somber mood, I led Mijung down the street to Trafalgar Square, in search of a statue of Charles astride a horse. Trafalgar Square was built on what used to be Charing Cross, where various regicides, after the restoration of Charles II, were drawn and quartered and disemboweled. Neighbors complained of the stench, and eventually those as well as other executions were conducted elsewhere. The square, with its towering column commemorating Lord Nelson's naval triumph over Napoleon in 1805, is a massive display of empire. Four lions guard the bottom of the monument. Days later, on a bus tour, I was told that the lions were modeled on the sculptor's dog after the dead lion he initially used as a model got too decayed and stinky.

Although Mijung and I had to look up at Charles on his horse, he still seemed dwarfed by Nelson's monument, rather a petite king. Cast in 1633 by Hubert Le Sueur, the statue was placed where it now stands in 1678, eighteen years after John Dixwell had fled the country. As we stood staring at the whole scene I noticed that Nelson's column was in the background and in the foreground was a modern walk signal, red at the moment, telling us to stop.

Would that we could be stopped, I thought, remembering my own country's wars in Iraq and Afghanistan. Fatigue settled over me as we walked all the way back to the Penn Club. I felt homesick for the quiet woods of Amherst and the wide fields of Hadley.

13

John Dixwell's Roots

MONDAY WAS DAY ONE of my rigorous interviewing schedule. I was supposed to take the train from Euston station to Rugby, traveling about an hour and a half northwest of London to meet Roger Hailwood, the math teacher who wrote a book about Broome Park.

Over the weekend, we had figured out how to get to Roger, even taking a dry run to Euston a day early, Mijung's idea. Not surprisingly, she was a marvelous traveling companion. When we were too tired, those first days, to drag ourselves out of the Penn Club in search of something to eat, it turned out she had brought a generous supply of readymade Korean food in her two suitcases. We sat in the Penn Club's dining room eating prepackaged porridge—a mix of winter squash, rice, beans, and bits of clam. Salvation.

On Monday morning we walked through Russell Square, then Tavistock Square Garden, where a bronze statue of Gandhi sits not far from a bust of Virginia Woolf. Then our problems began. At the station we discovered Mijung's ticket would not put her on my Britrail pass train. We waited endlessly in a long line (it was a Bank Holiday) to change it, then realized we needed to pee and got kerflummoxed by having to come up with the precise British coinage even to get past the turnstiles into the women's room, let alone relieve ourselves. An attendant yelled at Mijung for attempting to put pence instead of whatever was required in the slot. Shaken, we raced back to the cavernous waiting room only to discover our train was delayed.

And delayed. And delayed, the announcer's plummy voice told us every five minutes while the growing Bank Holiday crowd, which included the world's most authentically English giant sheep dog, was increasingly antsy. I began discussing our sorrows with nearby strangers. Would the trains ever travel? No, an Australian said, give up now. Mijung suggested I try out my new cellphone. I called Roger's home. His wife answered, instantly stressed. "I can't reach him. He left hours ago. He's waiting for you in Rugby."

"Does he have a cell phone?" I asked after a moment of stunned embarrassment at so inconveniencing these people I'd never met.

"Well yes but we never turn it on, of course. It's just for emergencies."

Despair set in. Mijung decided to cash in her ticket and return to the Penn Club. Suddenly alone, I stood staring at the sheepdog, my mind racing. Just then, a vibration. What? My tiny new phone was ringing. It was Roger! He sounded big and calm and reassuring. I must go to a different train station, St. Pancras, and find a train to Market Harborough, and call him when I knew which one.

"Where is St. Pancras?" I started asking anyone who would listen. I ran. St. Pancras, like Euston, was enormous and crowded. I couldn't figure out how to get from the underground Tube to the trains and ran here and there, the key to Dover Castle beating out a rhythm on my spine through the thin blue nylon of my backpack. I was wiped out by the time I collapsed into my train seat. It was already well past noon and I hadn't brought lunch. "I'm too old for this," I thought as I bought a packet of shortbread from the cart traveling down the aisle. I wolfed down one piece, then the other. It was so late! Would Roger politely wait until 2:30 to have lunch with me? I hoped not. If so, would we have time to visit Churchover?

Roger's plan was to take me to the church I had visited in 1980, to see the Dixwell monument described in John Burke's *Extinct Baronetcies*, the one with all those noses just like mine. I hadn't told him I'd already seen it, and didn't at all mind seeing it again, but my biggest mission was asking Roger, face to face, what was truth and what was fabrication in his account of John Dixwell's life.

On the train to Market Harborough I sat cramming Roger's section on my seven greats grandfather as if I were about to take a particularly scary exam. The thought of asking Roger how much he had made up out of the whole cloth made me quail. How might he react to being caught in the act of concocting stories that weren't based on established facts? This was pretty silly of me because Roger admits to it right in his introduction: "Since the early events are somewhat sketchily documented a little imagination has been used to put them into context and to paint a picture for the reader."[1]

Roger wanted to tell a good story, but I had come all the way to England in order to find as many actual facts about John Dixwell as I could in the space of two weeks. Roger's stories about him are so vivid I wanted to ask him which ones were figments. Two seemed particularly unlikely. One was that John had sat with his dying brother Mark after they had fought on opposite sides in a civil war battle at Arundel Castle. Mark, Roger wrote, had been on the Royalist side (loyal to Charles I) and John on the Parliamentarian. Was Roger right that the brothers were thus divided? I also planned to ask Jason Peacey, the historian at University College London, on Thursday.

But what a powerfully painful story if it were true! In his book, Roger makes the most of it, telling the story in the first person, from John Dixwell's point of view:

"When I arrived at the castle I found Mark among the wounded prisoners; he had been carried into the great hall where he lay on his cloak. The musket ball had penetrated deeply into his chest, and blood trickled from his mouth as he coughed."[2]

I had smiled at this purple passage when I'd first read it several months ago. Now, it resonated with emotional truth even if the facts might be wrong. I wondered if Roger was aware that Mark and John were very young when they lost their father. I wouldn't know exactly how young until I could check the parish records in the far north of England on Saturday. Roger may not have known, either, that Mark and John were the only two of Edward and Mary's six kids to be sent south to elegant Uncle Basil in Kent. But somehow Roger had divined how close they probably were as brothers. This time I found myself moved to tears by the death scene as the train chugged toward Market Harborough:

> We had done so much together as we had grown up and no one was a closer friend, but this conflict over who should rule the country had cruelly forced us apart as we followed our own beliefs . . . As I had taken his hand in mine his eyes had looked deep into mine with a desperate earnestness; we were not soldiers any more but brothers once again. But he was not thinking of himself but of his family. He had asked that I should be a guardian to his boys until they were of an age to look after themselves and to look after Elizabeth his wife.
>
> I had sat beside him during the night and as time went by his breathing had become more and more labored, beads of sweat gathered on his brow, and I had continued to wipe the blood from his mouth until the moment came when he breathed no more and the hand I held become lifeless and fell away.[3]

My nose prickled at the awfulness of losing a sibling. Had Roger made it all up? The scene is presented as part of John's thoughts as he sneaks away from Broome Park, in the near darkness of early dawn, accompanied by his faithful manservant Robert, bound for a ship that will take them across the English Channel to France. It's early summer, 1660. John is supposed to appear in court, in London, for his role in Charles's execution, but he is escaping to the Continent instead. This much, for sure, is true. Not the manservant Robert, that is, but the escape to Europe to avoid standing trial and almost certain death by drawing and quartering at Charing Cross.

The other part of Roger's story that I questioned was his description of John's time in Hanau, Germany. After the professor in Germany wondered whether Dixwell had been there at all, I found good evidence that he was in Hanau for some time and became a burgher there. The source is fellow regicide Edmund Ludlow's massive memoir, initially titled *A Voyce from the Watch Tower.*

Ludlow was the last surviving regicide (Dixwell was the second to last), dying in Switzerland in 1692 after successfully evading several assassination attempts. His memoir, in its entirety, is online, and states that four of the regicides escaped to Germany. Ludlow lists Dixwell as the fourth:

"Colonel John Barkstead and Colonel Okey, with Colonel Walton and Colonel Dixwel [*sic*], who had been commissioners in the High Court of Justice at the trial of the late King, having made their escape from England into Germany, were received into protection at Hanaw [*sic*], and made burgesses of the town."[4]

Colonel Valentine Walton died of natural causes, probably in Flanders, some time after Barkstead and Okey were taken into custody and brought back to England. Ludlow describes in detail how the latter were captured.

> Of these Colonel Barkstead and Colonel Okey took a journey to Holland, to meet some relations who were contented to banish themselves with them, and to conduct them to the place which they had chosen for their residence. But one Mr. George Downing, who was agent for the King in Holland, and had formerly been a preacher and chaplain to Colonel Okey's regiment, having received information that such persons were in that country, obtained an order from the States General for their seizure; by 1662 virtue of which they were taken, together with Mr. Miles Corbet, one of the King's judges also, sent into England in a ship of war, and committed prisoners to the Tower.[5]

It's pretty hard not to hate Downing. He was so traitorous to Okey, who'd not only sponsored Downing's education in the New World but also, Ludlow writes, hired him as chaplain of his regiment! Downing's bio doesn't explain how he became such an opportunist. Born in Dublin, he moved to Salem, Massachusetts with his family. His mother, Lucy Winthrop, was Governor John Winthrop's sister. While in the colony

Downing went to Harvard, graduating in 1642 with the other eight members of his class. In 1645, he sailed for the West Indies as a teacher and preacher to the sailors. The cargo was enslaved people. Throughout his life, Downing contrived to benefit from the constantly changing politics of his times. London's Downing Street is named in honor of him. Samuel Pepys termed him a "perfidious rogue."

I won't go into the scene of the deaths of the three regicides Downing turned in. You can easily find it, if you wish to be horrified. John Dixwell must have heard of their fate and felt anger, grief, and fear. He had spent the first two years of his exile with them. How intense to be, as far as I can see, the only survivor of the regicides who had gone to Hanau.

I glanced at my watch. In half an hour I'd arrive at Market Harborough. I leafed to Roger's version of John Dixwell's life in Hanau. In it, Dixwell learns to be a silversmith from Col. John Barkstead. This had so surprised me, when I read it back home, that I Googled "John Barkstead, regicide" and discovered he was, in fact, a silversmith before he became the custodian of the Tower of London. I also knew Dixwell's and Bathsheba's son John, born in New Haven in 1680, had become a noted silver and goldsmith in Boston. How had Roger come up with regicide John learning to work silver in Germany?

There was some plausibility to his tale, even though it seemed unlikely that a man who'd spent seven years studying the law and then lived for nearly two decades in the opulent mansion built by his uncle Basil, would learn a trade. Roger writes of the Hanau years: "The newcomers [i.e., the regicides] quickly became a part of the community, and since he had to find some way of making a living John Dixwell learned the skills of the silversmiths trade, giving an opportunity to display the artistic temperament that he had shown as a boy. His skills as a lawyer and administrator were also quickly recognized and he became a Burgher of the town."[6] A few pages later, Roger has Dixwell managing, before his death, to impart silversmith skills to his son John, only nine when his father died. Could this be? But now my train was pulling into the station. I stuffed the little book into my blue backpack, got off, and there was Roger Hailwood, looking exactly like the person his voice suggested he was: big, calm, reliable, and kind. If he was annoyed by his long wait for me, he didn't say so. He'd had a sandwich at a Subway. I didn't admit I was hungry. We climbed into his little Ford Focus and off he went down tiny lanes with me trying not to feel queasy as he zipped along the left side of the road.

14

A Church Full of Dixwells

ALTHOUGH ROGER TOLD ME, toward the end of our afternoon together, that he was "on the wrong side of seventy-five," he looked much younger and was very sharp in a kindly, unruffled way. He'd brought a sheaf of information he'd printed off the internet that he thought might be of interest to me, and as we drove along I realized he knew a great many of the things I'd wanted to ask about at breakfast in the Penn Club the day before.

As we headed for Churchover, he explained the difference between villages and hamlets. A hamlet is smaller. Coton, in the time of John Dixwell's grandparents, was a village and Coton Hall was the manor house in which they lived. The Dixwells, he explained, were the largest landowners and as such were members of the yeomanry. This meant they were untitled commoners.

They were, he said, the most important family in Churchover, all those years ago, though they have since disappeared. We arrived at Holy Trinity Church, which looked just as it had in 1980. Its walls are golden-brown stone, and parts of it date back to the 1100s. As we walked down the path to the entrance he wanted me to notice the land to the right was higher than that on the left, because of many layers of bodies buried beneath it. Only people in the topmost layer got tombstones.

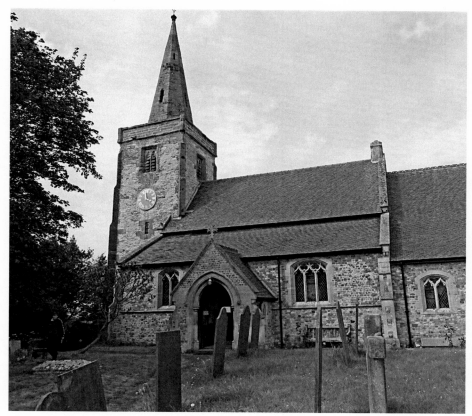

Holy Trinity Church, Churchover.

But the Dixwells weren't in the churchyard. Being wealthy, Roger said, meant you got buried inside the church. As we entered, there on our left was the Dixwell monument, in perfect condition. The inscription above it reads:

> This monument was erected Anno Domini 1641 in the memorie of Charles Dixwell of Cotton Esqr and of Abigail his wife, he dying in the yeare of our Lord 1591, and she in the year 1635. And of 4 sonns and one daughter that issued from them viz William Dixwell, Esqr, Edward Dixwell, Humphrey Dixwell, Sir Basill Dixwell, Knight and Baronet, and Barbara Dixwell, all whose figures this work doth represent

Dixwell monument.

I stood staring at my nine greats grandfather and grandmother, still kneeling in prayer with their five children arranged in a row beneath them. The only shadow on my joy was my realization that two nearly identical monuments not far away, memorializing other rich families, depicted pious people very similar to my Dixwells. It must have been the fashion, I thought to myself, and those are generic noses.

Still, it was thrilling. There were so many Dixwells—Dixwells to right of me, Dixwells to left of me, Dixwells beneath my feet, silently decomposing. The pipe organ, said Roger, was built into what used to be a private Dixwell chapel. A series of matching diamond-shaped Dixwell stones were set in the floor immediately in front of the altar, where fewer footsteps could wear away the lettering. They looked brand new, but on the far right was one with a different surname. "Abigail Harcourt," the last one said, "d. 1635."

Same first name, same death date. Could John Dixwell's grandmother have remarried? Maybe she hadn't spent the forty-four years of her widowhood alone after Charles died in 1591. If she had remarried, and it looked as if she had, would that have made it easier or harder for her to help Mary and her six children after Edward died up in Ponteland? Roger thought she would have stayed involved with her children and her orphaned grandchildren. Because she was buried in the same church that bore her monument with Charles and their five children, she must have stayed in Churchover. I wondered if John Dixwell had known her. Did he visit her and his various aunts and uncles? Might he have known some of these people? Then I noticed that several Dixwells beneath those diamonds had died a few years or decades after John's 1689 death in New Haven.

What did they know of his life there? What did they think about him?

Wouldn't they have been terrified of being executed if they were caught helping him? I suspect they simply went on with their lives. Back home, before I left for England, I had found a little online information

Dixwell floor tiles.

about two of them. A different Abigail Dixwell Harcourt is mentioned in Volume 21, Part 1 of the Parliamentary Papers of the House of Commons and Command: "Abigail Dixwell Harcourt, in 1672, gave £50, for which certain lands were conveyed to trustees for the use of the poor."[1] Who is she? Maybe this Abigail was Edward and Mary's fourth child, born in Ponteland in 1611, just two years before her little brother John came along. Could her grandmother have adopted her? Might the granddaughter never have married, but wound up with enough money, at the age of sixty-one, to give such a generous gift?

Before my arrival in England, I had found many snippets suggesting the Dixwells in Churchover took care of Edward's children after his death. When William died, only four years after his mother Abigail, in 1639, his will mentioned John's little brother Charles, the baby of the family: "Charles DIXWELL one of the sons of my brother Edward, deceased."

Standing there, gazing at all those diamond-shaped stones, I had a felt understanding of where John's father had come from. Roger and I walked down the nave to look again at Charles and Abigail's five children arranged in a neat row in order of birth. When I asked him about how primogeniture would have affected them, he reeled off what usually happened. William would have got the estate. The second son, in this case John's father Edward, often went into the church, the third (Humphrey) into the law or the army, and the fourth—I broke in and shared what I'd learned about Basil's tiny annuity of six pounds. That amount, Roger assured me, was enough to live on. What? Yes, he assured me, and Barbara probably got married.

We agreed that Basil was lucky to have inherited his Uncle John Herdson's entire estate, thirty thousand pounds. I asked him where all that money had come from. We knew that his mother Abigail and her brother John had a father named Henry Herdson, who was in trade, but we'd read differing reports. Some said Henry was in the business of ropemaking; others said the fur trade. It's possible "Herdson" was a variant of Hudson, and the Herdsons were related to the explorer Henry Hudson after whom Hudson Bay is named. We also knew Henry was an alderman in London, which meant he was a man of power and wealth, whether from rope or from fur.

"Either way," said Roger, "it was big business. There were miles and miles of rope on any ship in those days." Alternatively, we thought about beaver pelts coming by the shipload from the New World.

Had Herdson money paid for all these elegant stones and monuments? Not knowing, we returned to the subject of Edward. He wouldn't have inherited any money, Roger said, but being a vicar was a good enough job.

"Wasn't Ponteland in the middle of nowhere, way up north of Newcastle upon Tyne? What was that like for Edward?" I asked.

Roger thought it was fine, and not remote at all, for one of the four routes from England to Scotland ran through Ponteland. "There was a lot of traffic." Plus, Ponteland was connected with Oxford University's Merton College. "Merton College owned land up there, which gave them the right to appoint a vicar."

Edward must have been a decent student, I said proudly, or Merton wouldn't have given him that appointment. I told him there was evidence at Eton College that he had won a scholarship and become a King's Scholar for four of his five years at Eton. Then he spent seven years at Oxford. That adds up to twelve years at very good schools. Roger nodded politely.

After my tour of Holy Trinity Church we got back in the Ford Focus and drove to the Dixwell estate, now government property. Both the manor house and its gatehouse were rebuilt in the nineteenth century by whoever owned the place then. I admitted I was famished. Roger knew just the place. It had a KFC, a Subway and a Burger King, he said with satisfaction. Why wouldn't he assume an American would prefer such fare? Resigned, I chose Subway, where I bought a turkey sub for me, tea and a cookie for Roger, and we sat. Refreshed, I peppered him with more questions.

I began with asking him about Oliver Cromwell. Roger explained that one reason Cromwell was so successful in the English Civil Wars was he figured out a new way to fight. Before, he said, "the cavalry dashed about, slashing swords, but Oliver Cromwell realized it wasn't effective." He trained "pike men" to stand in formation with their pikes planted firmly in the ground and angled forward in such a way that the metal spikes on top drove into the advancing horses' bodies. The poor horses were impaled, then Cromwell's soldiers pulled off the horsemen and killed them. "Cromwell was the beginning of the British Army."

It seemed a good moment to bring up Roger's touching scene of John Dixwell's brother Mark's death. Where did Roger find his evidence that the brothers were together for that tragic event? Roger was sure Mark was killed at Arundel Castle, and he added that Lorraine Sencicle, a history buff whom I planned to meet in Dover, would be able to give me the source. Although he did not know that John was present when Mark was killed, he felt it was a reasonable conjecture that he was.

I gave Roger a Hadley maple sugar leaf. It was cracked from my wild run through St. Pancras Station, but he accepted it graciously. Then I pulled my key out of my backpack. We looked reverently at my great great grandfather Epes Sargent Dixwell's tiny handwriting on the label. When Roger read "in Command," he explained that John, during the interregnum, commanded the foot soldiers of the Kent Militia. These would have been farmers and farmworkers—people conscripted to fight.

We talked about John Dixwell's 1660 flight from England and his years in Germany. Roger felt sure that John, knowing King Charles II's commissioners were on the lookout for regicides trying to leave the country, would not have sailed from Dover. The king had put a watch on all the ports. Instead, Dixwell might have sailed from Folkestone, which Roger said was not a recognized port but a little fishing village.

At long last, I asked about Hanau. Was there any evidence that John had learned to be a silversmith? Well, no, but Hanau was famous for silversmithing. How about John teaching his little son the art in New Haven? That, too, was conjecture. When you're writing a story, he said simply, you have some facts and you hang the story on them as best you can. Clearly my concern about how it would feel for Roger to have a Dixwell descendant appear, carrying an ancient key to Dover Castle, asking for corroboration of facts, was unnecessary. He was entirely comfortable. I'd say he enjoyed the whole afternoon. So did I.

At the train station, we shook hands and parted, both of us forgetting the sheaf of photocopies about Churchover and Dixwells he had prepared for me. And that is why, a few days later, I received a package from him. There was more inside than just the photocopies. He had given me a copy of the book he had written about his father, *A Dedicated Man, The Life of the Reverend Richard Hailwood B.D.* His father had been a missionary in China, where Roger was born.

When I arrived back in London I walked from Euston Station to the Penn Club, full of gratitude to Roger Hailwood, who for no reason other than kindness had taught me so much about my family. More kindness awaited me. Mijung was sitting in the dining room with hot Korean food and a cup of tea.

15

Entering Eton College

EXACTLY A WEEK LATER I took a train to Eton College to meet archivist Eleanor Cracknell. Eton is the next step in the chronology of John Dixwell's ancestry. At Churchover, I'd seen his grandparents and father and uncles and aunt. Now I wanted to visit the school his father had attended.

I was feeling a bit bereft, for Mijung had left at 7 a.m., bound for Amherst, Massachusetts, her big solo vacation without her husband or any of her three sons being over. She had been the best of travel partners, independent yet wonderfully supportive of my endeavors. The day before, we had had separate itineraries. She had gone on a Korean bus tour to the Cotswolds and Oxford while I'd taken in a Quaker Meeting near Euston station in the morning, Chinese paintings at the British Museum in the afternoon, then St. Martin in the Fields' evensong service. We chose an Indian restaurant in Bloomsbury for our last meal together. It turned out Mijung had never had Indian cuisine. She liked it.

It would be strange not having Mijung in the tiny room beside mine at the Penn Club, watching her Korean soap operas on her laptop in the evenings and sharing her suitcase's stash whenever I needed a snack. I always knew when she went to bed because my little sink, back-to-back with hers, gurgled loudly when she turned on her tap. I would miss that companionable noise.

Now I was alone. I took the Tube to Paddington, yet another gigantic London railroad station. In my haste to grab a train, any train, to Eton and Windsor, I inadvertently landed on the slowest one. This gave me a full hour to prepare myself to set foot on the ancient and hallowed premises of Eton College and interview archivist Eleanor Cracknell.

How on earth had second son Edward Dixwell wound up at such a prestigious school? Maybe it wasn't prestigious at its outset, for Henry VI founded it in 1440 to provide free education to seventy poor boys. His plan was for them to continue on to King's College at Cambridge, which he also founded, one year later.

Interesting. In the beginning, you had to be poor to go to Eton. I thought about all those expensive memorials Roger Hailwood had shown me inside the church at Churchover and felt confused. The Dixwells weren't poor. But because of primogeniture, Edward was entitled to nothing.

Being American, and also lucky enough to have parents who were scrupulous, in their wills, about dividing their assets equally among their four children, I find primogeniture weird beyond comprehension.

The British do not. P.G. Wodehouse, in *Something New* (1915), one of his comic novels mocking the British landed gentry, has a passage about primogeniture and its difficulties for parents of especially stupid sons.

> Like many fathers in his rank of life, the Earl of Emsworth had suffered much through that problem which, with the exception of Lloyd George, is practically the only fly in the British aristocratic amber—the problem of what to do with younger sons.
>
> It is useless to try to gloss over the fact—in the aristocratic families of Great Britain the younger son is not required.[1]

Ah Edward, you were not needed. You were packed off to the charity school of Eton when you were pretty little, maybe only twelve or thirteen. You probably weren't even home, three years later, when your father died.

It could be that being a younger son, though, had advantages. Younger son David Lloyd George (1863–1945) is the only Welshman ever to become Prime Minister. His first language wasn't English; it was Welsh. Did this help him bring an outsider's perspective to politics? And aren't younger sons, within the system of primogeniture, outsiders too? As a younger son perhaps he was particularly aware of injustice. He spearheaded the introduction of Britain's social welfare system and felt the British Empire needed to be based on freedom, not "racial arrogance."

Lloyd George's thinking was often ahead of his time and who knows, maybe being able to think creatively was an occasional side effect, during primogeniture's long heyday, for younger sons. Perhaps John Dixwell, having nothing to gain from the status quo of primogeniture, was forced to be better at thinking outside the box, at questioning the divine rights of kings.

I stared out the train window at a scene alternating between green pastures dotted with sheep and vividly yellow fields of oilseed rape. Then I looked at my watch. Half an hour to go. All this thinking about second sons and the unfairness of primogeniture was not helping me get calmer about visiting Eton. It was just stirring me up. The Eton of today, from everything I had read online, is a school for the highly intelligent but also the über wealthy and the super snobby. I wasn't even there yet, and already my hackles were rising.

Much later, in my peaceful study in Amherst, I have the time and space to ponder the intensity of my feelings. How ironic to have had such resentment against an exclusive private school in England when I myself am the beneficiary of an exclusive private school in Milton, Massachusetts. I went to Milton Academy for thirteen years because I lived in the town and my parents had enough money to send all four of us to private school. Our father had gone there too, and both his parents. When we were graduating, in the 1960s, it was common for many Milton students, most of whom were white, upper-middle-class protestants, to be admitted to top schools. What right had I to be so judgmental of Eton College?

What right indeed given that after I went to Milton I went on to get my B.A. at Harvard University? As a general rule, people haven't heard of Milton Academy, but just about everyone, everywhere, has heard of Harvard. I cannot even say its name, whenever I am asked where I went to college, without the inquirer having some sort of reaction, often intense. And I squirm, hating and loving being seen, suddenly, as—and here my fingers come to a standstill on the keyboard. As what? As smart? As unforgivably privileged? As guilty of thinking I'm special when of course I'm not? The possibilities are endless not only for what goes through the asker's mind but for what, if I'm feeling overly sensitive or paranoid, goes on in mine.

"Harvard," I say, amazed myself that I went there after not only flunking sixth grade history, but having trouble in every attempt at history or science since. The only possible major for me was English, which, thank God, I could do.

You would think that going to Harvard would have convinced me that I had a functioning brain, but old stories die hard. They can morph into an unkind voice inside your head that's hard to shut up. Mine is quick to tell me I know less than anyone else in the room and will shortly fall from grace when someone like Sir Paterson notices and broadcasts my inferiority.

This tendency wasn't helped by being the youngest of four and therefore always the one who knew and understood the least. Was this another engine driving my anxiety about going to Eton? I think so. I was afraid I wasn't smart enough to accomplish the sprawling Dixwell task I'd set myself, and Eleanor Cracknell would know it the minute she met me.

As my train chugged past towns with wonderful names like Bisham, Maidenhead, or Slough, I thought about how unfair it is that some children get to go to Eton College and Milton Academy when so many more go to ill-equipped schools or no school at all. Like primogeniture, the bestowing of an elite high school education is random. I was given so much by being born into a family that not only had money but valued education. I wondered how aware Eton college students are of their extraordinary privilege.

Would Eleanor Cracknell be the sort of person who bought into the high-status world of Eton? Despite knowing next to nothing about her other than her name, her job title, and what she had written in response to my emails, I had formed all sorts of theories about her. She would be scary smart. She would find my ignorance annoying.

Some of my anticipatory anxiety had been heightened in the months leading up to my trip to England by her relaxed response to emails. Maybe it's a cultural difference. In the U.S. we expect instant responses. In England, I observed, people dawdle. They take their time. For weeks and weeks I didn't know if I'd get interviews with people or not, just as I hadn't known whether Mijung would actually purchase a plane ticket. In the same way as Mijung likes to take her time, the British, when it comes to email, refuse to be rushed. Eleanor Cracknell waited ten days to answer my first email, an enthusiastic gush with too much information and too many questions:

At the time, in my excitement over having actually decided to go to England, I couldn't see how over-the-top my letter was. Perhaps Eleanor Cracknell could. Here is what I got back. She wasn't at all sure it would be worth my while to visit Eton:

Dear Ms Dixwell Brown,

Thank you for your recent enquiry regarding Dixwells at Eton.

Unfortunately our knowledge of boys before 1792 is very patchy, unless they were a King's Scholar, and even then our records are only complete from 1600 onwards. It is therefore not possible to say 100% accurately that someone was not at Eton, as the records just do not survive. The Dyxwell you mention is the only entry we have of a Dixwell/Dyxwell at Eton.

You are very welcome to come and use the readers' room to conduct your own research, but I am afraid that there would be little to see. If you would like to come anyway, we are open by appointment only Monday to Friday, 9.30am - 1pm, 2pm - 5pm. I am afraid that we are closed 27th, 28th and 30th May.

I am sorry that we cannot be of more assistance,

Yours sincerely,

Eleanor Cracknell

Eleanor Cracknell (Miss)

College Archivist

Eton College Library

Eton College

Windsor

Berkshire

How disappointing. She didn't sound excited at all. I began seeing (Miss) Cracknell in my mind's eye as a fiftyish single woman living out her life at the nation's most prestigious prep school surrounded by teenage boys, every one of them in the throes of serious hormonal maelstroms. This was surely a problem when she was first hired, perhaps straight out of a university much more distinguished than Harvard, unless she'd had no interest in fending them off. But she sounded so proper in her email I thought she'd probably resisted all those passionate advances and was now gently aging, as was I, towards her retirement years. She would be fit from daily, bracing walks in her sensible shoes through the fields and woods around Eton.

I even imagined her hair, which, like mine, would be undyed, but not my short mass of mostly white. Hers would be long, and still partly chestnut brown, pulled back in a simple but attractive bun. She would have wire-rimmed spectacles and have attended Oxford or Cambridge. She would speak Latin and possibly a little Greek, and she certainly wouldn't have flunked sixth grade history or indeed any other history course since.

Underneath all my imagining, of course, was the conviction that Miss Cracknell, thousands of miles across the Atlantic, had already dismissed me and my project, but in a calmer moment I managed to email her back that I wanted to come, scant materials notwithstanding. She continued to be polite and mildly discouraging.

"Dear Sarah [if I may]" began her next email, and it ended with a reiteration of the paucity of her resources: "I should say though, that there will be very little to add to the information which you have seen online. There are very few records from that period . . ."

Pleased that she was answering my emails with less lag time, I began asking her questions. What did it mean, in the records I'd found on the internet, when it said Edward Dixwell was "commensal at the third table"?

She wrote back, "His description as being 'commensal' means that he was not a scholar; commensals received free education but had to pay for their board." I was still confused. Why weren't all the students "scholars"? I would have to admit to Eleanor Cracknell, when I met her, that this was Greek to me.

I looked again at my watch. Fifteen minutes to go. I began reviewing pages I'd printed out from the school's website. Happily, just reading again what it said about life at Eton during Edward's times took my mind off of Eleanor and into the grim reality of life at a British boarding school in the 1500s.

"The earliest records of school life date from the 16th century and paint a picture of a regimented and Spartan life. Scholars were awakened at 5 a.m., chanted prayers whilst they dressed, and were at work in Lower School by 6 a.m. All teaching was in Latin and lessons were supervised by 'praepostors,' senior boys appointed by the headmaster."[2] Poor little Edward, I thought just as the conductor's voice called out, "Windsor-Eton." Like it or not, I had arrived.

I stuffed the papers into a folder and stuffed that into my backpack, pushing my hand down to the bottom to wrap my fingers around the key. Its solidity was curiously reassuring and grounding.

I had imagined the train would let me out at the foot of the campus, but I was on the wrong side of the river. Here, instead, was Windsor Castle, gray and forbidding. Maybe Queen Elizabeth was inside, but I'd lost all desire to be invited to tea. How strange to spend much of one's life in castles, behind thick walls. I straightened my shoulders, suddenly glad to be American. I was no tourist; I was a direct descendant of John Dixwell with a key to Dover Castle in my backpack. Good for him for taking a stand against the tyrannical Charles I.

Fortified by thoughts of my lineage, I asked a bystander how to get to Eton College and was directed to walk across the Thames. The bridge was gently arched and beautiful. I stopped to admire the wide river, complete with ducks and swans, and thought of Charles in his happier, early years being carried in various boats and barges on the Thames from London to Windsor and back.

Once across the bridge I entered the town of Eton. Some of the buildings lining its little streets were half-timbered and looked medieval. They were lovely, but what really caught my attention was the back of a young man in unusually formal attire, half a block ahead of me. Was it someone who had just been at a wedding or was this an Eton student in his school uniform? It had to be a student. If I weren't already convinced, a glance in the shop window beside me gave me the answer. "School Uniforms," read the sign. A headless manikin sported a black tailcoat, gray trousers with a narrow lighter gray stripe, a black vest, and a white shirt with a stiff detachable collar. Crowning the whole affair was a white butterfly of a bowtie.

I shook my head involuntarily, as if to dislodge this new and astonishing image of imperialism. Eton, training the future leaders of nations, is clothing them in such a way as to set them apart from the hoi polloi the moment they arrive. Two more boys in the elaborate getup were coming down the sidewalk. One looked South Asian, the other African, and both were so handsome it was practically blinding to behold them. Something about their beauty made my fear return. What was I doing in this rarefied atmosphere? I quickened my pace.

Getting inside Eton involved being cleared by security. I had to go into an office at the entrance, show my passport, then be photographed and issued a day visitor badge, which I clipped to my jacket. It had Eton's coat of arms on the upper left, and me, looking frozen, on the lower right. It listed my host as Eleanor Cracknell.

To my surprise, once I'd been issued my pass, the porter told me how to find the archives and then let me go off alone. As I headed numbly across a deserted courtyard, I forgot the handsome penguins and I seemed to be going backwards in time. Edward was here in 1588, I thought, awed by how ancient everything looked, and nothing has changed. Everything was made of brick or smooth, light gray stone. Was this the architecture he had seen? Was I walking where he had walked? I hesitated in front of the entrance to Eleanor's lair, the Archives. A thick wooden door with a rounded top was framed by a stone arch. To one side was a narrow, leaded glass window. Looking around to see if anyone was watching me, I pulled out my camera and pressed the shutter. Hurriedly, I hid the camera inside my backpack.

I inhaled slowly through my nose and tapped on the door, which was barely taller than I. Silence. Footsteps. I stepped back, clutching my backpack. Out came, stooping to get under the low doorframe, a woman no more than twenty-five. I blinked.

It couldn't be. "Hello," she said. "You must be Dixie Brown. I'm Eleanor Cracknell." She held out her hand. I took it.

What? She was younger than my children. She had a sweet smile. She was wearing an engagement ring. She wasn't in the least snobbish. If anything, she was friendly and apologetic as she told me that she had only been at Eton for six months, but she would answer my questions as best she could. "Come in," she said, ducking back through the tiny doorway, as if it were entirely ordinary to work in a place dating from the fifteenth century. I followed.

We went into a room with a table as she began telling me what evidence she had of Edward Dixwell. "Prior to 1792, they didn't keep lists of students. So we're lucky. The reason we have a record of Edward is that he was a 'commensal.'"

It was easy to confess to this entirely friendly young woman that I still didn't understand the term. She wanted to help. There were three categories of students back then, she explained. First were the King's Scholars. Seventy were elected to receive full scholarships after an examination by faculty from King's College, Cambridge. This still happens today. In Edward's time, said Eleanor, in order to be eligible you needed to be legitimate, "whole in body" and "poor and indigent." Poor and indigent! What about that huge Dixwell manor in Churchover, I wanted to protest. But I knew Edward, as a second son, qualified just fine.

The second category was that of the "oppidans" ("Oppidum" is the Latin word for "town"). Oppidans were students who paid for their education and lived in the town. The third was the "commensals" (from the Latin for "eating at the same table"). "They received free education but paid for their lodging in the town and were charged for meals at the school. Thus, commensals are listed in the audit books that survive." She left the room and came back with an outsized audit book from the sixteenth century. My jaw dropped.

"Can I take a picture of Edward's entry?" I asked, eyes wide.

Yes, she said calmly, and laid the book in a sort of cradle. We can be pretty sure, she added, that Edward became a King's Scholar after his first year at Eton, because his name is only listed as a commensal for 1588. After that, as a King's Scholar, he would have had no bills to pay.

She leafed through the book to the bill pictured below.

There was Edward's surname, "Dickswell." Much of the rest was indecipherable, but Eleanor could read not only the Latin, but what to me were impossibly illegible Roman numerals. Edward had paid fifteen shillings and two pence for six and a half weeks of meals at the third table in "College Hall," which is still used today by King's Scholars and was built between 1443 and 1450. If it wasn't occupied when we finished, Eleanor would take me there. She turned to a later entry that noted Edward had paid thirty shillings and four pence for another thirteen weeks of board. Then she showed me pages detailing how much meat and beer had been purchased, how much staff and provost were paid, how much rent the

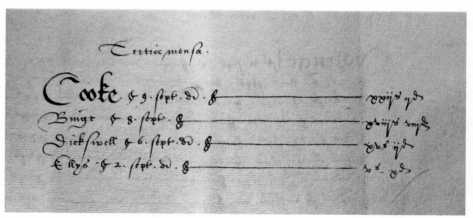

Edward Dixwell's Eton College bill from 1588.

school took in from each property it owned, and the cost of repairs to the buildings.

She deduced, from a more modern, published book that stated when Edward arrived at Oxford University, that he probably was a student at Eton for five years, from age thirteen to eighteen. In a 1911 history of Eton, by Sir H.C. Maxwell-Lyte, she showed me a black and white etching of "Long Chamber," the dormitory in which all seventy King's Scholars, and perhaps forebears of Sir Maxwell-Lyte, had slept, sometimes three to a bed, from 1443–1846.[3] It looked drab and depressing. Boxy wooden beds, each with a sort of lip, presumably to keep young sleepers from rolling out, ran the length of a vast, high-ceilinged room that had, down each side, deeply recessed Tudor windows with interior wooden shutters. The beds on the left were slightly larger and more elaborate than those on the right. Were they for the older boys? Here and there, but not that often, small cupboards were attached to the walls. It looked as if you had to share your cupboard with several other boys. Perhaps those scholarship boys had the minimum of clothes. Two fireplaces, each on the side with the smaller, simpler beds, must have had to heat the whole barnlike room.

Eleanor had located for me, in Eton's museum on the curriculum, a description of life at Eton in Edward's time that was more detailed than what I'd found online. It said the boys had two vacations a year, each lasting three weeks, but they were only allowed to go home for the summer one. So Edward, at thirteen, was already essentially out of the nest, and nothing in his new life was easy. Nevertheless, it would equip him to be self-supporting. The curriculum was minimal. Everything was taught in Latin, the language of the Church, the law, and business. No other subject was taught. In short, the boys were required to write Latin verses and memorize them. This was what an Eton education meant, in the sixteenth century.

I was intrigued to learn that not until the eighteenth century were subjects like modern languages, music, art, dancing, fencing, and arithmetic available, and even then, they were to be studied as extras in the boys' free time. Mathematics did not become part of the regular curriculum until 1851.

All in all, it looked as if, in Edward's day, students needed only to master understanding, speaking, reading, and writing Latin. Not much else would be taught or was needed to go on to a university or get a job as a secretary or any other position requiring literacy. Still, there was moral instruction. Edward learned to be disciplined and self-denying. "Boys were marched in double file to College Hall for the two meals supplied each day," Eleanor told me, adding that there was no food at all on Fridays, a day of fasting.

Though Edward had to go hungry every Friday, College Hall was and is a feast for the eyes. Eleanor showed me a picture of it from over a century ago, and it was dazzling even in black and white. Then she looked at her watch and said there was time to walk down to see, before anyone arrived for lunch, what College Hall looks like now.

College Hall.

When she pushed open the double doors in the tall doorway, I was so astonished by the grandeur I almost started to laugh. Teenage boys eat here, surrounded by gold leaf and famous oil portraits? I fought for a respectful facial expression as we entered the room and she explained that only the seventy King's scholars eat here. The rest of the 1400 boys currently enrolled at Eton eat elsewhere. Eleanor said that "Fellows" (who are adults) sit down at the far end on upholstered blue chairs, and are given nicer silverware and better food than their young charges. The students sit on long benches at the tables on the sides. She told me to turn around and look up at numerous coats of arms above the entrance we'd just used. Below them stood a curious little desk where a boy sits and records, in Latin, how much bread, as a total, is eaten daily. Boys have been doing this since the 1440s. I tried not to murmur, "Why stop now?" but it came out anyway. Our eyes met, and Eleanor's twinkled. She didn't say a word, but I suddenly felt solidarity with her. There we were, two women in all this male splendor, amused.

The moment passed. It was time for Eleanor to return to her duties, but she told me to ask the porter, on my way out, to let me into the Lower School, a classroom that, like so many other parts and practices of Eton, dates from the 1440s. I thanked her over and over for her help, and gave her a maple sugar leaf from Hadley, MA. I hope she loved it.

Back in the office where I had been photographed, the porter opened a little door on the wall. Behind it were rows and rows of keys looking very like the one inside my backpack. He selected one, took me to the left across the courtyard, turned the key in an ancient lock, and then graciously left me alone to soak in Edward's classroom.

I was stunned. How could all this still be here? Edward had filed in at 6 a.m. every morning, to be taught in Latin. He must have had to be so perfectly behaved, in this long, serious room with its battered dark wood benches and long slanted writing surfaces. I pictured the boys elbow to elbow, struggling with feather pens, trying not to knock over inkwells. Like the dormitory in the picture Eleanor had shown me, Lower School had recessed windows down both sides of the room, each with a wooden shutter you could close from the inside.

Lower School classroom.

What were Edward's thoughts as he sat in this room? Was he homesick? Did he envy his brother William back in Churchover not having to do all this endless studying because he would inherit the entire family estate? Or did Edward realize how very lucky he was to get an education? I hoped he loved learning Latin, as I had in high school. But did he have any fun at Eton?

Gradually, as I stood gazing and imagining, my eyes took in something that proved he must have. What have schoolboys done since time immemorial with their penknives? Graffiti were carved into every available surface. Gorgeous letters worthy of tombstones adorned practically every square inch of ancient wood. When had they done it? Did they sneak down from their horrid dormitory in the middle of the night?

The columns, the desktops, and even the window shutters were covered with names. Had they come in their nightshirts with stolen stubs of candles to shed flickering light on their work? Here are closeups of a shutter and a desktop:

Classroom shutter, classroom desktop.

It was awe-inspiring.

It was also remarkably silent. In my hour at Eton I had yet to hear or see a single student. Reluctantly, I left the classroom, pulling the door to behind me. The porter and I waved at each other as I left the campus, then I spotted two Etonites right across the street from me, looking as though their next stop would be the House of Lords. There they stood, in their black tails and white bowties, while in the background a mere mortal of a mother pushed her child in a stroller. She wore a baggy sweater and jeans. There's normal life, and then there's Eton.

Back across the river I walked around two sides of Windsor Castle. I'd been interested to learn, in the archives, that it had been captured by Parliamentary forces during the first Civil War. This meant the side John Dixwell chose had managed not only to take Windsor Castle in 1642, but also to defend it from Prince Rupert's bombardment, fired from Eton College's grounds. What would Edward have thought of his son John?

I knew I should visit the castle but I was worn out. I had loved experiencing so much of the Eton Edward had known, but I couldn't wrap my mind around the Eton of today with its young men being groomed to rule. The thought of being inside Queen Elizabeth's hulking home was equally off-putting. I caught a fast train to London, and in no time I was walking past the massive British Museum. More empire. But then something caught my eye.

A diminutive plant with tiny leaves and purple flowers was thriving in a crevice between two blocks of granite supporting the iron fence around the museum. I stopped to admire it, so perfect and ephemeral, a brief and beautiful thing. I wished I knew its name.

"Ivy-leaved toadflax," a voice murmured in my ear. I turned, startled. A small, tidy English woman had stopped beside me. She said it again, enunciating each syllable, "Ivy-leaved toadflax." Then, without another word, she headed on down the street.

16

On to Oxford University

TO GO FORWARD in the chronology of Edward Dixwell's education, I need to rewind a few days of my time in England. When I visited Oxford University, where he earned both his bachelor's and his master's degrees, for my appointment with archivist Julian Reid, Mijung came too. It was actually the only day trip we took together, and it was lucky she could come because I woke up feeling awful. I had caught a brand new British cold. I needed her calm and sensible self beside me to guide me. She had been amazing, right away, at figuring out the best buses, most efficient trains, and most delicious Korean restaurants. I knew she would get my stuffed-up self safely to Oxford with time to spare.

But back in Amherst trying to write about it, I discovered that not only could I not remember Oxford clearly at all, perhaps due to having been so congested, but my notes from that excursion are, as Eleanor Cracknell would put it, very patchy.

I couldn't recollect whole chunks of the day. Were we required to go through security? What had the library looked like? I wasn't sure. After all that time, effort, and money! I had to take a day off from writing.

The next morning, feeling better, I realized I could ask Mijung for help. I was missing her company, as we weren't planning to resume our studies together until the fall. She was too busy with all three of her sons plus her husband home for the entire summer. I'd been too obsessed with writing up England.

I texted her. "Good morning!" I typed, then: "Do you remember our day in Oxford?"

Scarcely a minute went by before a gold mine began appearing on my phone's screen. Mijung is always critical of her English, but I have loved her way of expressing herself since the moment I met her in my ESL class many years ago. Here's what she texted me:

"I remember the day like a movie or picture. Which scenes do you want to remember?" My heart leapt up. Then:

"That day morning, we took a train. The weather was gloomy." Then:

"We saw the outside through the window. There was lambs on the moor and so English style houses."

Oh my God. How fabulous. Would she be able to come over so I could take notes on all her observations? She would. Within the hour, she arrived.

We sat at my kitchen table not only reconstructing our day in Oxford, but talking about our trip, about England, about colonialism, about what it had been like for Korea after Japan took over in 1910 and did terrible things, as foreign invaders and colonizers always have.

Mijung perfectly remembered our Oxford day. She told me we had caught the number 7 bus in front of the Penn Club and gone to Paddington Station for our train to Oxford. And on the train, she said, people had looked "white collar and well educated."

Since I had noticed none of this I asked her how she knew they were white collar. Well, "the men had on tweed jackets and khaki pants. They were semi-formal," she said. I felt sure she was right.

We had walked from the station to Oxford's Merton College, crossing a narrow stream, which was, she said, the Thames. I didn't believe her, thinking of the huge river behind the houses of Parliament or the wide expanse of water between Eton and Windsor Castle. I ran upstairs to get the little map of Oxford I'd bought that day, and we spread it out on the kitchen table.

The Thames. I beamed at Mijung. What else had she noticed that had flown right by me? A lot.

We looked at the photos we had taken as she helped me reconstruct the day. We had bought sandwiches at a tiny restaurant and eaten in the more-or-less basement where the tables were. As she said it, I remembered that her sandwich was more delicious than mine.

Because Oxford University has thirty-eight colleges, it had taken some map-studying to find Merton. When we arrived, we didn't go in the college gate at first, but explored, marveling at the juxtaposition of old and new. All the buildings were made of a light-colored stone, a glowing brownish yellow, which contrasted beautifully with ancient timbers and dark shingled roofs. The grass was a vivid spring green, and every leaf seemed newly unfurled and perfect.

To get into Merton College, Mijung remembered, we went into the porter's office beside the entrance and I had to show a picture I.D. Then we waited for Julian Reid to come and escort us to the library. I asked her to remind me what he looked like, and as she did, I could picture him again. "He looked young. He was a little tiny chubby," she said. "He had a round face." She went on to describe his jacket, his pants, his leather shoes. He wasn't wearing a tie.

But best of all, Mijung had seen, in Julian's face, something which I had missed. "So nice, so gentle," she said. "His eyes looked like a little scared—like he doesn't know well about something. He really wanted to help you but didn't know how. His eyes were puzzled. He was shy."

Mijung's observations were a gift. They helped me see that it might have been every bit as challenging for archivists to meet with me as it was for me to meet with them.

She went on. We had crossed a courtyard, following Julian Reid, who pulled out a key and unlocked the library door. The place was very old and very small and, she said, our footsteps made a clicking sound on the wood floor. But the building, despite being ancient, had new window frames and many computers.

We passed students studying and walked into an even smaller room where two students left as soon as we arrived, then Julian put on gloves and brought an old book over to a foam cradle on a table and turned the pages to the Edward Dixwell entry. At that point, Mijung went back to the regular part of the library, to allow me to be alone with Julian while he showed me what he had and answered my questions.

Mijung had sat there thinking about how everything in Oxford looked so old, but once inside the library she had found it alive with students from all over the world. Since so many of Korea's beautiful old buildings were lost to war, she was especially struck by the way, all over England, she saw very old structures not only preserved, but made to work well in modern times.

After Mijung went home that day I kept thinking of how much richer my trip to England keeps becoming, because of her. Her habits of thought, her ways of being, widen my perspective. Refreshed, I went back to writing.

Julian Reid, to be fair, did not fit my stereotype of the English being slow to answer emails. Not only was he prompt in his first response to my questions back in April, but he also took the time to answer them in detail. I had asked about Edward's seven years at Oxford, curious to know what he had studied and if his master's degree, since he'd gone on to be a vicar, was in theology. The answer, surprisingly, was no:

Odd though it may sound, the study of theology did not play a very large part in the official studies of Masters students in the seventeenth-century. The seventeenth-century curriculum still followed quite closely the medieval practice of a broad education in the 'Liberal Arts', although those arts also included some science; technically the Master's degree included philosophy, mathematics, astronomy and the theory of music, although some subjects may have been covered more than others. The formal study of theology was reserved for students who went on to specialised degrees in theology, such as the Bachelor of Divinity and the Doctor of Divinity. However, students were required to attend chapel daily where they would have heard scripture read and doctrine taught through sermons so there was a strong religious environment in the colleges.

My task with Julian, as with everyone in England whom I asked for help, was to put Edward and then John in their historical contexts, and to set aside my twenty-first century American one. Julian had politely prefaced his paragraph about Edward's education with "Odd though it may sound." Absolutely.

The night before we went to Oxford, Mijung and I had the good fortune to eat our microwaved dinners in the Penn Club at the same time as a friendly Brit and Scot. They immediately got interested in my project. The Brit, John Corden, had not only graduated from Oxford University but was, like John Dixwell, the son of a vicar. Was it possible, I asked him, that Oxford's Merton College had appointed Edward to a far-distant vicarage in Ponteland? Of course, he replied at once. What seemed "odd" to me was natural to John Corden. "The Oxford colleges," he said, "along with wealthy individuals, became patrons of Church of England parishes, which gave them the right to appoint the vicar."

He was eating an enviable salad he'd bought at a supermarket called Sainsbury's. When he had told us about the place earlier that evening, we had dashed over, but the salads were all gone. Now, we wrapped spoonfuls of Mijung's Korean rice in crisp squares of green seaweed.

John chewed a tomato slice meditatively. "Your ancestor may have had to pull a lot of strings to get to go to Ponteland."

I felt a little defensive. Edward, pull strings? That seemed out of character. Besides, I'd already decided Ponteland was a depressing spot. "It's so far north," I said. "Perhaps it was a place he wouldn't have wanted to go. Wasn't it pretty isolated?"

"Not at all," he said, "and Merton may still, nominally, be a patron of Ponteland. It's not such a backwater. It's a fashionable suburb of Newcastle now."

Roger Hailwood had said the same thing. Why was I so set on dismissing Ponteland? I suppose because it was the place where I might soon find sad evidence that Edward had died and had left little John fatherless at the age of three.

I can't remember what the Scot, who introduced himself as Colin, was eating for supper, but both he and the Englishman made much of the fact that Merton was and remains one of Oxford's wealthiest colleges. Then Colin told us there was plenty of money as well in the vicarage Edward was sent to, just below the Scottish border. He said that Northumberland (the county which comprises Ponteland and Newcastle) is in many ways unchanged from Edward Dixwell's time. "Northumberland is a very feudal place," he said. "Dukes and earls still own a lot of land."

Mijung's and my eyes widened. Mijung, as a history major, knows a lot about feudalism, but I predicted she wouldn't say a word. She didn't trust her English skills enough to do anything but listen. So I said, "Feudal? Are you kidding?"

He was not. He said it's still possible to find "tenant farmers vying to tell stories of how kind their earl is." What?

At Oxford, Julian Reid essentially said the same thing. In Edward Dixwell's day, Merton functioned like the modern earls and dukes Colin had described. The college leased "its landholdings out to local tenant farmers," and if the land generated more income "than the vicar needed, Merton took the balance."

I wondered if Merton and the various vicars of Ponteland had always agreed on how much "the vicar needed." What if Edward had had a hard time? In his first email to me, Julian had mentioned original notations of Edward's doings that were in Merton's archives. In a college register dating from the late fifteenth century he had found:

> a couple of entries for July and August 1611 recording that the college issued "Letters Testimonial" as to his moral integrity, and it may be that Edward Dixwell was seeking appointment to another church and needed a letter of recommendation; that is just a suggestion. The register does not, however, record either Dixwell's death or the appointment of his immediate successor; the next reference to Ponteland does not occur until 1655 when a Master Hurst was appointed to succeed Dr Thomas Gray. Gray's earlier appointment is not recorded.

Back in April, I had emailed Julian asking if Edward were in trouble or simply asking for a letter of recommendation. Julian, in his careful, gentle way, said it was the latter:

> I realise now that my reference to the Letters Testimonial as to Edward Dixwell's 'moral integrity' may not have given quite the right impression. Letters Testimonial were, as you suggest, issued routinely for candidates for ordination; ministers seeking appointment to a new church; schoolmasters, and a number of other occupations. The phrase used in the College Register is "pro morum integritate', but "character reference" might be a better translation.

The day Mijung and I met Julian, an ancient register was the first thing he laid in the foam cradle and opened with gloved hands. In Latin, it says that Edward was seeking a letter testifying to his moral integrity. As I gazed at the beautiful penmanship of some unknown Mertonian in 1611, I thought about Edward's situation in Ponteland. The babies were coming so thick and fast, maybe he asked for a "pro morum integritate" because he needed a parish that would pay him more.

In 1610 (a year before his request to Oxford) Edward Dixwell, his wife Mary, and several other people in Ponteland were fined twenty shillings each for watering their hemp (which was used to make rope) after the third of September "in a river called the Ponte in which beasts were wont to drink, and they are to forfeit 20s to the king."[1] Had Edward been struggling financially? Did the fine intensify that struggle and had Merton refused to increase his income? In the next five years he and Mary would have three more children and then, if what Julian had written me in his first email was true, Edward died:

"I have found one online source that records that Edward Dixwell was buried 10 January 1616/17, but I have no evidence here for that, and I think you would need to check the Ponteland register of burials."

Though he doesn't know it, I have Julian to thank for my realizing I did want to check—in person, if possible. The day his email arrived, I contacted the Woodhorn Museum and Northumberland Archives, which has Ponteland's parish records, and set up a meeting with an archivist. I would go to the far north of England on Friday and I was already praying that my cold would get better, and fast, before then. It was such a long journey to and fro that Mijung had opted not to come. I didn't want to go alone, but I felt compelled. I had to see for myself proof that Edward really was the vicar of Ponteland's church, and proof of John's birth and the births of his five siblings. If the documentation was there, it made John's life such a study in contrasts. When he fled England he was a man who'd been responsible for so much: an estate with thousands of acres of land, a huge mansion, his brother's widow and her five children, and Dover Castle, not to mention the judgment to put a king to death. Yet he had begun life as the son of a man who owned nothing but his appointment as a vicar. I wanted to set foot in the place John was born. And in those archives I wanted to see the entry, if it was there, of Edward's death.

It was helpful to have visited Oxford University before I headed north to Ponteland, so I could think about the differences between them. I loved Oxford. I suppose I am biased by my own happy college years, but I imagine Edward had a wonderful time in that rich intellectual atmosphere and those beautiful buildings full of books. During my hour in the archives, Julian Reid showed me another book, *Registrum Annalium Collegii Mertonensis* (the register of Merton College), with an entry confirming that after his three years at Merton, Edward had spent four more getting a master's degree at St. Alban Hall. There were other Dixwells on the same page, including the Basil Dixwell (John's great nephew) who welcomed John's son, the silversmith from Boston, when he visited in 1710. His address was Broome Park, where I planned to spend two nights the following week in the big house that is now a golf resort and timeshare. The entry noted that Basil, too, served as governor of Dover Castle and was a member of the House of Commons.

Julian explained that Edward would have spent three years at Merton, then four at St. Alban, which would have been, he said, "the equivalent of an apprenticeship in a trade. Seven years were needed." It sounded luxurious, getting to study for such a long time, and in such an intimate setting. Merton, at the time Edward attended, was smaller than Eton. It had twenty or thirty fellows and ten or twenty undergraduates. St. Alban was probably even smaller.

Sitting in Merton's library made me wonder if becoming the vicar in Ponteland wasn't a shock for Edward. He'd had twelve years, if you include Eton, of rigorous schooling, and many good friendships and late-night discussions. Everyone, teachers as well as students, was male. Then he wound up in the far north of England with a brand-new wife, endless responsibilities as a church leader, and a new baby every two years. I concede I am bringing a modern sensibility to thinking about Edward, but mightn't it have been a difficult adjustment?

When I was an undergraduate, I loved not only my studies and my own late-night discussions, but also the delightful fact that living in a dorm meant I didn't have to cook or shop or scrub the bathroom. I could

Edward Dixwell's dormitory, Merton College, Oxford.

spend my days reveling in the life of the mind. In this respect, Edward's time at Oxford was similar. His job up north was in sharp contrast to his life as a student and may have been a financial struggle. Another book I saw in England, a slim 1920 volume entitled *Vicars of Ponteland,* by Mr. H. M. Wood, explained that Merton got more of the money from its parishes than the vicars did: "In the early days the great tithes on corn went to Merton as rector, while the vicar was able to claim the small tithes which included flax, hay, hemp, geese, ducks, pullets, etc., the tithes on mills and fisheries, Easter offerings and the grass of the churchyard."[2] Was there enough to feed and clothe Edward's family adequately?

Finally, Julian showed us the building where Edward had lived while he was at Merton. It was well over four hundred years old, and he assured us it looked just as it had in Edward's day. "They lived here, two or three to a room, more comfortably, often, than they had at home," he said, calling our attention to the double windows of the living area and the single windows of the attached studies.

Julian had to go back to the archives, but said we could explore as long as we liked. After thanking him I stood quietly, taking in Edward's ancient dorm, glad that Edward, despite his early death, had gotten to live and study behind those handsome walls. For that part of his life, I hoped it had been more fun to gossip in Latin late into the night with his roommates, than to be firstborn William chained to the ancestral manor in Churchover.

17

Birth and Death

IT WAS TIME TO GO NORTH. The high-speed train from London to New-castle upon Tyne takes three hours. It's such a long trip it didn't make sense to do it in a day, so even though Mijung and I hated being parted for thirty-six hours, we agreed it had to be. The night before, we had met one of Mijung's fondest desires by seeing the musical *Mama Mia!* The show was nearly sold out and the audience, which Mijung told me was largely Korean and Japanese tourists, was wild with enthusiasm. While I was gone, Mijung thought she might take a Korean bus tour to Stone-henge or visit a British mall quite far from the city. She was, as usual, calmly keeping her options open.

On the train, I noticed my cold was considerably better, and I was used to the time change. I sat next to a man who liked to talk. He was going much farther than I, for he was on his way to the spiritual community of Findhorn in the north of Scotland. He had been there several times and now, in early middle age, was considering moving there altogether.

He spoke with an upper-class British accent he said he had picked up from an ex-girlfriend, the daughter of a peer. He had spent a lot of time in the region I was visiting, during their long relationship. They had not married, and were no longer a couple, but had children together. Mijung and I had had trouble believing the Scotsman Colin when he said the place was still feudal, but here was direct evidence to prove his point. My seatmate's girlfriend's family sounded wealthy beyond imagining. I wondered if they were dukes or earls as he described their thousands of acres in Northumberland, their hunting preserves and tenant farmers. He had gone on hunts. In essence, her family was living the way John Dixwell must have lived at Broome Park, a lifestyle exponentially wealthier than anything John would have known if his father hadn't died. Had Edward lived, John would have been an impecunious third son of a vicar and might not have become a regicide. How strange life is.

I told my seatmate a little about my project. Part of my mission in visiting Ponteland, I said, was to confirm that John Dixwell really had lost his father when he was very small. I wondered how such a loss had affected him. We agreed it must have been traumatic. He was quiet for a while, then said his own father had died recently, in India, where he had returned toward the end of his life after decades in England. As the oldest son, my companion had gone at once to India to prepare the body, buy special presents for his relatives, light the funeral pyre, and spend a month engaged in the traditional mourning activities of his Hindu heritage.

He was grateful for the prescribed cultural container that held them as they grieved. Washing his father's body had felt holy. Hearing him say this made me remember the day my father died in the retirement community where he lived. I had visited him the day before, but it didn't surprise me that he died without any of his children with him. He was a private person. The sole witness to his death was a young woman named Sylvia, a home health aide. When Sylvia called to tell me, she was in tears. All morning, when she looked out his third-floor window, a female house finch was sitting on the edge of the nearby roof. One of my parents' friends who stopped by said, "It's Sarah. She's waiting for him."

Sylvia kept noticing the bird, as Dad's breathing got shallower. Finally, he took three deep breaths, and he was gone. Just then, a male finch came flying toward the waiting bird, whereupon she flew up to join him and they went off together.

When I got there, my siblings had not yet arrived so I sat alone with

Dad for a while. He lay there, tucked into his bed, his big, competent surgeon hands folded on his middle. He looked beautiful, not ravaged by
cancer. I kept imagining I saw him breathing. His hands were still warm.

Edward Dixwell must have died at home. I hope he went quickly. I
wonder how aware his six children were of his dying process. I picture
him being laid out in their house. Would Mary have lifted up each child
too short to reach, to kiss the father in his coffin?

My seatmate got off before we reached Newcastle. As I came out of the
station into the busy city, I was struck by how cold it was. It was much
colder than London, up beside the North Sea, and people's accents were
so distinctive I had trouble understanding what was being said when I
asked for directions.

I dragged my suitcase around construction projects and over cobble-
stoned roads to the Premier Inn. Newcastle felt industrial, pragmatic and
working class. People I passed seemed both tough and kind. A woman
sitting on the edge of a massive war memorial asked if I was lost. I nodded, whereupon she ground out her cigarette and walked with me to
make sure I found my hotel.

During check-in I had to ask the woman at the desk to repeat everything. It wasn't just her accent, it was her turn of phrase and her vocabulary. There's a name for inhabitants of Newcastle and for their accent, too.
It's "Geordie," and Geordies can trace the roots of their dialect back to the
Anglo Saxon spoken in the fifth century. Edward Dixwell may have felt
like a foreigner when he arrived to start his first and only job.

I put my suitcase in my room and raced to Newcastle University's
Robinson Library, where I stashed my backpack (the key was inside) in a
locker and worked with a pencil as I studied books from their archives. I
asked the librarian, Ruth Sheret, to help me understand, in a list she had
found of the vicars of Ponteland, why, after Edward's name, it said "p.m.
Hancock." She couldn't find the answer before closing time, but before I
went to bed that night she emailed her findings. I love librarians.

The "p.m." was a Merton College thing. It stands for "postmaster," but
has nothing to do with the mail (an aside: one of the good things King
Charles did, fourteen years before he lost his head, was to open the first

general post office in London). Ruth thought "postmaster" might be a title for a Merton College scholar. I later learned from Julian Reid that Merton is the only Oxford college that calls the money granted to students postmasterships instead of scholarships.

Ruth Sheret's email had more tips for interpreting the list of vicars we'd consulted, "p.m. doesn't seem to be linked to the new vicar, but seems to be linked to the surname which always comes immediately afterwards. I don't know if you noticed but the p.m. name is always the name of the retiring vicar."

Sure enough, the vicar preceding Edward Dixwell in Ponteland was a man named Richard Hancock. Ruth then wrote something poignant: "Your ancestor doesn't go on to confirm the new vicar in this way, assumedly because he died unexpectedly? So wasn't able to be present at the ceremony for the new vicar and be named as the person conferring the title."

As I read Ruth's words, scenes flashed in my mind's eye—Edward in his coffin, Mary and her six children weeping as he was lowered into the grave in the churchyard, the man on the train washing his father's body, me touching Dad's still-warm hand.

The next morning, in a somber mood, I took a cab to the Woodhorn Archives in Ashington, which has the original parish records of the Ponteland church where Edward Dixwell was vicar. It was pouring rain and the driver could not find the place. He kept calling his dispatcher for help. When we arrived, we weren't sure we had, for it looked deserted, being an abandoned coal mining operation on a flat landscape seemingly in the middle of nowhere.

Woodhorn Archives.

To my relief, there were people inside, and I was directed up long ramps and around corners to the archives, where patrons were hunched in front of screens studying microfilms or poring over books at long tables. I had made an arrangement to pay fifty-two pounds for two hours of help from a "mentor."

Mine was named June. After I put everything but my notebook in a locker and was given the obligatory pencil (no cameras, alas) June showed me the restored *Ponteland Register 1602–1729*, which has the parish records kept by various vicars as the decades went by. Some clever person had attached each fragile page to new, flexible material. The originals had so crumbled around the edges that they had a lacy look where they joined the sturdy new pages.

I wasn't allowed to touch the register, but June, turning the pages with gloved hands, showed me the births of each of Edward's six children, starting in 1605. In between were births and deaths of other parishioners, and June said the beautiful handwriting was likely Edward's. She especially wanted me to notice the content in the entries for his children. Other birth entries listed the child's name but not the father's profession or home address. Here is what Edward, proud papa, wrote for his firstborn: "Jacobus Dyxwell filius primus Edwardi Dixwell de Ponteland natus [some illegible words] die 13 January 1605 baptizat 23 Jan ejus anno."

Commas would help, but the gist is this: James Dixwell, first son of Edward Dixwell, of Ponteland, was born on the thirteenth of January 1605 and baptized on January 23 of that year.

For their next child, Anna, born in 1607, Edward put in even more information, as if buoyant at her safe arrival. The remnants of my high school Latin helped me translate her entry: Anna Dixwell, daughter of Edward Dixwell, minister of the church of Ponteland, born May 14 between the third and fourth hour and baptized—the rest is illegible.

Marcus, the brother who went with John to Uncle Basil hundreds of miles south, came along in February of 1608, but because of the seventeenth century dating system, it was actually 1609. The Dixwell babies were arriving at two-year intervals. Next came Abigail, likely named for her grandmother in Churchover, and then, as June's gloved finger moved down the page, we came to my seven greats grandfather: "Johannes Dix-well filius tertius Edwardi Dixwell pastoris ecclesia de Ponteland natus 21 Marti et baptizat 6 April."

There it was, concrete evidence that he'd reinvented not only his name but also his age. John was born in 1613, Dixwell baby number five. He wasn't born in 1607, despite his 1689 tombstone in New Haven, Connecticut stating that he died "in the 82nd year of his age." He was seventy-six when his life came to a close. I gazed at the entry. Remarkably, every word Edward wrote was legible. Not one letter of the birth entry of the Dixwell who would be expunged from the family tree was missing. Who could have known, in March of 1613, that this baby was a future regicide and fugitive from justice? How improbable that I, his seven greats grandchild, had stashed his key to Dover Castle in the bank of lockers around the corner and now marveled at his father's notation of his arrival.

June glanced at my penciled notes and noticed I had forgotten, for several Dixwells, to include the year. I shook my head at my omissions. We went back and found the dates. Then June went carefully down the succeeding entries until she arrived at the final Dixwell baby, "Carolus filius quartus," Edward and Mary's fourth son, probably named for grandfather Charles, born in 1615 on March 20, one day before his big brother John turned two.

The next Dixwell entry was a year later, and in a different penmanship: "Edward Dixwell vicarius pochia de Ponteland sepulte Jan. 10." Sepulte. Buried. June and I looked at each other. How terrible. The children were so young. James, the eldest, turned eleven three days after his father's death. Charles was less than a year, and John just a few months shy of his third birthday. Would he have had memories of his father or was he too little to remember? Sepulte.

June sifted through the next few pages. She wanted to check every year up to 1621 to see if any Dixwells had died. There wasn't a single Dixwell entry. This, she said, told us something important. The Dixwells probably left Ponteland. In the wake of her disastrous loss, Mary must have packed up her household and her six children and headed for Churchover and her mother-in-law Abigail Dixwell's big house. How else would

John and Mark have ended up in Kent, living off the giant inheritance of Abigail's brother, their great uncle John Herdson? Also there was Abigail's son Basil, who got all that money after John Herdson died. How fickle fate is. The middle two of Mary Dixwell's four sons tapped into enormous wealth in County Kent because Edward died prematurely in the wild and chilly north of England.

My two hours with June were up, but she had gotten so interested herself she gave me extra time. We looked at the criminal records from 1594 to 1630 that had the indictments of Edward and Mary for watering their hemp. June explained it was dangerous for cattle to drink water after hemp was washed in it, as it could be contaminated. She called my attention to an outsized, 1926 volume called *A History of Northumberland* she'd found for me, and went off to have her lunch. I was in a hurry because I'd arranged a ride to Edward's church in Ponteland in less than an hour. I scrambled to take notes: "The position of the vicar of Ponteland in the first half of the 17th century must have been difficult, as among the principal landowners in the parish, the Erringtons of Ponteland were Roman Catholics, while the Ogles of Kirkley and the Horsleys of Milbourne Grange were ardent dissenters."[1]

The names are fabulous, but I soon learned how easily a vicar could be hurt not only by rich landowners who didn't like his ways, but also by a single parishioner. Thomas Gray, who was installed in Ponteland a decade after Edward Dixwell died, was accused by a woman of being a "base rascal, base roague, base bastardly roague."[2] What had he done? It didn't say, but his punishment was severe:

> He was sent for as a delinquent by the Serjeant at Arms . . . He lost his place and he was plundered of all his moveables, money, linen, household furniture and corn; of which he had a vast stock, having farmed the whole corn tithe of the parish; in all, to the value of £1,500. He had seven children at home, no beds were left him for their use. The charity of kind neighbours supplied the loan of substitutes which, that they might not be taken away, were brought in every night and carried out every morning. The soldiers first took away all the children's shirts which were not actu-

ally on their backs; but they came a second time and stript them of these that were left. Of these last however, a captain in pity for their nakedness, compelled the restoration. Gray himself was carried to Newcastle, where he met with very harsh usage; and during his constraint was with difficulty allowed a visit from his wife. At last he was rescued by a Right Honourable person of his own name, who maintained him at one of his own seats till his death.[3]

What a nightmare. I looked at my watch—only twenty more minutes. I hurried through the history book, looking for more tidbits about the place where John Dixwell was born. I learned that Ponteland, then as now, was wet. "The low-lying land of each side of the Pont [the river] is liable to floods after heavy rain, and until the beginning of the 19th century, much of it was undrained marsh. The slightly rising ground on which Ponteland Church and the oldest buildings of the village stand was called Pont Island."[4]

My time was up. Blearily, I found my way back down various ramps to the parking lot. It was still raining, fitfully. My driver pointed out the gray and forbidding North Sea as we drove along. "It's cold all year 'round," he said.

The land around Edward's ancient stone church sloped down to the swirling waters of the River Pont. It bristled with tombstones, but none of them dated from Edward Dixwell's time. Still, he must have been buried here. Had any other Dixwell descendants visited his church over the centuries?

Happily, it was unlocked and I went in. On the wall hung a framed list of all the vicars of Ponteland. At the top, in blue calligraphy, it said, "The Church of Ponteland was granted by Walter de Merton in 1274, to Merton College, Oxford, to which it was impropriated and a vicarage ordained therein and to that Society the rectory still belongs with the right to present the Vicars." Below, it listed vicars starting in 1154 and continuing to 2008.

There was Edward Dixwell and his dates of service: 1602-1616. A few vicars later, Thomas Gray's entry described his troubles: "Sequestered and put out of Ponteland vicarage by the Puritans. Suffered great hardships and died in 1661."

As I emerged from the church it began to pour, so we drove through torrential rain to Newcastle, barely arriving in time. I dashed to the train and collapsed in my seat. "I've done it," I wrote in my journal as soaked green fields flashed by. "I've visited the place where John's life began. I've seen the book where his father recorded his birth."

I wanted to tell my father. I wanted to tell my grandmother and her mother Mary Catherine Dixwell Wigglesworth and her father Epes Sargent Dixwell. I wanted everyone who had had the luck to own the key, all the way back to John Dixwell himself, to know that I was here, in England, learning all I could about the man who had been erased from the family tree.

18

Learning the Law at Lincoln's Inn

NOW WE ARRIVE at a fifteen-year gap between documents I was able to track down in England confirming the events of John Dixwell's life. These are the years between the Ponteland Register entry noting Edward's 1616 death, and the handwritten record of John's arrival at Lincoln's Inn in 1631 to study the law. They comprise his childhood from age three to eighteen. I wish I knew more, but I do have pieces of the puzzle, some of them quite traumatic. John and his older brother Mark, having lost their father, were at some point separated from their mother and four siblings as well, and sent to County Kent, 300-plus miles south of Ponteland. Their Uncle Basil, the youngest of Charles and Abigail's four sons, became their guardian. Surely Grandmother Abigail made that happen, for she outlived Charles by forty-four years. When Edward died, Basil was living with her rich bachelor brother, John Herdson, who passed away in the early 1620s. Now Basil inherited his big estate. He too was a bachelor, and needed an heir. Enter his nephews Mark and John. They were lucky there was so much money in their new family unit. Still, what was it like for them, already uprooted from Ponteland, to be transplanted once again, this time to someone who had never had a wife or children? What kind of a person was Basil?

Because he was in the House of Commons, I learned quite a lot about him from a detailed biography in the *History of Parliament*. He lost his father when he was six. "As the youngest of his family he was not afforded an education at university or the inns of court, and on his father's death in 1591 he was granted an annuity of just £6 13s. 4d. However, in June 1620 (at which time he was living in Canterbury), he had the good fortune to be adopted by his maternal uncle as heir to an estate near Folkestone worth 2,500 pounds a year and 30,000 pounds in money."[1]

Oh British understatement. Good fortune? It was a fabulous inheritance, many millions if it were today. Basil made the most of it. Once he was elected to Parliament, in 1626, observers thought him, "in respect of his quotidian new suits of apparel, to be the bravest man in the House of Commons."[2]

And when Charles I made him a baronet, the fee was waived because of family connections. Usually, new baronets had to purchase baronetcies at great expense—a nice income stream for Charles. Soon enough that same kingly connection got Basil out of a serious crime: "As a consequence of a minor traffic accident in Moorgate in 1631, he was involved in a brawl with 'a drunken fellow in his doublet and hose out of an alehouse', whose head he broke with his sword. Unfortunately for Dixwell, the man died under the surgeon's hands, and it was expected that 'it will cost him many thousands of pounds ere he get clear of the business'. However, his fortune was not seriously impaired, as one month later he received a royal pardon."[3]

As if killing someone doesn't matter, which then as now it might not if you're rich, the next sentence of the entry skips to the building of the mansion. "Between 1635 and 1638 Dixwell built Broome Park, Barham, situated midway between Folkestone and Canterbury, at a cost of 8,000 pounds. At around the same time he also had his portrait painted by Van Dyck."[4] Anthony Van Dyck was the best and most sought-after portraitist of his day.

What were John's thoughts when his uncle mortally wounded a man? He was learning the law when it happened, and must have observed his uncle not only emerging unscathed from a manslaughter charge, but also finding more ways to spend money. Basil was, after all, one of the wealthiest men in Kent, and Kent was a wealthy county. When construction began on Broome Park, John was four years into his seven-year stint at Lincoln's Inn, but probably watched it being built when he was home, just as Roger Hailwood had imagined. And perhaps, in his final year, John met the great artist Basil commissioned for a self-portrait worthy to hang in their magnificent new mansion.

I hoped to have time, when I stayed at Broome Park, to visit the museum in Canterbury where the painting hangs. It was recently purchased for a million pounds from an anonymous American. It's ironic that Anthony Van Dyck was the artist who painted Basil Dixwell, because he was Charles I's choice for many royal portraits. Basil, in such good graces with the King that he slipped neatly away from a murder charge, commissioned the king's portraitist. Eleven years later his nephew signed Charles's death warrant.

A month before I left Massachusetts for London, I happened upon a Van Dyck portrait in Boston's Museum of Fine Arts. I winced when I realized the elegant child was Princess Mary, Charles's firstborn, resplendent in pale blue satin. She was painted in 1637, just a year before Basil Dixwell sat for the same great artist.

I gazed at her serious little face. There she hung, even at ten so stiff and queenly, being studied by a direct descendant of one of the men who had condemned her father to death. The caption said she married William Prince of Orange in 1641, when she was fourteen. She had been living across the English Channel in the Low Countries for eight years when Charles was beheaded.

But let's leave the royal family. The year Edward Dixwell died, John was almost three, Mark seven. I now knew they hadn't stayed long in Ponteland. They probably went as soon as possible to Churchover, to Grandmother Dixwell and Uncle William, the firstborn son who had inherited the entire manor. When were Mark and John separated from their mother and siblings and sent, two little preacher's kids, into the moneyed world of their man-about-town Uncle Basil?

I hope they spent a few years after their father's death living in County

Warwick with their mother, cousins, aunts and uncles, and their grandmother, attending the church where so many Dixwells are buried inside
the sanctuary. I know some of Edward's family stayed in Churchover, for
although I found no paper trail for John and Mark's early years, I did discover one for two of their siblings.

In the 1619 Warwickshire Visitation (visitations were periodic inspec-
tions of the temporal and spiritual affairs of the dioceses, regulated by ecclesiastical councils), Edward and Mary Dixwell's firstborn James is listed
as being under the care of his Uncle William and being thirteen years old.
Also, William left money in his will to Charles, the youngest. I presume
he took the two girls, Anna and Abigail, as well. Since Mark and John are
not mentioned in the visitation, it suggests that by 1619 they were already
living in County Kent. In that year John turned six, Mark ten.

Kent was a place where landed gentry families had been tending their
sprawling manors for generations, enjoying their relative freedom from a
centralized government. When rich newcomers from the mercantile class
like John Herdson, then his nephew Basil, arrived and bought big estates,
they were privately viewed as upstarts who didn't appreciate Kent's ancient ways.

It seems possible the two boys sensed their uncle, a newly-rich man
who liked to spend lavishly, was seen as inferior by the established peck-
ing order. I wonder who cared for them while Basil was wearing a new
outfit every day in the House of Commons? Was it like Frances Hodg-
son Burnett's *The Secret Garden*, where orphaned Mary Lenox, coming
all the way from India, arrives at her uncle's Yorkshire manor house only
to find he isn't there to meet her? It's likely Uncle Basil left Mark and John
in the care of servants, as Mary's uncle did. I'd been picturing them in the
sprawling splendor of Broome Park, but Basil didn't start building it until
1635, when John was up in London, halfway through his legal studies at
Lincoln's Inn. The family must have lived in Uncle John Herdson's house
a few miles away. It wasn't as grand, but it was a fine manor house nonetheless. When Broome Park was finished in 1639, Basil lived in it for just
three years. He died in December of 1642, the day after his fifty-seventh
birthday. John was only twenty-nine.

Basil's wealth stayed in the family, the Dixwells having provided him a nephew to inherit his giant estate. I say nephew, not nephews, because, as you know, primogeniture meant Mark would get everything. No doubt Abigail sent John along to serve as a replacement, should Mark die childless. John could be the spare heir, a financially precarious position. No wonder he spent seven years studying law and was called to the bar. He needed a profession.

It was good for my research that John did, because Lincoln's Inn is the only place in England where I found tangible evidence of his education. Unlike his father Edward, John did not go to Eton or Oxford. Neither did his brother Mark. Uncle Basil must have hired private, in-house tutors for them.

Lincoln's Inn is the private, clubby place for lawyers Mijung and I had explored on our first jet-lagged Saturday in London. The fact that John Dixwell went there is key to understanding his later actions. The more I read about seventeenth-century England and Lincoln's Inn, the more convinced I become that his decision to judge a king and mete out the death penalty was substantially influenced by his stint in the heady atmosphere of London and the even headier atmosphere of Lincoln's Inn when he was still in his teens. For years, I'd been thinking of him as twenty-four when he began. I knew now, having been to the Woodhorn Archives, that when he was admitted on February 3, 1631, he was about to turn eighteen, an impressionable age.

The day of my interview with librarian Guy Holborn, I spent the morning reviewing two dense books he had emailed me about, in the months before I visited England: *The Inns of Court under Elizabeth I and the Early Stuarts 1590–1640* and *The Rise of the Barristers—A Social History of the English Bar 1590–1640*.[5] I couldn't believe my good fortune that Mr. Prest had written not one but two books about the specific years and places that helped form John Dixwell's character.

While I was cramming, Mijung was serenely taking in the British Museum, one exhibit at a time. It had never occurred to me, dutiful New England Puritan that I am, that you could, as she did, go to a museum, look carefully and calmly at one thing for a while, then leave. So halfway through the morning I treated myself by taking a one-hour break to visit the museum's Korean Room. Mijung led me to the place then left me alone to take in its orderly loveliness.

Back in my little room at the Penn Club I fortified myself with peanut butter and a rice cake, then walked over to Lincoln's Inn. Now that I knew the way, it seemed close. Once again, I went past the Holborn Town Hall and down High Holborn Street. At the Inn's entrance, a different porter said, "Turn left at the second lamp post." As if I were Lucy in C. S. Lewis's *The Lion, the Witch and the Wardrobe,* off I trotted.

The library was to one side of the Great Hall, where barristers and law students eat, I presume, very good food. Both were as elaborate and soaring as cathedrals. I crept up an interior flight of stairs. At the top was a big oil painting of Charles the Second looking very like his father. Avoiding his gaze, I turned right to enter a high-ceilinged room lined with old books, some behind glass or wire screens. Tall, narrow, leaded-glass windows let light in through diamond-shaped, softly colored panes. Iron stairs and catwalks gave patrons access to the upper shelves. Studious young men and women, some in black robes, worked at long tables.

I had told Guy Holborn I was short and had white hair so it was no problem for him to spot me through the glass front of his office. Out he came, a slender man of indeterminate middle age, his dark blond hair parted neatly on one side, his glasses rimless. He wore a suit and tie.

He motioned for me to enter his office. Oh horror, a cat was curled up on the floor. I stopped abruptly. "Oh no," I said. "I'm allergic to cats."

"This one is probably all right," he said. "He sleeps a lot."

I have been hearing this nonsense all my life from people who want you to just get over your asthma and stop refusing to come to their dinner parties. I balked. "No, really," I said, poised in the doorway. "Is there another place . . ."

The man was bending over. He was picking up the cat.

The cat came up all of a piece, as if it had rigor mortis. I stared. Guy Holborn stood poker-faced, holding his frozen cat.

Our eyes met. He was too reserved to grin, but I thought I detected the slightest upward movement of the left side of his mouth as he bent back down and replaced his taxidermied cat on the floor. I sat in the chair before his desk and we began.

Guy Holborn was terrific. He gave me a full hour of wonderful teaching about the particularities of Lincoln's Inn in the years that John Dixwell studied there. But first I'll explain a few things about England's Inns of Court. I think of law school as a graduate school where you spend three years after you get your bachelor's degree. But if you look into the history of law instruction, you discover this wasn't the case for a long time, either in England or in the United States.

In John Dixwell's England, you needed no piece of parchment to begin studying the law. You just gained admission to one of London's four inns of court (Lincoln's Inn, Gray's Inn, Middle Temple or Inner Temple) by having two members of the inn sign as your "manucaptors." The word "manucaptor" is Latin for "led by the hand," and your manucaptors agreed, in essence, to stand surety for you. They would pay your bills and supposedly ensure that your conduct at the inn be respectable.

Fast forward to my great great grandfather Epes Sargent Dixwell, who was admitted to Harvard in 1823, when he was only fifteen. He earned his bachelor's degree by age nineteen, then he too became a lawyer, but without attending law school. Harvard Law School had been founded in 1817, but by 1827 was struggling so badly it had only one faculty member and one student. Epes instead "read the law" in a law office for several years, was admitted to the Massachusetts Bar in 1833, then hung out his shingle. As it turned out, he got almost no business and fairly quickly decided to be an educator instead. In his unfinished autobiography he describes the haphazard and flawed law education he got.[6]

In John Dixwell's era, England's great universities saw the education of common lawyers (that is, practitioners of common law, not civil or canon law) as beneath them. And this had much to do, like so many aspects of life in the U.K., with social class, with keeping clear boundaries between people possessed of wealth and prestige and those who had to work for their bread.

In other words, being a lawyer was more or less a trade—good for younger sons like John Dixwell—not necessary for firstborn sons. John's brother Mark was one of his manucaptors. He, too, had been admitted to Lincoln's Inn but spent little time there. When Uncle Basil died he'd inherit a lot of money and property. He didn't need to tax his brain with difficult legal concepts.

John Dixwell's other manucaptor, a man named John Clarke, was a bigwig. He was not only a barrister but also a bencher, which means he held the coveted position of being a member of the King's Council. Only the most brilliant and successful barristers, then and now, get to do this. The evening Mijung and I had snooped around Lincoln's Inn we'd seen the names of various Queen's Council barristers (as England is currently headed by a queen) on a sign posted at the entryway of their chambers.

Not long into our interview Guy Holborn politely excused himself, disappeared through a tiny stone-arched door and returned with the original 1631 document confirming John's arrival at Lincoln's Inn. There it was, in perfect condition nearly 400 years later.

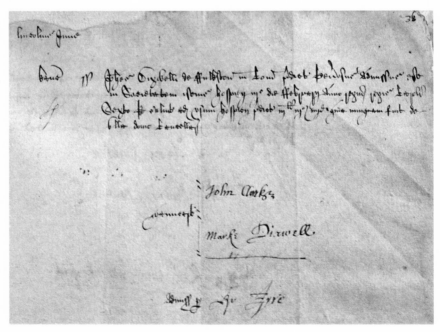

John Dixwell's admission to Lincoln's Inn.

Holborn also brought me a printed edition of the Lincoln's Inn Admission Register, which describes my man as follows: "John Dixwell, of Folkestone, gen." Then I launched into my questions about the Inn itself. I knew, from Wilfrid Prest's book, that the place was pretty small back then, though not as small as Merton College when Edward was an undergraduate. The year John arrived (1631), seventy-five students were admitted. In 1636 only twenty-four were admitted, but in general some sixty students came each of his years. Prest's tables of how many men actually passed the bar are intriguing, for they show a big increase in the number called to the bar from Edward's generation (380 among the four inns of court from 1590 to 1599) to John's—511 from 1630 to 1639. A hundred years earlier there had been only a handful each year. How did this increase affect the balance of power between the crown and the people?

Maybe a lot. These men were dangerously well educated. To pass the bar they had to spend seven years studying and practicing the art and presentation of well-reasoned, carefully supported arguments. If they continued to practice the law, to teach it, and to be promoted in the country's elaborate legal system they became ever more adept at questioning the status quo.

Lincoln's Inn, I learned from Prest, was the inn most strongly allied with puritan thinking. It "maintained the longest succession of puritan preachers and the leading reputation as a hotbed of militant puritanism."[7]

"There it is," I had written in my notes from the book while I was still in Amherst. Now that I was here, I could ask Guy Holborn whether my hunch was correct. Was Lincoln's Inn, in John Dixwell's time, a place where you could get radicalized?

"Wasn't it," I began my question, overcome with excitement to be in the very place where John may have begun his transformation into a person who would agree to judge a king. I paused and reframed the question in my head. Guy Holborn was clearly not, like me, someone who jumped to conclusions. I tried to sound calm, but out gushed my enthusiasm: "Do you think it might have started him on the road towards becoming a regicide to be at a place with such a heady atmosphere of intellectual thought and such fabulous opportunities to learn a lot?"

He took a moment to think. I suspect "fabulous" is not a word he often employs, but then he surprised me. "Yes," he said. "It's fair to say it was heady and fabulous." He actually smiled, then changed the subject to the obstreperous nature of adolescents everywhere. "They got into trouble, behaving like young men."

I was thinking only about Charles's execution. "Trouble?" I echoed vaguely.

"Drink," said Guy Holborn. "Women."

But the students also, he told me, had an elaborate curriculum. In the Great Hall, after dinner, "moots" or mock trials would be held which mirrored the arguments in the courts of Westminster. Students listened carefully, for eventually they would have to argue themselves. There was a moot-book containing moot-cases that were assigned to students. Some of them were used for over 200 years, and they were fiendishly complicated and difficult.

Holborn said you needed both Latin and what was called "Law French," a bastardized form of the language. During the Protectorate, Oliver Cromwell banned both. He wanted lawyers to function in plain English.

In Dixwell's time, Holborn told me, "Once you'd been deemed eligible you'd be called to the bar. Benchers acted the part of judges, and students acted the part of the barristers."

When our hour was up, he took me to a table where I could study as long as I liked. He brought me a big book called *A Portrait of Lincoln's Inn*. It was coedited and had a piece by him, which he did not mention, instead directing me to an article called "Learning the Law," by Nicholas Le Poidevin. I photocopied both, as well as an entry on regicides in the *Oxford Dictionary of National Biography* he thought would be useful to me. Then I sat reading while he had another meeting. I was in the blissful state that can come over me in libraries, particularly when librarians have given me more than I imagined was possible.

It didn't hurt that Nicholas Le Poidevin's article was funny. In his opening paragraph he describes the antics of many centuries of students: "they played ball in the Old Hall and broke the windows; they indulged in absurd pranks; they gambled at cards—some of which have been found under the floorboards—and at dice; they committed casual violence, and they were found introducing women into chambers."

It sounded way more fun than Cambridge or Oxford. "Nowhere but the Inns offered the glitter and variety of metropolitan life alongside the discipline of learning." But it was rigorous, too: "For those willing to take advantage of it, the legal instruction the Inns provided was anything but superficial."[8]

My seven greats grandfather must have been one of the students who took full advantage, I thought loyally, then was startled by Guy Holborn arriving silently at my table. "I remembered I had not shown you the locations of the oldest parts of Lincoln's Inn," he said.

I had forgotten I'd asked him which of the buildings in today's Lincoln's Inn were there in John Dixwell's time. He unfolded a long, pleated paper depicting all the manifestations of Lincoln's Inn back to the 1500s, and pointed out the chapel. The building attached to it had served as the Great Hall in Dixwell's era. Both still stand.

He told me to explore the chapel and the grounds for as long as I wished and we said goodbye. Did I give him a Hadley maple sugar leaf? I cannot remember. What I do remember is my delight at finding, inside the chapel, that John Donne was the inn's preacher from 1616 to 1622. He is one of my favorite poets.

Lincoln's Inn Chapel, with the former Great Hall to its right.

The scene beneath the chapel, Lincoln's Inn.

When I came outside, I discovered that the chapel is supported by lovely rib vaulting under which John Dixwell must have walked countless times. It reminded me of a forest of bare-branched maple trees in winter.

Except for a man in the distance, I was entirely alone, so I recited a little Donne. "No man is an island entire of itself; every man is a piece of the continent, a part of the main. If a clod be washed away by the sea, Europe is the less, as well as if a promontory were, as well as if a manor of thy friend's or of thine own were . . ."[9]

How interconnected we all are: Charles the First, John Dixwell, Guy Holborn, Mijung Kim, Dixie Brown, branching off and intersecting in patterns flung across oceans and centuries.

19

Lawyers vs. the Status Quo

BACK IN AMHERST, I kept thinking about my interview with Guy Holborn. He had told me that individuals entering the legal profession in John Dixwell's era "tended to be younger sons." Because of primogeniture, there was such a difference between the trajectory of firstborn sons and that of their younger brothers. Did primogeniture create class division within families? It certainly created haves and have-nots in each generation.

Second son Edward Dixwell became a vicar so he would be able to support his family, because the wealthy estate at Churchover would go to firstborn William. The situation was the same for his son John. Despite Uncle Basil being one of the richest men in Kent, John, like Edward, would need a profession. Mark would inherit everything.

Then something new occurred to me. Wouldn't going to the Inns of Court, especially if you put in seven years and passed the bar, have given second sons a way to get back more than a little power? I got a vicarious pleasure from imagining my seven greats grandfather impressing his family with his legal expertise. It was satisfying to think of a younger child coming out on top. I remembered how it felt to be the youngest of four and a girl to boot. "Your poor parents," some dreadful adult said to me when I was maybe six years old. "Three girls!" she whispered, as if telling me an important secret, then she smiled. Was I supposed to smile? I didn't feel like it. I had not known, before, that girls were a disappointment.

But now that I did, evidence mounted. Quite often grownups said matter-of-factly to me, "You should have been a boy. That would have balanced things out." One of my mother's friends said to me, "Your poor brother! Three sisters! You should have been a boy." It was a kind of refrain, when people first met the Brown family with its abundance of daughters. And I took it in, absorbing the idea that I was not as valuable as a son would have been.

Any second son, in John Dixwell's time, was early aware that he was less valuable than his big brother. Unless death took that brother, the second son would get nothing. Cain and Abel. Jacob and Esau. Brothers can behave badly when land and money are involved. But in the England of the 1600s, at least there was the compensation, for second sons, of educational opportunities if the family had some wealth. Perhaps that created a different kind of friction between brothers. Couldn't feelings have gotten pretty complicated between wealthy but perhaps less sophisticated first sons and their highly educated kid brothers? I doubt it was easy for either group.

What was it like for John, toiling away at Lincoln's Inn, to watch Mark spend those same seven years getting married, becoming a father and living off the income of land worked by tenant farmers? I'd figured out the simultaneity of Mark's babies and John's studies before I got to England, when I found online a list of Mark's children's births. Elizabeth, the eldest, arrived in 1636, when John was twenty-three. Take note of Elizabeth, for she was a major character in the drama of his life in exile. Alice came along in 1638, the year John passed the bar. Basil arrived in 1640, closely followed by Heardson, 1641, and finally William, born just weeks before Uncle Basil's death at the tail end of 1642. I found out later there was another daughter named Bennet who wasn't listed so I don't know her birth year.

On the other hand, what was it like for Mark to watch his younger brother soak up the culture, the intellectual intensity, the politics and countless other aspects of the great city of London? Was he intimidated, jealous? Wilfrid Prest quotes a seventeenth-century contemporary who described the barristers as "'the most knowing men in business or any profession . . . They know the nature of estates and the condition of their owners and can thereby pleasure themselves more and surer than other men can.'"[1]

"It would be surprising," Prest writes, "if migrating barristers did not often encounter contempt, fear, jealousy, and resentment."[2]

John had only migrated to London and returned to Kent, but I wonder if it changed the dynamics between him and Mark that he was now so highly educated. Nevertheless, unquestioning duty to one's family was very much the norm in John Dixwell's day. There's no evidence that John did anything but the right and dutiful thing when Mark was killed in the first civil war. Basil had died only a year earlier. John was barely thirty when he became responsible for Mark's widow, her five surviving children, and the sprawling estate that would go to three-year-old Basil. He did what needed to be done for the next eighteen years. If Charles II hadn't ascended the throne in 1660 and John hadn't fled for his life, perhaps he would have spent the rest of his days caring for his dead brother's family and managing their assets.

If so, I wouldn't be here in Amherst, Massachusetts, marveling at his key, exploring what it meant to be a lawyer in the seventeenth century. Everything I've read convinces me that his seven years at Lincoln's Inn were transformational. Studying the law must have honed John's intelligence to an extraordinary sharpness.

It was grueling. A man who passed the bar at Lincoln's Inn a decade before John did, complained to the benchers hearing his "reading" (the equivalent of a final oral exam) that learning the law was "so hard, so unsavoury, so rude and barbarous . . . that it requires a very strong and healthy body to endure it."[3]

John Dixwell had such a strong and healthy body he was able to marry and have children in his late sixties and seventies, thousands of miles from home, more than thirty years after he'd laid Mark to rest in Kent. A man with that much energy even in old age must have been a force to be reckoned with when he returned to Kent in 1638, not yet twenty-five years old. He had been successfully called to the bar on January 30, the same day King Charles, twelve years hence, would be beheaded.

How radical had he become while reading the law? What if Mark and Basil were more conservative? Maybe John, fresh from Lincoln's Inn, now questioned things Mark and Basil held dear. Prest, in his chapter entitled "Religion," writes that being friends with and respecting "individual clergymen in their spiritual capacity hardly inhibited common lawyers from vigorously asserting the subordination of the Church to the lay magistracy and the common law."[4] What were the conversations at the dinner table between Uncle Basil, Mark and John?

A history professor friend, whom I've been peppering with questions like these, suggested I read "The Winning of the Initiative by the House of Commons," by Wallace Notestein. I found it in the bowels of Amherst College's library, down in those scary stacks that threaten to slide together and turn you into a pancake even as the automatic lights click off.

For some reason (is it because I am short?), the lights went off every time I mounted a round step stool provided for people who can't reach the higher shelves. I had to keep hopping up and down in alternately inky dark and sudden bright light but at last I spied a slender thing nearly hidden between its bulkier neighbors and fished it out just as I was again plunged into darkness. I clambered carefully off the stool and the lights clicked on. Inside cardboard covers bound with gray library tape was Wallace Notestein's 1924 "Raleigh Lecture." The Raleigh lectures, I read, were founded by the British Academy "on the occasion of the Raleigh Tercentenary, October 29, 1918."[5]

"Walter Raleigh?" I said aloud to the silent books on either side of me. Sir Walter Raleigh was John Dixwell's hero. Raleigh's *History of the World*, which he wrote in prison, was one of the books John Dixwell owned during his years in New Haven. On his deathbed he gave it to his minister and next-door-neighbor James Pierpont.

As soon as I got home with Notestein's little pamphlet, I looked up Walter Raleigh and learned why John Dixwell must have admired him. Raleigh was beheaded on October 19, 1618 for his plots against James I, father of Charles I. Then I got curious about the writer of the pamphlet.

Wallace Notestein (1878-1969) spent the bulk of his academic career at Yale University, where his specialty was early modern English history. I hope he enjoyed New Haven's three streets named after regicides Whalley, Goffe, and Dixwell. I leafed through his lecture, printed on acid-degraded paper marked with many penciled notes from students past, and found it to be brilliant. He looks at how the House of Commons gradually arrived at the kind of thinking that got them their Bill of Rights—adopted in 1689, the year of John Dixwell's death, 102 years before the drafting of the American Bill of Rights. Charles the First would have been appalled, the more so because his grandson was at the helm when it happened. William III of Orange and his wife Mary ascended the English throne in 1689 in the Glorious Revolution and ushered in the changes that John Dixwell had dreamed of. They signed a contract that forbade them being absolute monarchs and a Bill of Rights which granted individual liberties and permitted a degree of religious toleration.

Lawyers, Notestein contends, had a lot to do with these profound changes. Toward the end of his lecture he writes, "The influence of lawyers upon the new developments in the Commons can hardly be overestimated . . . One has only to read the debates in the Elizabethan House to realize that it was filled with men who bandied with one another in Latin phrases, who rejoiced in legal subtleties, and throve upon the finer points of land custom."[6]

Then this: "By virtue of their manner of education and discipline, they had become almost a class in society, a class with which the Government had to reckon as with the nobility and the gentry."[7]

Yes, I thought to myself. Basil and Mark were landed gentry. John was something else, a lawyer trained to think deeply. Notestein argues eloquently that power for the people grew organically, primarily through lawyers, without anyone really seeing what was happening, let alone predicting the execution of a king: "Lawyers it was more than any others that hit upon new ways of doing business in the Commons. In the Common Law, an old institution, they had seen a growing and changing thing, adapting itself to new conditions and new times." Then Notestein captures what I experienced over and over during my two weeks in England, namely the intriguing blend, in that society, of creativity and conservatism: "they had learned that the new was not to be rejected but to be grafted upon the old. What more natural than that they should come to see in Commons procedure another living thing, whose growth might be directed, pruned here, and there led along a garden wall."[8]

Notestein helped me understand how someone from as wealthy a family as John Dixwell could wind up risking all by signing Charles's death warrant. It wasn't, it couldn't have been for anyone, a premeditated thing. Rather, it grew out of a multiplicity of converging events, many of them played out in the House of Commons: "Not that they were definitely out to change its constitution. Rather, as leaders of opposition, they were full of devices to overcome particular difficulties, and when these devices led on to new custom they saw in it nothing out of the way."[9]

Notestein concludes his lecture with the argument that the first part of the seventeenth century, in which John Dixwell was born, lost his father and became a lawyer, was the seedbed of the English Bill of Rights that arrived just as John Dixwell was breathing his last. "No doubt the Civil Wars had to be fought," Notestein says. Then, as if he has to tread carefully as an American addressing a British audience, touches as lightly as possible on the beheading, "the scene outside the Banqueting Hall had perhaps to be enacted . . ."

It's nearly a century since he delivered his talk, but here I am, fascinated. I'm thinking about how Notestein, a forty-year-old American academic, has been invited to explain the evolution of Parliament's seventeenth century House of Commons to a British audience. He's analyzing the processes that would lead to the birth of his own nation, and his touch is so deft: "but before any of those more celebrated events could have the chance of occurring, the Commons had to gain control of their own parliamentary processes . . . The years that revealed the splendor of English literature, that gave us Shakespeare and Ben Jonson, Richard Hooker and the King James version, gave us in politics a new kind of Commons that was by and by to make inevitable a new constitution."[10]

Nicely done. He gives those British academics a paean to their literature, their Bible, and their House of Commons, but he also honors his own government without saying a word.

20

The Ultimate Dixwell Expert

BREAKFAST AT THE PENN CLUB, that Quaker gem of a boarding house, could be huge if you so chose. I invariably did. Mijung, never. She'd have a plate of fresh fruit and yoghurt, the former arranged in beautiful little lines of kiwi, banana, strawberries, grapes, and honeydew melon, the latter in a parfait glass. Then she'd insist on giving a sample of each to me, who was devouring two poached eggs, gently burned toast, a slice of fried to-mato, baked beans, and mushrooms. She always refused to take any of my breakfast. She felt I needed to be strengthened for the next rigorous day of research. She was just going to go shopping, she said. No need for eggs.

On the morning after my visit to Lincoln's Inn a gray-haired woman at our table, who had just returned from a peacekeepers visit to the Mid-dle East, asked me politely what I was doing in London. Was I here as a tourist?

She was sawing away at a black sausage, so my mind went straight to Charles's beheading. I hesitated. Every time an English man or woman inquired about the purpose of my visit I felt as if I ought to apologize for being descended from a regicide. After all, here they were, 364 years later, still adoring their queen. And who was paying for the upkeep of those palaces all over the place?

"I'm sorry to say that I'm writing a book about—" and on I blundered. Oh no, she looked annoyed.

She *was* annoyed. "Don't be so self-conscious!" she said quite loudly. Startled, I hung my head.

"Oh for goodness sake," she went on. "There was another Charles. It wasn't the end of the world."

She gave me a stern look, then the tiniest smile, and popped another bite of black sausage into her mouth. It was like an absolution. I felt washed clean. She was right. I *was* being insanely self-conscious, about everything. Life went on after John Dixwell signed the death warrant.

I finished the last triangle of toast, climbed the many flights of stairs to my room, and said goodbye to Mijung who was headed off to Harrod's. Then I sat at the little desk and reread all the articles by Professor Jason Peacey that I'd brought with me. I would meet him in a few hours at University College London.

Peacey wrote the entry on John Dixwell in the 2004 *Oxford Dictionary of National Biography*. Years before it occurred to me to visit England, his entry caught my attention because it was so much more positive than the one Mr. Firth had written in the 1908 edition. Inspired, I emailed him about my interest in researching Dixwell's life. He responded immediately, then sent me several other, even more detailed and helpful articles he'd written about my man. More than anyone, he helped me start seeing Dixwell as a rounded human being instead of as someone who'd done something shockingly violent.

And he's the one who wrote me, "I must confess that I found it hard not to empathise with Dixwell. I'm sure historians are supposed to be a bit more detached!"

His Hadley maple sugar leaf was already in my backpack.

It was raining when I stepped outside the Penn Club, headed for University College London. I opened up the umbrella Mijung had picked out at Marshall's and set off through Bloomsbury. I made my way through Tavistock Square with its bust of Virginia Woolf, coaching myself fiercely to summon up courage for this most important of interviews. There was so much I couldn't understand in Peacey's scholarly articles, and I wanted to grasp every word, for no one in the world but he has spent as much time, and spent it as carefully, learning all there is to know about John Dixwell.

I arrived at the gate and told the porter my business. In a moment, Jason Peacey himself, under his own umbrella, strode across the courtyard to meet me. He was an entirely friendly, unpretentious, regular guy. He took me to a faculty common room, bought me a cup of tea, and we sat down. I pulled out the key and placed it before him. He was satisfyingly delighted.

I know this can't be true, but it felt as if Jason Peacey knew everything. I couldn't take notes fast enough. I started with Edward. Did it put Edward in a different social class from the one occupied by his older brother William when he went to Oxford's Merton College and became a vicar?

"Class in the seventeenth century is strange," said Jason, "because it's not strictly about parentage but a mix of that and birth order." He went on to explain that it was clear the Dixwell family, after Edward's untimely death, was "trying to ensure that Mark and John could overcome the problem of being orphaned and being younger sons." Theirs was not "a well-funded family."

In short, early on, Mark and John had three strikes against them: they were fatherless, younger sons, and poor. How strange that John ended up judging a king.

I looked down at my list of questions.

Had John and Mark been on opposite sides in the first civil war? That was what Roger Hailwood had conjectured. Peacey was emphatic. "Mark was not a royalist. There's *no* evidence of this. Kent was overwhelmingly parliamentarian. You'd have to be brave to be a royalist there."

He went on teaching me about the events that led up to the regicide, getting so involved in telling the tale that he used the pronoun "we" and the present tense. In the second civil war, in Kent, "We've defeated the King in 1646—we've offered terms to him. This fails, because of Charles's nature. He escapes and goes on dividing and conquering. He goes into league with the Scots and starts another war. This makes the parliamentarians particularly angry.

"However gentlemanly the war has been, it gets more bloody and nasty in 1646. Kent was a theatre of war then. Kent and Essex are the main places." I knew that less than a year before the king was put to death there was a fierce battle at Maidstone, in Kent, where parliamentarians under Lord Fairfax triumphed over royalists despite having fewer men. Fairfax pursued them into County Essex where they endured several months of famine and deprivation before surrendering.

The country was in chaos. "It hardened the hearts of a lot of people. We can't prove that Dixwell was hardened or very radical. There's no clear evidence. But he signs the death warrant. He loses patience."

I wanted to know what it was like, deciding to judge a king. "Clearly, people had doubts. Lots walked away from it or got jitters on the last days of the trial." I mentioned that some sources suggest people were coerced and had signed on different occasions, not all at once.

"It doesn't stand up that people were physically forced to sign. The warrant may have been signed over a couple of days—we don't know."

We returned to John Dixwell, who was "a lesser player. But the trial made him grow in stature, for his involvement at that stage raises his profile. He has very clearly indicated he is willing to take this bold, momentous step. At the very least he seems to be one of the people who is enthusiastic for the republican regime once it's in place."

I asked for more clarification. From 1649 to 1653 the country was a republic, governed by the Rump Parliament. The "Rump" consisted of the limited number of members of the House of Commons who were allowed into Westminster Hall during what soon thereafter became known as Pride's Purge. On December 6, 1648 Colonel Thomas Pride, checking his list of members deemed enemies of the New Model Army, turned away 140 MPs, about a third of whom were placed under a sort of house arrest in two inns in the Strand. Excluded were all the members who disagreed with the plan to try the king for treason against his own people. Many felt it wasn't a legitimate parliament anymore. The Army made sure it got its way.

The Rump, in the weeks after Charles's execution, had to scramble to put a new government in place. They created a Council of State to act as the executive branch, a function previously served by the king and his Privy Council. Dixwell was elected to the Council of State in November 1651. But in 1653, Peacey told me, "things got messy because Oliver Cromwell wants more, and then the army steps in."

Dixwell, he said, "doesn't seem to want to have any truck with that."

Under Cromwell, the ideal of a republic gave way to the quasi-monarchical system of the Protectorate. Jason effortlessly reeled off the dates of Dixwell's political activities, "In '54 and '56 he is a kind of moderate republican who gets elected on an anti-Cromwell ticket, but he's not kicked out. Some are, but not Dixwell. But neither is he active. He's anti-military."

I had no interest in drinking my tea. Interviewing Peacey felt as if I were talking to one of John Dixwell's contemporaries, someone who knew and rather liked him.

The Republic, in the early years, consisted only of the House of Commons and the Council of State, for the Rump abolished the House of Lords. It sounded to me like a wildly confusing and exciting time. Peacey went on painting the scene, still in the present tense, "it isn't clear that anyone has a program for what the government would look like. They abolish the monarchy, but not straightaway. They are thinking clearly by May."

"And Dixwell?" I asked. "Where was Dixwell in all this?"

"He's happy from 1649 to 1653, and not so happy thereafter." Before the civil wars, England had not had a standing army. Oliver Cromwell, in contrast, maintained one in peacetime, and professionalized it. "This was unprecedented and controversial and he abused that power, creating a legacy of distrust." Dixwell, he said, "looks like a committed civilian republican. His is a position of principle. He's opposed to the military having too much power."

There was so much to learn, and my hour was disappearing. I wanted to know more about Dixwell's political activities, the ones Peacey enumerates in his articles. Here was my chance to ask what the various committees were on which Dixwell had served. Some had names that were foreign to me, like "sequestrations," or "oyer and terminer." Others were self-explanatory: "ejecting scandalous ministers," "relief of poor prisoners," or the ultimate one on which he served in 1659, the last year he was a trusted public servant before the Restoration, "sewers."

No. I could figure those things out by myself. I touched the key, lying there between our teacups, and asked what it meant to be the governor of Dover Castle. It meant a lot, Jason said. Dover was one of England's five cinqueports, a string of ports in Kent. Then, and for many centuries, Dover was one of the most important castles of defense in the country, and the center for the military in Kent. From it, you can look across the English Channel towards the city of Calais in France and spot anyone invading by sea. You keep watch for England.

What did he know about Dixwell's first few years after the 1660 restoration of Charles II, when so many regicides fled for their lives? I told him I'd been unable to find much information about his time in Germany. Peacey thought records had probably been lost in the Second World War. The best source we have is Edmund Ludlow's *A Voyce from the Watch Tower*. Ludlow was the only regicide who lived longer than Dixwell, dying of natural causes in 1692 in Vevey, Switzerland, despite numerous attempts on his life. I made a mental note to look into Ludlow's book when I got home.

Abruptly, I moved my inquiry back two decades when I realized I hadn't asked how spending seven years at Lincoln's Inn might have influenced John Dixwell. All four Inns of Court were exciting places to be, he said, "but Lincoln's Inn is a bit special because of interesting debates and ideas floating around. The best legal and political minds are at Lincoln's Inn in the 1630s." He began listing names: John Selden, Oliver St. John, Henry Parker. I scribbled as fast as I could.

We hurried on to John Dixwell's life after he got himself to New Haven, Connecticut and changed his name to James Davids. Jason had read the letters Dixwell received in exile and was fascinated by Dixwell's connection with John Wildman. "To be still in touch with him is amazing."

Wildman, though not a regicide, was a brilliant and outspoken critic of powermongers from kings to Cromwell. After the Restoration, in the years that John Dixwell was in Germany and then in Connecticut, Wild-man was in the "most radical wing of opposition to Charles II."

Our hour was up and Jason Peacey had a meeting to attend. I could hardly bear stopping when there was so much still to learn. I pulled out his maple leaf and made sure he noticed it was from Hadley, refuge for Major Generals Edward Whalley and William Goffe. Then I was back in the rain, so happy with that interview I practically danced back to the Penn Club.

21

Broome Park: Uncle Basil Dixwell's Big Idea

WHEN I AWAKENED on the morning I was to travel to Broome Park, I listened for water gurgling in Mijung's sink next door, remembered she was back in Massachusetts, and felt bereft. Having her with me for the first ten days had been so helpful. She knew how to stay calm, eat well, and rest when tired. These are seemingly simple things, but I often forgot them all in the rush of trying to find and learn and photograph every possible scrap of evidence of John Dixwell and his extended family. Then Mijung came to the rescue. She had discovered another Korean restaurant or grocery store. She had new snacks or yet another surprise treat hidden in her suitcase.

I felt grateful for her good sense as I loaded up the smaller of the two suitcases she'd insisted I buy at Macy's. It would be easier to bring it to County Kent for the last leg of my journey and leave the big one at the Penn Club.

I wished she could be with me for the upcoming highlights of my trip. Still to be visited were Uncle Basil's Broome Park and, biggest destination of all, Dover Castle. The key that had spent hundreds of years an ocean away from where it was made, was going to put in an appearance at its original home.

As my subway car rumbled through the Charing Cross station, I thought of the regicides who were drawn and quartered there. Several were astonishingly calm and centered throughout their ordeals. What sort of faith in divine love made that possible, or was it adrenaline? On the day of his execution, John Cook comforted his distraught wife with gentle humor when she came to Newgate Prison to say goodbye: "My dear lamb, let us not part in a shower." Just before he began the protracted process of being hanged almost to the point of death then cut down so they could eviscerate him while he was still aware, he asked Charles II to accept his death as payment so as to spare other condemned men.

The train to Canterbury took a while, for without Mijung to guide me, I had gotten on a slow one by mistake. But I didn't mind. It gave me more time to study. As we passed a station called "Hither Green," then "Pluckley," I dug in my backpack for an article about Broome Park written by a fourth cousin I'd met in the course of my research, Caroline Dixwell Cabot. She'd visited it, loved it, and encouraged me to go there too. I'd also brought Roger Hailwood's *Looking Back at Broome Park*.

The construction, Caroline writes, began in 1635. "By 1639 the house was completed using 2,700,000 bricks made with clay dug from the marl pits on the estate." An inconceivably large number of bricks! There were also stables, a brew house, and gardens. The cost was 8,000 pounds sterling. It wasn't yet the fashion to use an architect. "The Carolean style of Broome Park is mainly Flemish because brick buildings of the period were often constructed by Dutch craftsmen who worked in the area at this time."[1]

I turned to Roger's description of the brick-making process, told from young John Dixwell's point of view. "With so many bricks needed, the puddling process of the clay, which had been done by treading it with bare feet, was greatly speeded up with the use of the new invention of the pug-mill driven by a donkey walking in a circle. The acrid smell of the wood smoke from the brick kilns firing the thousands of bricks drifted down the valley and often lingered on John's clothing as he rode home again to Terlingham at the end of his visits."[2]

Because of my recent visit to Lincoln's Inn, I now knew that Roger's "conjecture," as he had put it, was likely true. John may well have watched the construction when he came home from London. Guy Holborn, the librarian with the stuffed cat, had told me law students in that era got one "proper vacation" a year, in summer. Because it took years to build Broome Park, Dixwell must have seen it at various stages each summer.

I leafed to Roger's version of what John thought of Anthony Van Dyck's portrait of Basil. "John had often felt that it was a somewhat severe picture with his uncle unusually dressed in black. He felt it would have been more appropriate if it had shown the more flamboyant and stylish nature of the way his uncle normally wore his apparel, and for which he was well known, especially when appearing in the House of Commons."[3] "Canterbury," a voice announced. Startled, I got a pit in my stomach. A wrong-side-of the-Atlantic Dixwell was having the temerity to visit the manor and spend two nights. Equally uncomfortable was the realization that some part of me wanted to stake my claim. How absurd. I stood up and gathered my things. But after I disembarked and began looking for a taxi, I found myself wishing there might be some fanfare to welcome me, a bona fide Dixwell, returning to the ancestral seat with a key to Dover Castle in my backpack.

Soon I was being driven across the Barham Downs where Charles the First had welcomed his betrothed. I had just read Roger's lively description: "The celebrations had taken place not far away from Broome House. Henrietta Maria, daughter of the French King, had landed at Dover and had then taken the road to Canterbury, pausing for a picnic with her husband to be on the Barham Downs. The picnic had taken days to prepare with hundreds of servants and men pitching tents, building kitchens in which were roasted whole animals over open fires, tables had been covered with the most sumptuous of foods, the whole scene decked out with extravagant banners and finery." It was 1625. John and Mark, aged twelve and sixteen, were living nearby in Folkestone with Uncle Basil. Might they have attended the celebration?[4]

Now, stretching to the horizon in every direction, were fields dotted with sheep and clusters of woodlands. The word "downs" is derived from the Celtic word for "hill." The Barham Downs are made of chalk, hence the white cliffs of Dover. Geologically speaking, there's lots of chalk in the southeast corner of England where John and Mark went to live after Edward died. It's a good place to graze sheep, because chalk hills provide the substratum for well-drained grassland. Chalk is also great for digging secret tunnels and bunkers. Dover Castle sits on a labyrinth of them, many from the twentieth century but some dating back to medieval times.

It took quite a while to get to Broome Park. We passed miles of sheep but almost no houses. At last the taxi turned down a long drive and there stood the most amazing pile of bricks, Basil Dixwell's stately home.

The reality of the building's in-your-face grandeur gave me a physical shock. I stared out the taxi's window. Basil, Basil, I thought, you were such a show-off. I felt embarrassed to be related to him. The driver announced the hefty fare. I gave him an alarming portion of my remaining cash, got out, and tried unsuccessfully to drag my suitcase over impossibly thick gravel. Its wheels got mired at once. I had to carry it to that impressive front door. Just inside was a vast room so ornate I was stunned again. The white ceiling was a mass of stylized bas-relief petals and what looked like small white stalactites.

Broome Park.

Beneath it were numerous comfortable sofas and chairs in which golfers rested from their labors on what remains of Basil's acreage. At intervals around the walls were big portraits of First Earl Kitchener of Khartoum (1850-1916), who was the last private owner of Broome Park and died in the First World War when his ship went down in the North Sea after it struck a German mine. After gazing at some length, I made my way over to the reception desk. Checking in was complicated, because Broome Park is jointly owned by a golf resort and a timeshare company. I was told that only someone from the latter could help me. Eventually a young woman appeared from a back room.

As she asked for my credit card I thought, "What the heck," and identified myself. "I'm here," I said, "because I'm directly descended from John Dixwell the regicide and I'm researching his life for a book I'm writing."

She lit up. "Really? That is so exciting!" She launched into stories she had been told about the Dixwells of Broome Park.

"Wait!" I said. "Let me get my journal so I can take notes." She stopped abruptly. She didn't want me to do that. She might get it wrong—she was just a local girl who had grown up hearing stories.

"But that's exactly what I want!" I exclaimed. "Please, please. Will you tell me your stories if I promise not to use your name?"

Now her cheeks were pink. "Let me think. Oh dear. You should talk to Gillian Matthews. She's the manager of the Broome Park Owners' Club. She knows ever so much more than I do."

By now I'd found pen and notebook and opened to a blank page. I gazed at her imploringly.

"Oh, all right. But you mustn't use my name."

I shook my head solemnly and she began.

"The story is, there was a highwayman named Black Robin who used to rob people on the road where the A2 is now. Basil Dixwell had the road moved because it was on his boundary and highwaymen were stopping coaches."

I scribbled as fast as I could. "There's still a pub called Black Robin. It's in Kingston, two villages away, just after Barham.

"Once Black Robin was caught, he needed to be punished. He was to be hanged on the Barham Downs—the area as you come down to the estate—it was quite high up." Her eyes shone. "So he was about to be hanged and he was asked what his last words were and he said, 'I will curse the House of Dixwell for one hundred years, and there will be no male heir for a hundred years.'"

I stared at her, dumbfounded, for as far as I know the name Dixwell only exists in people's middle names. In a sample database of 88.7 million names surveyed in the U.S. in 1997, the surname Dixwell appeared only twice. The last John Dixwell in my branch of the family died childless in 1931. Meanwhile, the young woman was telling me about Lord Horatio Herbert Kitchener.[5] "When he bought the house, in 1901, it was derelict. There was much less land by then. It had been twelve parishes under Basil. 5,000 acres. It's only 250 now."

She said Kitchener had torn out all Basil Dixwell's blue marble in the Great Hall where we were standing, and replaced it with carved wood paneling. He also replaced the massive original roof trusses and used the beams for the staircase I would take to go up to my room.

When she came to the end of her story, I asked if she knew where I could find Anthony Van Dyck's portrait of Sir Basil Dixwell. "It's at the Beaney," she answered promptly.

"The Beaney?" I said. "What's that?"

"It's Canterbury's library, on High Street. Upstairs is a museum. Basil is up there. He's wearing black silk, which says he was a rich man. You could not dye silk black unless you had a lot of money."

But now there was another guest behind me, waiting to be checked in. She handed me my key. "Thank you, thank you," I said, and headed off, buoyant.

22

Walking in Green Pastures

THE DOOR WAS SMALL, cunningly camouflaged by the dark wood panel-ing, but the staircase! Craftsmen had put the original roof trusses to good use. It was a phantasmagoria. A winged griffin sat on one newel post, a dragon on another. Carved curlicues adorned each baluster. When I got to the landing, Gillian Matthews came hurrying in my direction. She has been the manager of the Broome Park Owners' Club for many years. She was excited to meet me, in the nicest gushy way, and full of facts. She adores Broome Park, which she thinks of as a she. "She either likes you or not—if she doesn't, it's not a good thing!"

Briskly, she brought me down a long corridor and a couple of steps to my room. The leaded glass windows went from the floor to the high ceil-ing and were framed by yards and yards of drapery.

I went over to the window and gazed out, imagining the greensward outside wasn't a driving range for the golfers who'd arrived in their Volvos that day, but a lawn John Dixwell strolled on all the years that he lived at Broome Park.

"Does this house like you?" I asked, too mesmerized by the view to turn around. If I were Jane Eyre, I thought, I could hide from my mean cousins behind that curtain. The first sentence of the novel came to

My bedroom window at Broome Park.

me: "There was no possibility of taking a walk that day," then Charlotte Brontë's description of the room: "Folds of scarlet drapery shut in my view to the right hand; to the left were the clear panes of glass, protecting, but not separating me from the drear November day."[1]

Or maybe I was in Wuthering Heights and at any moment I'd see Heathcliff out there on the moor, crazed with passion and foaming at the mouth. I blinked and turned to Gillian, who was saying quietly that yes, the house did like her. It better like her, for she, meaning Gillian not Broome Park, has championed the house as no one else has.

"She's a Grade 1 listed Historic Building, like Windsor Castle," she said proudly, then launched into the difficulties of joint ownership and how in 2007 her employer, the Broome Park Owners Club, sued the golf resort company, Diamond Resorts International, headquartered in Las Vegas, because Broome Park was becoming derelict.

Gillian had served as a witness in the Royal Courts of Justice, the very place Mijung and I had seen when we were scoping out Lincoln's Inn on our first day in London. She remembered the experience vividly. "There were three barristers and one judge and eleven sets of lawyers. The judge said I was 'a transparently honest witness.' Diamond Resorts had to pay two million pounds to repair the place." I was impressed. That's three and a half million dollars to put the shine back on Basil's big idea.

Gillian Matthews excused herself and returned with a homemade tea loaf and extra tea bags to keep up my strength until dinner time. A gift! I had been dismayed, upon my arrival, to discover there was no food at Broome Park until suppertime, and the nearest grocery store was in Canterbury. She was saving me from hypoglycemia. But best of all was a green cardboard, book-shaped box Gillian was cradling in her arms. In it was her growing collection of articles and pamphlets about all things Broome Park and Dixwell. She presented it to me, both of us as solemn as if it were the Holy Grail. I could keep it until I checked out of Broome Park.

"It's your house, really," she said. This was such a charming remark I unzipped my backpack, pulled out the key to Dover Castle and handed it to her.

She caught her breath, and held it reverently for such a long time I forgot she had it. She continued to regale me with Broome Park stories while I interrupted her with burning questions like, "Can I walk on the grounds without getting hit by a golf ball?" or "Where is the church where Basil is buried?"

She said I could walk on the grounds, carefully, and then beyond them, through sheep pastures to the church. "You must go at once, before it gets dark. It isn't far. Ask for a map at the front desk," she told me as she gave me back my key and dashed off.

As soon as the door shut behind her I ripped off a hunk of the tea loaf, devoured it, then flopped on the bed. I closed my eyes and became aware of how tingly my body was. I was full of so much excitement and happiness, but also something else. I lay still and recognized an instinctive recoil, a gut dislike of places like Broome Park that goes back to my childhood. I had felt set apart and lonely in our massive house with no playmates nearby. On the few occasions when I had a little girl over, for I was too shy most of the time to ask anyone, I cringed if she reacted, as several did, with shock at the place where I lived. One burst out, the moment she came in, "How many bathrooms does this place have?"

I went on lying there, envying Gillian her unmixed pleasure in Broome Park, then I sat up, put on my sturdiest walking shoes, and went back down that fanciful staircase. At the bottom, a young man was carrying a round table with its legs folded against one side.

"This is quite a place," I said, hoping he would be as chatty as everyone else I'd met so far. He was. I told him my connection, and he invited me to tag along as he cleared away tables set up for a reception, talking steadily about Broome Park while he worked.

He seemed to have no love either for the mansion or the man who had it built. "Basil got his money in a shady way," he said darkly, "and this place is a folly." He told me the grounds were in a state of disrepair and the house has a leaky roof.

I was glad someone else found the place a bit much, but then I remembered I was supposed to be getting directions for my walk to Barham Church. I didn't just need to get there and back before dark, I needed to get into the dining room before it closed at 8 p.m. I hadn't had any serious protein since my two poached eggs at the Penn Club that morning.

A new woman at the desk gave me a sheet of directions for my hike, and told me where to start. I was so relieved to push open the heavy front door and get out of the place. I stood still, inhaling the fresh cool air and getting my bearings. There was still plenty of light, but the sun was getting low in the sky as I went across what felt like acres of golf course, then through a stile and a field, then another stile and a huge pasture with a scattering of sheep. Gentle hills stretched in every direction and there wasn't another soul to be seen.

It was utterly beautiful. He had been here, my John Dixwell, and so had his key. He must have known this land intimately for he was in charge of the entire 5,000 acres surrounding Broome Park from the time of Mark's death in 1642 to the day of his flight in 1660. And he was alone, as I was too, with no partner to keep him company. I stopped and looked all around me at the fields, the sheep, and the lengthening shadows. I could almost sense him. "Why do I feel so compelled to know you?" I said aloud. Had he described all this to Bathsheba, my seven greats grandmother? She had never gotten to see it but here I was, walking across the pastures he'd known, heading for what must have been his church.

Then it occurred to me that if I tripped and sprained my ankle no one would come looking for me. Also, there was no cell phone coverage. Why hadn't I told the woman at the desk what I was doing and asked her to expect me back at a particular hour? My daughter, thousands of miles away in Minnesota, would be worried if she knew—my son in Boston, too. How troublesome I'd been to them as a single parent for the last twenty-four years, always charging unaccompanied into places I wanted to explore.

A big lamb, his ears backlit an intense pink by the descending sun, left his mother and trotted over to check me out. He was so wonderful to behold it changed my mood at once. How lovely to be alone in such a place, communing with my namesake, unencumbered by other human beings as I continued my solitary quest. I resumed walking across the tussocky grass. Had John Dixwell taken any pleasure in his solitude after he fled to Germany? Had he managed to cling tightly to the belief that he had done the right thing for his country, and that the sacrifice of his well-heeled life in this beautiful place was worth it?

I walked and walked. At length, I came to a road so narrow that when a lone car drove toward me it took up the entire pavement and I had to leap into the bushes. The road went up and up. There were no road signs anywhere. Although the hill had seemed small, it went up relentlessly. I began panting and sweating.

Just as I was about to give up and turn back so as not to miss dinner, there was a small sign, "Barham Church," and an arrow. More walking. More gorgeous green hilly pastures in all directions. Then, eureka, a church, with a copper-covered spire weathered to a verdigris just the shade of the celadon pottery in the Korean Room at the British Museum.

In the churchyard were Oxinden gravestones from the eighteenth and nineteenth centuries. I knew Dixwells had married Oxindens after John's flight. "You're my cousins," I said to them.

Barham Church.

Basil and Mark must be inside. They'd had more than enough money to be out of the acid rain. John Dixwell would have ordered their monument. But the church was locked. A small sign beside the door read, "Welcome to Barham Church. Christians have prayed and worshipped here for over 1,000 years. As you come into the building we hope that you will feel nearer to God and know his blessing on you."

But there was no coming in. It was the only church, in my two weeks in England, that wasn't open. Maybe, with my bad attitude toward Broome Park and Basil's murderous past, I wasn't meant to see his grave.

Still, it was hard to walk away from John Dixwell's place of worship. At last hunger got me walking then trotting down the endless hill to the pastures, the stiles, the sheep, the golf course and, just in time, dinner.

"Pie and Pudding Night," said a sign in the Great Hall pointing to the dining room. I ordered lamb pie and apple and plum crumble, then sat at my table eating masses of deliciously greasy everything. The English are not shy about animal fat. The crumble was in a ramekin generous enough for three. I ate about half, and asked if I could take the rest up to my room, for breakfast. They said yes.

Back in my room I tried to read some of the papers Gillian had lent me but I was too tired. Also, I was freezing. Basil's giant windows didn't close all the way, and cold air poured through a wide crack. I got under the covers and struggled to get warm, longing for sleep but totally wired.

Mijung Kim in front of the Penn Club on our first day in London. William Penn (1644–1718) was a radical Quaker. He spent time imprisoned in the Tower of London, but by 1681 was creating a Quaker-style government for Pennsylvania. Eight years later, John Dixwell died in New Haven.

Edward Dixwell's church in Ponteland, where John Dixwell was baptized in 1613. I could not find Edward's tombstone in the graveyard.

Anthony Van Dyck's portrait of Sir Basil Dixwell, John's uncle who raised him and his older brother Mark after their father Edward died. *Courtesy of Canterbury Museums and Galleries, U.K.*

Broome Park, the mansion Basil built in the late 1630s and the home of John Dixwell until he fled England in 1660. My childhood home in Milton, Massachusetts, built in 1916, where four generations of Dixwell's descendants lived before it was sold.

Closeups of brickwork from each mansion. Broome Park was built with 2,700,000 bricks from clay dug and fired on the property. I don't how many bricks were used in my house.

The ramparts of Dover Castle, a military fortification overlooking the English Channel.

John Dixwell's monument in New Haven, Connecticut behind
Center Church on the Green. It displays the Dixwell coat of arms.
His original sandstone tombstone, on which only his initials
were carved to protect his identity, stands on the other side of
this nineteentho-century obelisk.

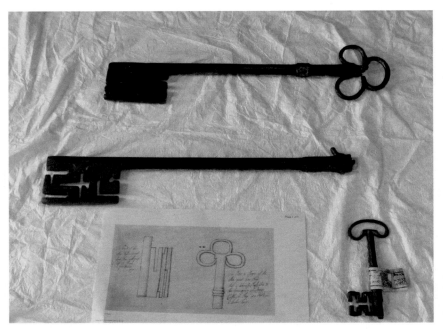

My key, on the day I visited the Castle's archives, laid next to the ancient keys (twenty-one and eighteen inches long) given, in a ceremony dating back to the thirteenth century, to the Lord Warden of the Cinque Ports Federation. When the warden is installed in his post, he also becomes the constable of Dover Castle. John Dixwell was the governor of the castle from late 1659 to 1660, when he escaped to Germany upon the restoration of Charles II.

23

The Key Returns to Dover Castle

FOR MOST OF THE NIGHT, sleep refused to come. I was tense about to-morrow's interview with Rowena Willard-Wright, the senior curator at Dover Castle, the expert with a special interest in Dover Castle keys, the one who'd agreed to "deal with Dixie." How could I prepare? I didn't have any books or articles by her. I just had the key, with its marvelous size and heft.

But as I tossed and turned in my chilly bedroom my mind was more occupied with my childhood home than with Dover Castle or my key. In some ways, being at Broome Park, with its big brick house and acres of land, felt strikingly similar to what I had grown up with. Our house was one of three my great grandfather George Wigglesworth (1853-1930) had built for his daughters on contiguous lots in Milton, Massachusetts. He and his wife Mary Catherine Dixwell raised their six kids in an even big-ger mansion in Milton, then kept their daughters close by building homes for them a few miles away.

George's wealth was extensive, though it may not have rivalled that of the seventeenth-century Dixwells of Broome Park. Roger Hailwood and I had speculated about whether their money, one generation back in the Herdson line, came from the fur trade, or maybe from rope. George's came from New England textile mills. He served as president of four of them, and grew so rich, during the Gilded Age, that both Harvard and Milton Academy have Wigglesworth buildings built with his donations. He'd been dead for twenty years by the time I arrived in 1951, but I grew up on the compound he had funded for his three daughters and their husbands. Even in elementary school I was acutely aware of my unusual situation. No other child I knew lived in as big a house as ours or had ancient great aunts and uncles as next-door neighbors across wide fields and formal gardens and acres of woods.

Then I began thinking about the similarities between John Dixwell's relationship to Broome Park and my father's to our home. Both of them wound up responsible for a sprawling property that was someone else's idea. Would Dad have chosen such a massive house if it hadn't already been in the family? Did he ever actually feel it was his? Perhaps he took care of it only because he had to, as a dutiful son. Could it be that this was even more the case for John Dixwell? Broome Park would never be his, and yet he had to take care of it for his nephew Basil after Mark was killed in the civil war. Basil, only three, was Mark's firstborn son. He would inherit everything.

John Dixwell and my father had the experience of war in common, too. John fought in the civil wars. Dad went to the South Pacific in World War Two. Both of them lived before the term post-traumatic stress disorder had been coined, yet they must have been traumatized. It was not possible, when Dad was a battalion surgeon in the midst of carnage, to airlift the wounded out. Often, he could do little but ease people's pain as they died.

They both came home from the horrors of war and went on with their lives. In another parallel, each was responsible for numerous small children. As I wrote earlier, after Mark died, John became the guardian for his widowed sister-in-law Elizabeth and her five children. They were already living with him at Broome Park. The four of us arrived in the first seven years after Dad returned from the South Pacific. My father and Dixwell, an ocean and centuries apart, were surrounded by people who had no real idea of what they'd been through. Both lived on generous pieces of land over which children could tumble, oblivious to bloody conflicts beyond their ken.

What was it like for my father, emotionally scarred by war, to have his kids grow up in his childhood home, explore the same woods, and run across the same fields, as if nothing had changed? He was the one who had changed. Maybe his Dixwell grandmother's "least said soonest mended" maxim helped him carry on. My father was adept at not talking about things.

I got out of bed, found a long-sleeved shirt, added a sweater and wool socks, and got back under the covers. Gradually I warmed up and lay perfectly still, taking in the essence of the gigantic house where John Dixwell had lived for nearly two decades. As the night crawled on, I kept feeling the thick pasture grass under my feet and the sense of limitless land and sky. In a way I didn't mind being unable to sleep.

In the morning, bleary-eyed, I ate the rest of the crumble and was about to dig into the remainder of Gillian's tea loaf when it occurred to me there might be as little to eat at Dover Castle as there was at Broome Park. I stuck it in my backpack, beside the key, then spent a couple of hours studying the contents of Gillian's box.

On top was a pale green, homemade-looking *History of Barham* (1959, 1966). Wonderfully, it described a visit by a twentieth-century American Basil Dixwell, the father of another cousin I'd met in the course of my research, Marcia Dixwell DiMambro. Basil's nickname, Marcia had told me, was Dixie: "On Sunday, October 11th, 1964, there were present at Matins in our Church Mr. Basil Dixwell . . . an American jet air-line pilot directly descended from Sir Basil Dixwell who built Broome Park (the eighth generation). After the service the Rector and Churchwardens showed the visitors the Dixwell monument, the funeral helm in the South Transept, and the entry in our oldest register of Sir Basil's death. The entry read: 'Sir Basil Dixwell was brought out of Folkestone and buried in the church at Barham, 1642.'"[1]

I was glad Basil "Dixie" Dixwell had gotten inside that church in 1964, but I felt envious until I remembered the internet could probably tell me everything I wanted to know about the monument I hadn't seen. It could.

The inscription brought home all the deaths John Dixwell experienced in the years leading up to his decision to judge a king. In the first five years after he passed the bar, he lost three members of his family.

> In the vault underneath are deposited the bodies of the under-mentioned persons, viz. Alice, daughter of Mark DIXWELL, gent. by Elizabeth his wife, who died in her infancy, and was buried Oct.16, 1639, also Sir Basil DIXWELL, knight and baronet, who was nephew and heir of Mr John HEARDSON, of the town of Folkestone, Esqr. and was buried Jan 12, 1642. Also Mark DIXWELL, above-mentioned, who was nephew and heir of the above said Sir Basil DIXWELL, and was buried Feb. 8, 1643.

They lost Alice when she was not quite two. A few months after her burial, baby Basil arrived in the spring of 1640, followed in rapid succession by two more boys—Heardson in August 1641 and William in December 1642. There were no more babies, for Mark was killed just a few weeks after William was born. John and his sister-in-law Elizabeth must have reeled in the wake of so much loss.

I sat there feeling the weight of it, but also the wonder that I was in the building where they had been so grief-stricken and so busy, she with many small children, he with the gargantuan estate he was legally bound to manage until three-year-old Basil came of age.

Maybe Broome Park's palatial elegance cheered them up. How big was it, anyway? It was hard to tell what the inside had been like before the time-share company turned it into condos. How many rooms had there been? Gillian's box had an advertisement from the June 7, 1902 "Supplement to Country Life" taken out by London Auctioneers Knight, Frank & Rutley. It said the place had "22 bed and dressing rooms." I smiled at the ad's smooth lies, namely that Inigo Jones had designed the place and that the "Residence is in good order throughout," and the grounds are "inexpensive to maintain."

How soon after this did Lord Kitchener purchase the estate? The answer was in a newspaper clipping. "Lord Kitchener bought Broome Park in 1911, with about 500 acres of land, for L14,000. His last day in England—before drowning in HMS Hampshire—was spent there. It was a

bright Sunday in June 1916, and he spent his time in the sunken rose garden. Next day the grey waters of the North Sea claimed him."[2] The North
Sea! Lord Kitchener, the last private person to own Broome Park, died
near John Dixwell's birthplace.

In ten minutes the taxi I'd hired to drive me to Dover Castle would arrive. I packed up the box and hurried down the carved staircase, across
the Great Hall and out the front door. My driver was waiting.

As we drove along I kept touching the key through the fabric of my
daypack. What if Rowena Willard-Wright, Senior Curator, expert authority on the keys of Dover Castle, told me it was too important an artifact to be wrapped in a plastic produce bag and kept in a desk drawer in
New England? Did it belong at the castle? Would I feel compelled to give
it to her? What if she tried to confiscate it?

I reviewed my printout of the last email she'd sent me just before I left
Amherst. After weeks of not replying she finally wrote:

Dear Dixie,

Would Wednesday (14) morning around 11 am be convenient for you to
meet at Dover Castle Stone Hut?

Kind regards,
Rowena Willard-Wright

Senior Curator
Stone Hut;
Dover Castle
Dover

"Stone Hut" sounded like a Roman ruin. The conquering Romans had
come through Dover in 43 A.D., but Dover Castle's website said the "Stone
Hut" was built in 1912 for the Royal Garrison Artillery. My taxi driver had
never heard of it. We entered the castle and drove past gray walls punc-
tuated with crenellated towers until he dropped me off at a place he did
know, a lunchroom featuring a massive cannon from some king's war.

The cashier directed me across the road but there were so many buildings it took me a while to figure out which was the one I wanted. I kept checking the time. It was already 11 and the Stone Hut was locked. Tentatively, I knocked on the big door. No answer. Several minutes went by while my adrenaline spiked. I was now late and I couldn't get into this forbidding pile of rock. I resorted to hammering and shouting "Hello! Hello?" Suddenly, the door opened. There stood a slender, casually dressed young man. He looked like a grad student, and when I told him of my interview he led me upstairs. I clambered after him, mortified. Who did I think I was, asking an archivist at Dover Castle to answer my elementary questions?

We entered a big cluttered room. It wasn't grand in the least. There was a motley assortment of desks, books, papers, posters, and bookcases, then archivists who drifted toward me and began introducing themselves: Rowena Willard-Wright herself, two women named Jo and Wendy, and two men—Connor, and the one who'd brought me upstairs, Rowan. "Don't be so self-conscious!" that woman at the Penn Club had scolded me. All right, I would try. I inhaled slowly through my nose. I'd survived Eton College, two universities and Lincoln's Inn. I could do this. It helped that not one archivist looked pretentious. They just seemed pleased to meet me and interested in my key. As they clustered around, I reached into my backpack and pulled out the key with something approaching a flourish.

"It's lovely!" exclaimed Rowena. She made no move to snatch it. Clearly, she thought it was mine and mine alone, for she didn't even touch it at first but had me bring it over to a table on which was spread special archival cloth. She put on gloves, took it as carefully as if it were made of glass and laid it at a right angle to two giant keys she'd brought from storage for my perusal. They were the ceremonial keys that are given, in a tradition dating back to the thirteenth century, to each successive constable of Dover Castle. The other archivists were clucking so joyfully, the embarrassment I'd felt at being caught pounding and shouting at the door morphed into delight that not only had I had the guts to take this extraordinary journey, but also the luck to intersect with so many people who were also captivated by John Dixwell's story.

All of us admired the three keys as Rowena told me about the big ones, which were eighteen and twenty-one inches long. "Part of the Castle's ceremony is that when the Lord Warden of the Cinque Ports Federation is installed in his post, he also becomes the constable of Dover Castle and he is given the keys to the castle. Usually he carries the position for life. He's given them, then we take them back to store them."

My big key was dwarfed in comparison. (See the last plate in the colored insert.)

Rowena fell into a ruminative silence. Finally she said, "Dover Castle has been called the Key to England, so these are important objects." It's the key because Dover is the perfect place to invade England, as the Romans did. The country has often needed the military protection of Dover Castle.

The moment felt sacred. Considerable time went by before I roused myself, opened my notebook and began asking questions. What did it mean that John Dixwell had been the castle's governor? What were his responsibilities? Rowena said he would have been in charge of securing the castle and in charge of the local military. He had been appointed governor in October of 1659, so did not serve very long before he had to flee the country. I asked if she had a theory about why he had chosen to take the key with him when he fled.

"You'd have thought he'd have taken away something more personal, so perhaps this is the key to his chambers. He would have had a place to stay here. Very few people did."

Rowan, the young man who had opened the door for me, came over with a book that helped place my key in the right century, then Rowena explained its three parts: the "ward," which is the square part that turns inside the lock, the "shank," which is the stem or shaft of the key, and the "bow," which is the circular part at the top. Rowan pointed out that my key's bow has a distinctive kidney shape, just like the book's illustration of a seventeenth-century key.

We again fell into a worshipful silence, then Jo asked if I wanted tea. Soon the six of us were seated at the far end of the long table that held the keys, dipping into an ample supply of cookies and chocolate-covered biscuits. We poured milk into our steaming mugs from a bottle Connor fetched from a half-fridge. Once again, I had the sense that Rowena, that all of them, took their time to study and try to understand and fully appreciate whatever came their way. It was so wonderful being with them I lost all track of time. They were funny and smart, and now that I was relaxing over tea I noticed their room was a place where they enjoyed themselves tremendously. On a nearby shelf were a Barbie doll on her own little sofa, a beaming nun puppet brandishing boxing gloves, and a teddy bear. A diminutive jar of Nutella sat beside someone's computer, and a gold-toned, life-sized ceramic bunny lay on another desk.

I ate a lot of cookies, and so did everyone else. Rowena dabbed briefly at crumbs that had landed on her chest, but it was clear they didn't bother her a bit. There they remained, clinging to her sweater. We talked and talked while people pulled various books on keys out of the bookcases and gradually came to conclusions about mine and what vanished door it had probably unlocked. Best of all, Rowena thought it was the real thing.

"I'm pretty sure it is a Dover Castle key because it's not made out of brass, which you might expect from a fine gentleman's lock for his home, but rather it's made out of a more rich, heavy iron alloy," she said. "It's cheaper metal and plainer as well."

They all felt it would have unlocked the governor's lodging in the Constable's Tower, which is at the entrance of Dover Castle. "It's the most important and impressive lodging in the castle. The head of the army for the south of England, the Brigadier, lives there now, so we can't go in," Rowena told me, but she said we could stroll over and look at the outside of it after we'd finished eating.

Everyone had nice things to say about John Dixwell, and Wendy must have noticed my sensitivity about my seven greats grandfather's role, for she said: "I don't think any of us have a problem with your relative being a regicide, because it was a long and slow process to becoming a constitutional monarchy."

Is that affirming or what?

Next, I asked how they thought he got out of England. "It's not too long a leap to imagine him commissioning an escape. It's dead easy from here—only twenty-one miles from France. Fishing boats were going back and forth all the time," said Connor.

Then I repeated the question I particularly cared about. "Why do you suppose John Dixwell chose a key to take with him when he fled?"

Gently, Rowena picked up his key again. "Why did he bring it with him? It's the key to England," she decided. "It's a memory of who he once was and what he once was."

As an answer, that felt right to me. In fact, it felt deeply satisfying, as if Rowena were honoring not only John Dixwell and his key but also me and my decision to come to England, bearing the key, trying to understand my radical ancestor.

I looked at my watch and was amazed to see that three hours had flown by. Everyone else seemed surprised as well, but Rowena wanted to do one more thing. She had to show me the place she was almost certain the key had unlocked, though the original keyhole was no more. We headed out to the apartment where John Dixwell had lived. She pointed out the Roman lighthouse, dating from around 50 A.D., then we arrived at the Constable's Gate, on which construction had begun in 1220. Above it rose the governor's lodging.

We went through massive wooden doors, then under the apartment to a bridge over a dry moat. Before us was the English Channel stretching to France. High behind us was a wooden balcony, which Rowena said has the date 1644 carved on it. Dixwell must have stood there, gazing off to sea, keeping watch. We stood in silence and gazed as well.

Balcony of Governor's Lodging overlooking the English Channel.

Chatting all the way, we walked back to the Stone Hut. I picked up my key and as I wrapped it in its plastic bag one of the archivists gently suggested I store it in a seal-tight container with a packet of silica gel to keep it dry. Another had the idea of sending a photo of it to the metalwork department of the Victoria and Albert Museum in London. "First, don't give them any background information and see what they say about it." At last, with considerable reluctance, I said goodbye.

"Be proud of him," Rowena called after me as I headed down the stairs.

24

Face-to-face with Uncle Basil

THERE WAS ONLY ONE DISAPPOINTMENT, the day I took the key back to Dover Castle, but it was a big one. I was hoping to see a woman named Lorraine Sencicle, who some years ago started a website called The Dover Historian. I'd read a number of articles she's written about her beloved city's history, including one about John Dixwell. We'd been emailing for a few years, and planned to meet when I came to visit the castle. However, in losing all track of time with the archivists, I ended up calling too late for her to be able to meet with me.

We were both upset. But to her credit, she took the time to answer some of my questions and suggested I consult a book, when I got back to London, in a special collection in the British Library, *The Oxinden and Peyton Letters, 1642-1670*. An excellent suggestion. My last day in England, I was able to get a British Library card and peruse not only that book but some seventeenth-century sworn affidavits pertaining to the seizure of various of John Dixwell's properties after he fled.

In the meantime, I had one more day in Kent, and I decided to spend the morning visiting Basil Dixwell's portrait by the great Anthony Van Dyck, the one the Beaney Institute had purchased from an anonymous American for a million pounds in 2004. After my second and final night in the ancestral mansion, this time with a full moon pouring light on me through that splendid, leaky window, I took a bus into Canterbury and quickly found the Beaney. It's a beautiful half-timbered building cheek by jowl with its neighbors. A sign under the peak of the roof reads "The Beaney Institute for the Education of Working Men, Public Library and Museum" and the gold-lettered sign above the doorway reads "Royal Museum and Free Library, founded 1858."

It wasn't hard to find Basil, as his portrait is one of the jewels of their collection, but what was hard was my emotional response. The painting is such a—what is the best word? I think it is "convincing"—portrait, I felt as if I were actually coming into Basil's presence. He seemed to look at me with a level gaze and I, gazing back, felt strangely shy.

There must have been other people in that gallery but I was lost in a visceral encounter with the man who'd raised John Dixwell. I stood still for a long time. To Basil's right was a nineteenth-century painting of Broome Park. Even in the twenty-first century, his moneyed, magnificent idea for a place to hang his hat is right beside him. If he was the kind of person who felt the need to dazzle, he's doing it to this day. The caption says that Sir Basil Dixwell was rich enough:

> to have his portrait painted by Van Dyck, one of the most famous portraitists of all time. The black silk clothes he wears indicate considerable wealth: it had just become possible to dye cloth black, rather than dark blue, using special wood imported from South America, and black cloth was very expensive.
>
> Dixwell inherited estates in Kent and also purchased land for a new house near Barham, on the outskirts of Canterbury. Broome Park, depicted in the painting on the right, took three years to build. Thousands of bricks were specially made and the project cost about £8,000—the equivalent of millions of pounds today.

Here were the dominant facts I already knew about his wealth and extravagant tastes, but Basil's face didn't match my stereotype of such a person at all. I studied him. His eyes, like so many eyes in my family, were a grayish blue. A wispy bit of beard under his lower lip, surely a fashionable touch, had a hint of gray. His hair, as lushly curly as my daughter's (if he wasn't wearing a wig), made him look as vulnerable as a teenager. There was something insecure and worried in his face. I took a close-up.

Basil! Impossible not to think about him intimately, this many greats uncle in whose gigantic mansion I had just spent two fairly sleepless nights. What had shaped him the most? He had lost his father when he was only six, and been given an annuity of six pounds a year. Was he less than fond of his oldest brother because William got everything? Or was he envious of the education his brother Edward got at Eton and then at Oxford when he, Basil, would get no formal education at all? He had kindly funded his nephews' educations, but why wouldn't he when he had become richer than anyone else in his family, wildly rich in his thirties after his Uncle John Herdson left him a fortune?

Detail of portrait of Sir Basil Dixwell by Anthony Van Dyck.

We continued to eye one another, Basil Dixwell and Sarah Dixwell Brown, there on the second floor of the Beaney. I thought about the description of him killing a man in his *History of Parliament* entry: "As a consequence of a minor traffic accident in Moorgate in 1631, he was involved in a brawl with 'a drunken fellow in his doublet and hose out of an alehouse', whose head he broke with his sword. Unfortunately for Dixwell, the man died under the surgeon's hands, and it was expected that 'it will cost him many thousands of pounds ere he get clear of the business'. However, his fortune was not seriously impaired, as one month later he received a royal pardon."[1]

Had Basil been indifferent to that "fellow," who sounds like someone considerably lower in social class, perhaps merely an impediment, one easily removed if you had a lot of money and the favor of the king? I gazed into his eyes. Were they a bit haunted? He was forty-six when he swung that sword. Surely it stayed with him, buried under the elaborate trappings of wealth. I contemplated the synchronicity of the murder and John Dixwell's arrival as an eighteen-year-old at Lincoln's Inn.

Was John, son of a vicar and brand-new law student, able to see the whole situation for what it was—a rich man with connections getting away with murder? Lincoln's Inn is a stone's throw from Moorgate. Did it shake John that this man, who had been a father to him, had ended someone's life in an impulsive, perhaps drunken, act of rage? Did various people at Lincoln's Inn help Basil "get clear of the business"? Did John, decades later in New Haven, tell Bathsheba about it, and was the story passed along to American Dixwells? I suspect not. I think they just associated the name Basil Dixwell with a dazzling gigantic estate that they might, with luck, have some claim to.

No one else was in the gallery, so I leaned closer. "Descendants of your black sheep nephew John in America were still naming their sons after you in the twentieth century," I whispered to him, "but maybe you're the real black sheep." Basil continued to regard me. His eyes now seemed sad, his mouth irresolute.

He was in his fifties when Van Dyck painted him. He'd provided for Mark and John, and now Mark and Elizabeth's growing family. Were those three young adults in the next generation, Mark, John, and Elizabeth, careful never to mention that nasty business at Moorgate? Was it a "least said soonest mended" situation? Everyone was living off Basil's money, after all, and there were plenty of distractions. In 1638, when Basil was sitting for Van Dyck and watching Broome Park's millions of bricks being assembled, Elizabeth was providing a steady stream of little Dixwells. She'd already had Elizabeth and Abigail, the child who died in 1639, and then, like clockwork, she gave birth to a daughter Bennet and three sons: Basil, Heardson, and finally William, who was baptized December 31, 1642, four days after his Great Uncle Basil's death.

The first English Civil War began in August of that same year. It was a terrible, tumultuous time, but Basil died in time to miss it, for the most part. I wondered, looking at him, if wearing a different outfit every day he served in the House of Commons and building the biggest, showiest house for miles around had taken his mind off his guilt for killing a man. On the other hand, maybe he never thought about it at all.

I walked slowly out of the gallery, then stood in the doorway for a long moment and sighed. There was so much I would never know.

It was disorienting to reenter the sunshine of a twenty-first century day in the ancient city of Canterbury. I wandered up a street to a church that had been converted into a tourist attraction featuring Chaucer's *Canterbury Tales*. I paid my money then wound through an odd labyrinth of dimly lit scenes peopled with manikins that popped in and out of windows and doors while I listened to an audio tour narrated by actors from *Fawlty Towers*. Finally a live actor, a very young man, gave a rousing description of Archbishop of Canterbury Thomas Becket's bloody murder in 1170. I'm never in the mood to hear about murder, but he was so young and enthusiastic I heard him out to the end of his spiel.

Then I rode the bus back to Broome Park, because I didn't want to miss its once-a-week tour. The tour guide told us a bit more about Basil's blue marble. Before Kitchener had it torn out of the Great Hall, it covered the columns and floor. The Dixwells had formal gardens, but the Oxindens, who married into the family not long after John Dixwell fled, used the land for farming until Kitchener put in formal, Italianate gardens. As we stood in them, she pointed out two statues that had been presented to Kitchener for his service in the Boer War. They are headless because soldiers housed at Broome Park in subsequent wars used them for target practice. Back inside the house, she showed us the magistrates' room, which was where the local court once met. In another room, a trapdoor was hidden under a rug. Somewhere, she said, there's a secret passageway, and there are "lots of ghosts."

Perhaps it was just as well I wasn't spending another night at Broome Park. Or perhaps I myself was a ghost, haunting the ancient premises, trying to understand the world John Dixwell had to flee.

It felt prosaic, but also like a relief, to take the bus back to Canterbury, catch a train to London, and end up at the Penn Club for my last two nights in England. The next day would be my final full day in England. I fell into my narrow bed, so relieved to be there instead of in Broome Park's chilly splendor, that sleep came at once.

25

Hearing John Dixwell's Voice

THE NEXT MORNING, I followed Lorraine Sencicle's sensible advice and went to the British Library, which houses what used to be in the Reading Room of the British Museum, that beautiful blue-domed room where I had discovered John Dixwell in 1980. This library, which opened in 1998, is spacious and imaginatively designed. One of the first things you see, upon entering, is a big bronze bench in the shape of an open book attached to a ball and chain. I was amused, but not that amused, for often that is how my Dixwell project feels to me. In the middle of a towering central space rises a great square glass column, filled with ancient leather-bound books, their spines alone a work of art.

In case I needed it, I was armed with a letter of introduction from an American professor, and maybe it helped, for I was quickly questioned, photographed and given a library card, good for three years. I stashed everything but a notebook in a locker, then various people helped me find and order Dixwell material. There was so much! When my first request was brought I sat and copied as much as I could from a hefty bound collection of original documents from the years after Charles II was restored to the monarchy. I wrote with a pink pencil given to me by the staff.

Just as at Eton College, or Oxford or Lincoln's Inn, I was in a state of awe not only that these paper artifacts had been so carefully saved, but also that I was allowed to examine them. The documents had been glued onto sturdy modern pages in such a way that you could leaf through the volume and see both the front and back of each without touching it. I soon learned that prior to his 1660 flight from justice, John Dixwell had purchased numerous parcels of land for his nephew Basil.

And I mean numerous. I had already been picturing Basil as the greedy uncle for whom having much meant getting more. Here was ample evidence John had carried on that tradition—busily increasing Dixwell lands as much as possible. One document, whose deponent described himself as "being a meniall servant to the said Mr. John Dixwell and privie to most of his transactions," said under oath that Dixwell "purchased the said manor of Outelmestone in trust to and for the use of his nephew, now Sir Basil Dixwell and the rest of his brother Mr. Marke Dixwell's children."[1]

But of course if you sign the death warrant for the king of England, and his son is restored to power, everything you own could be gone in a moment, even if you bought it for your brother's children. I turned page after page of proof that much of the land John bought for Basil was seized by the crown after he fled. One document described, "lands in the county of Kent late the possessions of John Dixwell forfeited into his Majestie for the treason of the said John . . ."[2] It was chilling to read, over and over, the words, "attainted of high treason." And what was it like for Basil, now a young man, to lose all those properties because of Uncle John's choice to judge Charles I?

I spent the afternoon going through the two-volume collection of *Oxinden Letters*, which Lorraine Sencicle had told me about. It's the most chattily vivid portrait of John Dixwell's times in County Kent that I could have hoped for. By some wonderful stroke of luck and/or genetically encoded hoarding habits, all the letters to and from a man named Henry Oxinden of Barham, the same Barham where I'd found that church after my sweaty hike through endless sheep pastures, have survived. Henry was born in 1608 and died in 1670. His correspondence was safely passed down in his family for hundreds of years.

Then, in the early 1930s, the brilliant and indefatigable Dorothy Gardiner transcribed and explained a batch of somewhere between two and three thousand letters dating from 1607 to 1670. Even though I was already tired, I could hardly wait to dive in.

The folios I had read before lunch were in a part of the library called "Manuscripts." Gardiner's 1933 chef d'oeuvre was in "Humanities," and it looked so brand new after the documents from the 1660s I had seen earlier, that I felt like breaking the rules and covertly photocopying every pertinent page with my iPhone, but I couldn't because I had obediently left it in a locker several floors beneath me. Instead, pink pencil in hand, I raced through as much as possible before the library closed.

Gardiner made me like Henry Oxinden right away. She says of him in her introduction: "The dislike of destroying old documents must have been in the blood, but it flowed most liberally in the veins of that untiring hoarder of the scrap of paper, Henry Oxinden of Barham. He had overwhelming respect for the written word, at times a lively sense of its mischievous possibilities, which yet could never bring him to tear up his old letters."[3] A man after my own heart! I have told you about the big house I grew up in, but I have not yet confessed that after my parents' deaths, I was the child who took all the letters and photos, thirty boxes of them, now taking up too much of my basement but as valuable to me as a Van Dyck.

In Volume 2, I discovered Dorothy Gardiner had nothing nice to say about John Dixwell. It turned out he had often acquired land that his neighbor Sir Henry had wanted to purchase. Gardiner says in her introduction, "Captain John Dixwell, schemer now, regicide yet to become, like the Londoners was too clever for his neighbor and competitor in the contest for episcopal woodland."[4] "Episcopal woodland" meant land that had once belonged to the Church of England, been confiscated by the new regime, and was now for sale.

Carefully, I copied her words with my pink pencil into my journal. Was John Dixwell a greedy land gobbler? I considered that possibility.

Well, yes, on young Basil's behalf he had used the family's fortune to buy acres and acres of land. On the other hand, I remembered what Wilfrid Prest, in his two books about the Inns of Court, wrote about less educated, perhaps less clever gentlemen feeling deeply threatened by men who'd passed the bar: "It would be surprising, if . . . barristers did not often encounter contempt, fear, jealousy and resentment."[5] As I studied Volume 2, flipping back and forth between the index and the letters in search of every reference to John Dixwell, I realized that Prest was right. John was a well-educated barrister, and Henry Oxinden, though he had "some knowledge of law acquired at Gray's Inn years before,"[6] ended up, when he and John wanted the same acreage, with the short end of the stick in numerous land deals.

John was too clever for Henry, and Henry hated this. He had private names for my ancestor. "Creeper," he called him, or "Crepentissimus," or "Secretissimus," favoring Latin superlatives. "You may be sure your J. D. will defeat you," he wrote his cousin, another Henry Oxinden, in 1646, "Crepentissimus is neither so faithfull to you or others as you judged him to bee."[7] In May of 1647 he wrote his wife, "Capt. Dixwell hath bought all Sir Thomas Soames his estate in Barham, but say nothing of it. I dined with him this Mooneday att Westminster where he told me of itt. Sure what ever others expect, by his paying out of his monie hee expects peace. I beeleeive in few yeares hee will have most of the land from thence to Folkston."[8]

Several times I almost laughed out loud at Henry's epithets, but they also upset me, especially because sixty pages earlier I'd been so touched not only by how torn Henry was by the civil war but also by the fact that he was present when Mark Dixwell was killed at Arundel Castle. On February 6, 1643 he wrote to Sir Thomas Peyton: "I was at Arundell, where though I was in great danger, I was not so much afrayd as grieved to see men of the same Religion, of the same Nation, so eagerlie engaged one against the other, as if they had beleft [believed] they had done Allmightie God good service in defacing his own image and destroying the workmanship of his owne hands."[9]

At the end of the same letter, Henry wrote, "That Almightie God whose counsels are of a great depth, hath taken my verie loving Friend, Colonell Dixwell and others to his mercie and spared mee the most unworthy of all his creatures."[10]

Oxinden seemed a sensitive and thoughtful man. I didn't like it that such a nice guy so resented my seven greats grandfather. I started to feel defensive. Henry should have been mad at Basil, I thought, that one-time murderer and builder of Broome Park. John risked everything to judge a king and spent twenty-nine years in exile. Come on! I went on consulting the index and found, to my shocked joy, letters to Henry from John himself. Here were his actual words to the neighbor who cut him up behind his back. On the last day of my trip, John Dixwell's voice came across the centuries to me.

There were letters between them in which they made arrangements to strengthen Dover Harbor's defenses with timber. Then Henry's young daughter's case of the measles meant they had to cancel dinner plans. Henry wrote John: "To have my house diseased is a misery, but to bee deprived of the societie of my friends (and such as you are) is one so great and grievous as transcends my abilitie to express."[11] Since I'd already been privy to his anger at John, I was annoyed. Give me a break, Henry, I thought. Must you lay it on so thick?

John wrote back, detailing how to repair the harbor and ends with this: "I am sorie for the sicknes of your young daughter, I hope there is noe such danger in that disease that wee should be debarred of your good companie, the which is verie much esteemed of by Your most affectionate friend and servant John Dixwell."[12]

Did he know Henry was angry with him? Another letter from him a few pages later suggests he did. Note that John's use of "sister" means his sister-in-law Elizabeth, Mark's widow, with whom he lived at Broome Park. Also, the "Covett" was land whose timber would be used to strengthen Dover Harbor. This letter gives the impression that he was skilled at smoothing feathers. "I must confess I was not satisfied when I came last from Broome what your intentions were concerning the Covett.

I did conjecture you did desire it wholy for your selfe; the which should have pleased me verie well . . ."[13]

Really? Perhaps John was way too clever for Henry, and generally got what he wanted. He ends his letter with this:

> Sir, I am verie glad if there were any discontent that might cause a differ-
> ence between you, my sister or myself that it is taken away. I hope there
> shall never be any; and that as wee are near neighboures wee shall alwaies
> continue loving friends; and truly for my parte I should be sorie to oc-
> casion the contrary, or in anything to be wanting that may express my-
> self to be
> Your affectionate friend and servant
John Dixwell
> January the 14th 1646[14]

There was a further complication that year. Henry got a crush on Elizabeth Dixwell. It was platonic, insisted Henry, a married man, but nevertheless Elizabeth sent him a polite reminder of his marital status, "I hope
I shall never covet what my neighbour possesses."[15]

Fascinating. They must have spent considerable time together, the
Oxindens and John and Elizabeth Dixwell. At one point, I got confused
because I found out that Elizabeth had remarried a man named Henry
Oxinden on February 18, 1661, less than a year after John's flight from justice. It was not Henry of Barham, however. It was his first cousin, Henry
of Deane. Deane is a few miles from Barham.

The collection had one more letter from John, dated February 24, 1647.
Henry had asked him for information about the Westminster School, as
he was thinking of sending his son there. John did careful research. "I had
given you an account the last weeke of Westminster schoole but that I was
unwilling to informe you with anything until I had spoken with the Master thereof myself."

How kind, I thought loyally. In his next paragraph John tells Henry
about how the forty King's Scholars at the school are given their room,

board, and an academic gown, but there are no open spaces left. He then details what fees the other students owe and describes other things to be had:

> if any gentleman have a desire his sonne shall learne to dance or play upon any Musicke, that is to be payed for alsoe; that is as punctuall an account I can give you about this matter. If there be any thing els you desire to know about this schoole that I can doe you any service in, you shall command
>
> Sir
Your affectionate friend and servant
JOHN DIXWELL[16]

A polite voice announcing the library would be closing shortly startled me out of my intense concentration. Hurriedly, I turned to the index. I had managed to look at every letter from John Dixwell.

I walked slowly all the way from the British Library to the Penn Club. Tomorrow I would be on a plane crossing the Atlantic. I moved in a kind of daze, avoiding the big streets in favor of side streets, scarcely noticing anything for I was down in seventeenth-century Kent, peering into the world of Henry, John and Elizabeth living in their big manor houses, John traveling to London to serve in the House of Commons. On the local stage were the dinners, the measles, Henry's crush on Elizabeth Dixwell. In the background, and all around was a country convulsed by civil war, no one yet imagining what extreme measures would soon be taken against the king.

Part Three

*The Lord will appear for people and the good
old cause for which I suffer, and there will be
those in power again that will relieve the injured
and oppressed.*

John Dixwell, New Haven Colony, 1682

26

Back in the U.S.A.

AS A GENERAL RULE I can't sleep on planes, which gives me ample time to think. As I crossed the Atlantic, I marveled at what I'd experienced in two weeks. All the places I had visited were part of me now. Henry Oxinden's letters had given me even more. They were helping me imagine life inside Broome Park. John Dixwell's references to "my sister," meaning his sister-in-law Elizabeth, made me realize how close they must have been, especially after death took three members of their family—two-year-old Alice, Uncle Basil, and Mark—in quick succession. Mark's death left John and Elizabeth as the only Dixwell adults in that huge brick mansion as five children grew up. The letters suggest they often discussed things. There was much to think about: maintaining the estate for firstborn son Basil, educating him and his siblings, approving and funding the marriage of the oldest daughter Elizabeth to a man named Thomas Westrowe.

People around me in the plane's cabin were sensibly dozing while my thoughts traveled from Broome Park to Ponteland and back again. I began comparing John's mother Mary to his sister-in-law, both widowed young. The situation for Elizabeth, after Mark's death, was so different from Mary's when Edward died. Mary was left with six children and slim resources. All I know of her is that she must have moved south, and that her children were parceled out to various in-laws. She lost her husband, then her home, and then her sons Mark and John were sent to Kent. You could argue, and you'd be right, that at least she had in-laws who made sure everyone was provided for. It could have been otherwise. But now that I had spent time in the chilly damp village of Ponteland and then in the opulence of Broome Park I had a sharp awareness of Mary's losses. Elizabeth, in contrast, went right on living at Broome Park and so did all her kids. She was lucky to have, under the same roof, a barrister brother-in-law to help her with her affairs and those of her children. I hope it was good for John Dixwell, too.

Before I went to England I had thought of him as a loner, but now I knew that wasn't true until he fled. From the time he became a barrister in 1638, until he escaped in 1660, he had lived in the midst of a big family. And because I'd witnessed his birth record written in Edward Dixwell's hand, I knew precisely how old he had been during those years—twenty-five to forty-seven—in the prime of adulthood. Did he feel especially attached to little Elizabeth, his niece, as one has special feelings for the first baby in the next generation, amazed by the miracle of it? He was twenty-three and still studying the law when she arrived, then he was admitted to the bar thirteen months later. When he came home to Broome Park, he hadn't missed much of her babyhood. Elizabeth was eight when her father was killed at Arundel Castle and John became her guardian. There's proof they were close—she was the only family member who wrote him letters all the years he was exiled in New Haven, and those letters have survived. For decades, she inquired after his needs and sent him what she could. The rest of the Dixwells, including his sister-in-law Elizabeth, disowned him.

I pulled out my folder of Jason Peacey's articles, interested to reread them now that I'd finished my trip. Parliament, Peacey writes, granted John the wardship of Mark's children in August 1644, six months after Mark died in the war. Mark's death led to John getting ownership of a Kent estate worth 200 pounds a year, and he had a share in the "Irish adventure." Rowena Willard-Wright had told me to be proud of him, and I was, but I wasn't proud of his investment in Ireland.

I had asked Peacey about the latter when I'd met with him in London, suspecting "Irish adventure" meant something bad. Peacey explained John was one of many Englishmen "banking on wholesale seizure of land . . . they seized the land, massacred, transplanted people elsewhere and started divvying up land. Alas, everyone was doing it."

Did Dixwell manage, as an investor, not to think about those atrocities? Perhaps, like his land purchases which so infuriated his neighbor Henry Oxinden, the "Irish adventure" was just another way he and many others got wealthier, and something he saw not as the moral outrage it was, but merely as a good investment for his nephew Basil.

On the other hand, I felt sure he did see as outrageous the ways King Charles's actions were affecting his country, particularly after Mark was killed. I rummaged in my backpack for Roger Hailwood's book about Broome Park, and leafed to his version of my ancestor's thoughts as he fled England:

John remembered how the first few years of Charles's reign had been full of incident. The king had come under the influence of George Villiers, the Duke of Buckingham who persuaded him into military actions against both Spain and France . . . which cost a great deal and achieved nothing. The king had tried to get Parliament to provide the funds for the wars but they had refused, so as a consequence Charles had resorted to other ways of getting money. It had been said that he used up his wife's dowry, and he had failed to pay his soldiers. Another way had been to extract money from his wealthier subjects by enabling them to purchase titles, offers they refused at their peril . . . The House of Commons had become increasingly irritated by the wayward approach of the king. He only called them together when he needed money and then totally ignored them. In an attempt to control the king's excesses they had drawn up a Petition of Rights. It had been designed to protect subjects from any taxation that had not been first authorised by Parliament, and from imprisonment without being first properly tried. The king had duly signed it, but then largely ignored it . . . after a few more verbal clashes with Parliament [the king] had adjourned the house. Parliament had stayed in recess for the following eleven years."[1]

Here were some of the policies that led, over a quarter century, to the trial and execution of a king. Roger, it seemed to me now that I'd been to England, was imagining John's thoughts pretty well. Kent grew resentful when goods coming in as well as going out of its harbors were levied. Money problems continued. During the two civil wars in the 1640s, Charles's troops were paid so infrequently they began defecting.

I returned to Jason Peacey's articles and read his detailed enumeration of Dixwell's political life up until his flight from England in 1660. A year after Mark's death, John was named a commissioner for the New Model Army, Oliver Cromwell's brainchild, the army that kept defeating Charles's troops. Alongside people like Henry Oxinden, Dixwell worked to protect Dover against the King's cavaliers. He sympathized with the political Independents, not the Presbyterians who hoped to compromise with Charles. When, in early January of 1649, Dixwell was appointed a commissioner for the High Court of Justice to try the king, he attended the majority of their meetings in the Painted Chamber, and all four days of the trial in Westminster Hall.

In other words, he was closely involved in the trial and execution of Charles I. If he was ambivalent, his actions don't bear that out. In the early 1650s, during the years of the republic, he was active in London. As a member of the Council of State, the new executive branch created after the abolition of the monarchy, he was one of the most consistent attenders. On the other hand, during Oliver Cromwell's Protectorate, Dixwell was more active in Kent, probably unhappy with Cromwell's increasingly army-dominated policies. He worked with Thomas Kelsey, governor of Dover Castle, years before he himself held that position.

When Cromwell died, in 1658, he passed the mantle of power to his son Richard, but Richard lacked his father's leadership abilities. In two years the Protectorate was no more. John Dixwell had to think fast, for soon, a rejoicing populace would welcome Charles II back from France. "It appears clear that by March 1660 he had detected the drift of political events, and that a restoration of the Stuarts was imminent. Accordingly, he sold his estate, or portions of it, to his kinsman Sir Thomas Peyton, for 3758 pounds."[2] He must have been trying to amass enough funds to support him wherever he settled in Europe, so he could wait until the situation in England became favorable for his return. He also did what he could to prevent other holdings from being confiscated by the Crown by putting them in trust for his nephews.

John Dixwell was pragmatic as he put his affairs in order prior to his flight, but he must have been terribly distressed that the cause he had worked for so passionately had failed. Cromwell had become, like Charles the First, another tyrant. His son, Richard Cromwell, was weak. The people wanted their monarchy back, but Dixwell wanted the fledgling republic he'd help hammer out in the early 1650s. In 1659, only about a year before Charles II would be restored, he met with, among others, the strongly republican Edmund Ludlow, the regicide who wrote his memoir during his long exile in Switzerland. The two men were on the same page politically. Ludlow had stood up to Cromwell for not honoring what was fought for in the civil wars, namely, that the nation might be governed by its own consent.

I do not know if they ever met again, after they fled, but decades later they ended up being the last surviving regicides. They would share the rare luck of dying of natural causes, never caught by Charles II's search parties.

I looked up, amazed to see that the plane was landing. I was back in New England and the twenty-first century. I turned on my cell phone and it rang immediately. My brother Eddy was waiting for me.

It felt surreal to be driven by my kind brother back to the house we'd both grown up in, where he still lived, that 1916 American version of an ancestral mansion. I spent the last night of my trip in a big brick house not nearly the size of Broome Park, but nevertheless reminiscent of it, even down to the fact that four generations of Dixwell descendants have lived there.

The next day, as I drove along the Mass Pike to western Massachusetts, I felt glad to be returning to my own ordinary home. Eddy had told me over breakfast that he and his wife were going to move into a smaller place and sell the old house. This did not make me sad at all. Hurrah for downsizing.

John Dixwell might not have agreed. One of Jason Peacey's articles argues convincingly that he never fully embraced his new life in New Haven. Evidence from the letters he received during his long exile and the legal documents he drafted show that he spent his last years trying to get everything lined up so his new little family, with or without him, could go back to Kent and live in the landed gentry manner to which he had been accustomed.[3]

But just as I was happy that my brother was moving out of our childhood home, I was happy our seven greats grandfather had to leave Broome Park, even though that was hard for him. He had to change everything in his life. For him, there were so many losses. For his descendants, though, so many gains because of his convictions. He couldn't have known that the New World, in which he lived with such limited funds that he couldn't imagine his family wanting to stay there, would before long become a country with no allegiance to kings or queens.

"Here we are," I said to him as I barreled down the highway. "Your children. Americans all."

27

Arriving in the New World, 1665

A FEW DAYS AFTER GETTING HOME I went into my study, pulled the key to Dover Castle out of its plastic produce bag, and held it between the fingers and thumb of each hand. It had let John Dixwell into the governor's lodging at Dover Castle so he could stand on that little balcony and gaze across the Channel to France, keeping watch for England. It had traveled to Germany, then to the New World and been safely passed down through multiple generations to me. How often had he held the key in his hands during the long decades of his exile?

My trip had given me many new ways to better imagine his life. Maybe, when he fled, he spent his last night, or perhaps only part of the night so he could leave under cover of darkness, not at Broome Park but in the governor's apartment. That way, his sister-in-law Elizabeth would know nothing, should she be questioned. Perhaps he brought the key with him because the last thing he did at Dover Castle was turn it in the lock before he found his way to the boat that would take him to safety. He had prepared quietly for months. The 3,758 pounds he freed up by selling one of his properties were the equivalent of close to a million dollars in today's economy. I wonder how long that money lasted him. Nearly five years went by before he turned up in Hadley, the next town over from mine.

I have two sources for that period in his life. One is the professor in Germany who confirmed that Dixwell was in Hanau for more than a year with fellow regicides. The other source is Edmund Ludlow, who was the last surviving regicide (Dixwell was the second to last), dying in Switzerland in 1692 after successfully evading several assassination attempts. His memoir says that four of the regicides escaped to Germany: "Colonel John Barkstead and Colonel Okey, with Colonel Walton and Colonel Dixwel [sic], who had been commissioners in the High Court of Justice at the trial of the late King, having made their escape from England into Germany, were received into protection at Hanaw [sic], and made burgesses of the town."[1] The fact that he and three other regicides became burghers in Hanau means the city recognized them as men of property, just as they had been in England. They lived openly at first, perhaps not yet grasping how profoundly and permanently their circumstances had changed. But then George Downing tricked Barkstead and Okey into coming to Holland to meet their wives so they could be captured, brought to trial, and killed.

Downing was so successful that prime ministers still live on the street named for him. He was also chillingly self-serving. After getting some of his schooling in John Dixwell's home county of Kent, George Downing crossed the Atlantic to the New World. His family was invited by his uncle, John Winthrop, the governor of the Massachusetts Bay Colony. The Downings settled in Salem, and George attended Harvard, sponsored by none other than John Okey. He was one of nine boys in Harvard's first graduating class of 1642. After a stint in the West Indies, profiting off the slave trade, Downing served as the chaplain for Okey's regiment in the civil war. He did not let personal connections stand in the way of what he could gain by ensnaring Okey and Barkstead for Charles the Second. Valentine Walton and John Dixwell lost no time getting out of Hanau when they heard the news.

Some time after, Walton died of natural causes in Flanders. I know he was with Dixwell at the time, for Ludlow describes his end with a tantalizingly tiny reference to Dixwell: "He retyred himself with Colonell Dixwell after the treachery of the Hollanders into—" There is a gap in the text at this point, and a little hand with a pointing finger, which seems to indicate Ludlow meant later to specify the place Dixwell and Walton went, unless he was choosing not to, to protect them. Then Ludlow writes of Walton's death: "where having finished his Course with much faithfulness & Integrity, some months since he breathed his last in the Armes of his friendly landlady, and according to his desire was buryed in his Landlords Garden, who there Erected a monument for him."[2]

That is all I have been able to learn about John Dixwell's time in Europe, but I can imagine what his reasoning may have been. He couldn't have known, when he first slipped out of England, how relentless the pursuit and punishment of the regicides would prove to be. He probably chose Europe, instead of New England where Major-generals William Goffe and Edward Whalley went, because he entertained hope that he'd be able to return home one day. Whalley and Goffe were too high up in Oliver Cromwell's chain of command to have a prayer of eventually living in England. As Cromwell's right-hand men, they had to get as far as possible from England. Dixwell, it seems to me, was a smaller fish and thus felt he could stay closer.

But my last day in the British Library had shown me how vulnerable he was once he took flight from the law and how long Charles's successors wanted revenge. I had leafed through pages of legal records about lands "late the possessions of John Dixwell forfeited into his Majestie for the treason of the said John and now part of the possessions of his Royall Highness James Duke of York."[3] James was Charles II's brother and succeeded to the throne after Charles II died in 1685, ruling for three years until he was deposed in the Glorious Revolution of 1688, a few months before John Dixwell's death in New Haven. James's nephew William of Orange became king. Even though William was a new and more tolerant king, under whom Dixwell might have been able to go home, who knows? William's mother was Charles I's daughter Mary. How sympathetic would William have been to one of his grandfather's killers?

Just after John Dixwell fled in 1660, his nephew Basil, now twenty, was created a baronet by Charles II on June 18. What timing. A few weeks before, John had feigned ill health to postpone appearing in court for his

186 REGICIDE IN THE FAMILY

role in the regicide. What were Basil's feelings toward the uncle who had
been his guardian since he was three? In fairness to Basil, it would have
been not only political suicide to help the uncle who'd raised him, but also
actual death for aiding a regicide. But I cannot help wondering what was
going through his mind as he became a baronet theoretically loyal to the
newly restored king.

Downing betrayed Okey and Barkstead in Holland in March of 1662,
so I assume it was later that year, or perhaps the next, that Valentine Walton died. Was Dixwell in the room as he breathed his last? Did he throw a
few handfuls of dirt on the coffin after they lowered it into a hole he may
have helped dig in the garden?

What should Dixwell do next? Wouldn't the New World be the last
place he'd want to go? To him it may have seemed a harsh and uncivi-
lized place, that distant continent where the zealous people who founded
Plymouth Planation had died in droves. Now, though, he understood he'd
never be safe in Europe. Perhaps he also was learning to accept the painful truth that his nephew Basil wasn't going to help him.

Was there anyone to consult for advice or lean on for emotional support before John Dixwell got on a boat bound for New England? He must
have been pretty isolated at this point, though the landlord and landlady
who were kind to the dying Walton were probably kind to him too. Were
his resources running low as the years dragged on? Perhaps he received
a letter from someone informing him that Whalley and Goffe had found
a safe haven in a remote new settlement in western Massachusetts, and
he could too. Whatever his reasoning, he left. He couldn't have known it
would be for good.

I've tried to find out which ship he took. Lists of passengers are available for the 1660s, and I came across several Dixwells who traveled to
Barbados, though none named John. The sad truth is that those Dixwells
likely invested in the lucrative sugar cane plantations where so many
people, first criminals and indentured men from the British Isles, and
then enslaved people from Africa, were worked to death. A history Ph.D.
friend said, "The Empire ran on sugar."[4]

One ship that might have carried John Dixwell to the New World was the *Thomas and Lewis*, captained by Richard Sicklemore. It sailed from London to France and then to Boston in 1664/5, stopping at Barbados on its return to England. John Dixwell, surely already using an alias, might have boarded that boat in France and then, once he arrived in Boston, gone overland to Hadley with Native American guides for what was largely a trackless wilderness. Alternatively, he may have gotten to Hadley by boarding a boat that sailed around Cape Cod and down the coast to New Haven. Could a smaller craft have carried him up the river to Hadley?

It was a very good time to get far away from his native land. In 1665 London would be decimated by the Great Plague, which killed about 100,000 in that city alone. Then in the fall of 1666 the Great Fire of London wiped out the entire downtown in the space of a week. John Dixwell was an escape artist. He escaped England just before he was to be brought to trial, he escaped the terrible fates of his fellow regicides in Hanau, and he escaped the natural disasters that befell the city where he studied the law, served as a politician, and judged a king.

Recently I stumbled across another escape he may or may not have engineered in 1660. He isn't included in a voluminous record published in London as the government took on the challenge of catching and punishing regicides. Did he or a friend have a hand in this, or was it luck? After twenty-nine regicides had been tried for treason someone, perhaps a Royalist named Heneage Finch, Earl of Nottingham, put together an account of their trials, hundreds of pages of transcriptions of what was said in court. A list of everyone who'd signed the death warrant was included, but it had fifty-eight instead of fifty-nine names. Only one person was missing: John Dixwell.[5]

It's another of many mysteries about the man, and one I doubt I'll ever solve. But I'm grateful that his key to Dover Castle isn't in the least elusive. It's solid and real. I own it. He chose to take it with him the day he fled and kept it with him until the day he died. There's no question he had it with him on that February day in 1665 noted in William Goffe's journal, the day he arrived in Hadley, Massachusetts at the home of the frontier town's minister John Russell.

His safe arrival was the best escape of all, for it was the beginning of a quarter century of his living a normal, civilian life, not an option for most of his fellow regicides. Much credit goes to John Russell and the people of Hadley, a stone's throw from where I live, who bravely kept the secret of the fugitives in their midst. The regicides were so well hidden that none was ever caught. All three died of natural causes. They were not drawn and quartered. Nor were their severed heads placed on pikes in the City of London. And one of them, the one I care about, got to slip undetected into the society of the Colony of New Haven, marry not once but twice, and live to a ripe old age. A complicated web of brave and helpful people in the New World made it possible for me, three centuries later, to be named Sarah Dixwell Brown.

28

Hiding in Hadley

ROUTE 9 runs the length of Massachusetts. The part that goes through Hadley, the first place we have a record of John Dixwell showing up in the New World, is called Russell Street, in honor of the courageous minister who sheltered major generals Edward Whalley and William Goffe. For years, they lived in an upstairs room in his house where they could hide behind the chimney if need be. By law, John Russell could have been killed for harboring them, and his willingness to do so put the whole town at risk of severe punishment.

When Dixwell arrived in Hadley, he hadn't seen another regicide since Valentine Walton, and here were two who'd been with him on that fateful day, sixteen years earlier, when they found a king guilty of betraying his own people and sentenced him to death. Who spoke first when Dixwell entered the room? There they were, alive and together, thousands of miles from their homeland. The regicides were dwindling in number. About a third had the good fortune to die during the interregnum. Thereafter, ten had been gruesomely executed, but these three who had made it to New England would never be caught, despite Charles the Second's efforts to track them down. It amazes me that they were sheltered just a few miles from my home. Evidence remains of their presence. I can easily visit

Reverend Russell's tabletop grave, first driving down Route 9 past Whalley and Goffe Streets on my way to the old cemetery close to the banks of the Connecticut River.

Seventeenth-century Hadley has to have seemed so strange to them. Founded in 1659 and incorporated in 1661, it was a tiny place, but ideal for men on the run. Some think Dixwell spent at least a year there, getting his bearings, though one of his granddaughters wrote Ezra Stiles that it was only six weeks. However long he stayed, it may have been difficult to live in such close quarters with men who'd been among Oliver Cromwell's closest associates. I imagine him experiencing a mix of gratitude for their hospitality, relief that his travels were over for a while, but also discomfort because of their significantly different politics and choices.

A history teacher at a high school in Connecticut wrote a book about Whalley and Goffe that came out in 2012. I read Christopher Pagliuco's *The Great Escape of Edward Whalley and Wiliam Goffe Smuggled through Connecticut* before I went to England and he was kind enough to meet me for tea. I reread his book and revisited my notes from our visit before tackling Dixwell's time in Hadley.

What emerged for me this time was how insignificant Dixwell was, compared to the major generals who shared their hiding place with him. They were at the heart of not only the civil wars but of the eleven years between the beheading and the restoration. Dixwell had distanced himself from Cromwell's increasingly tyrannical regime, whereas Whalley and Goffe had been deeply involved. Their ties to Cromwell were not just ties of conviction, but of family. Cromwell and Whalley were first cousins, and Goffe was Whalley's son-in-law.

As I went through Pagliuco's book, I thought about what I had learned in England, intrigued by the common ground I found in the major generals' and Dixwell's childhoods and then their divergences as England's world turned upside down. Edward Whalley, like John's father Edward, was a second son who got schooling (a B.A. from Cambridge) instead of an inheritance, just as John Dixwell went to Lincoln's Inn to learn the law while his brother Mark reaped the financial benefits of primogeniture.

William Goffe, like Dixwell, was the son of a vicar, in his case a fiery Puritan preacher. But then came interesting contrasts. Whalley was apprenticed to a London woolen draper, and Goffe to a grocer, also in London. Dixwell, on the other hand, instead of working as a barrister, ended up caring for the widowed Elizabeth Dixwell, his five nieces and nephews, thousands of acres, and a great deal of money.

During the early 1640s, as friction grew between Charles and his subjects, Whalley and Goffe suffered from the King's ruinous taxes. Dixwell did not suffer as much financially, but surely Mark's death at Arundel Castle, in the first civil war, contributed to his anger at the King. Also, he'd spent seven years at the most radical of the Inns of Court and had become a proficient legal thinker. He hated what Charles was doing, but I suspect he was too sophisticated and nuanced a thinker to be driven by Whalley and Goffe's certainty that God was on their side.

Pagliuco describes Whalley and Goffe as "exclusive, intransigent and fanatic in their religious conviction."[1] When I met him for tea, I was pleased when he said he didn't like them! Like Jason Peacey, he has a soft spot for my seven greats grandfather, whom he sees as "more pragmatic" in his approach.

And yet, would any of the extraordinary events that led to Dixwell's decision to judge his king have happened without the passionate fanaticism and superhuman courage of people like Whalley and Goffe? I think not. For example, Whalley was so skilled in battle that he rose through the ranks to command one of Cromwell's two personal cavalry regiments. In England's three civil wars, the last of which was fought after Charles's execution, he was a key part of numerous victories against seemingly impossible odds. In one battle, he fought on after being wounded in the hand and wrist and having his horse shot out from under him.

Goffe, too, was a successful soldier, but his particular strength was persuasion. As the army debated what to do with the endlessly duplicitous Charles, it was Goffe's ideas, perhaps more than anyone else's, that "began to change what was a constitutional dispute into a moral, religious fight." Goffe was convinced Charles was committing crimes against

God and their country. Later, in the famed Putney Debates, often cited "as being key to the development of modern concepts of democracy and liberalism," Goffe argued they were sinners themselves if they chose to continue negotiating with the king instead of bringing him to justice.[2]

At about this time, late in 1647, Whalley was given the hopeless task of holding King Charles prisoner at Hampton Court. The place has over 1,400 rooms and Whalley accurately predicted things would not go well, especially because the king continued to be treated with great deference. Sure enough, he escaped. Was it graciousness or gloating that prompted him to send Whalley a thank you note for his kind treatment? Charles fled to the Isle of Wight where he assumed Colonel Robert Hammond, the governor of the island, would protect him. Instead, he was taken into custody again. Undeterred, the king secretly arranged for a boat and horses to carry him to freedom, but got stuck between the bars of his window while trying to escape. Imprisoned in another room he hatched a new escape plan, bribing his guards, but two told on him. Freedom was not to be. Nevertheless, Charles successfully plotted with the Scots to invade England, throwing his country into war yet again.

After Charles's beheading, Whalley and Goffe continued to be at the center of things. Both were members of Parliament at various times in the 1650s, and were two of the eleven major generals in charge of the hated districts Cromwell created to control the populace.[3] When Cromwell established his "Other House," in place of the abolished House of Lords, Whalley and Goffe served in it for its brief existence. Actual peers sneered, of course, and refused to participate.

Wealth and privilege came their way. Oxford awarded Goffe an honorary master's degree, and he grew rich enough to buy one sixth of Newfoundland. Whalley bought or was given numerous valuable properties, including a house in London later used by Charles the Second for his dalliances with his mistresses. Throughout the interregnum Whalley and Goffe were in the middle of things. They were two of the seven men attending Cromwell on his deathbed.

They had been giants, Major Generals Whalley and Goffe, but now they were reduced to hiding in an alien wilderness. There is, though, a story that in 1675 one of them, no doubt Goffe because he was younger, miraculously appeared in the midst of a Native American attack on Hadley, brandished an ancient sword, organized the men, and drove off the invaders. To this day, Goffe is referred to as the Angel of Hadley, and various nineteenth-century painters depicted his dramatic appearance.

Colonel Dixwell's roles throughout the twenty years of England's tumults, while important, had been peripheral compared to those of his companions in that upstairs room. Much of his work was in Kent, where he was involved in naval affairs and served on many committees. Perhaps because he had fought for a republic and disapproved of the Protectorate, he rose in prominence after Cromwell's death. He was in Parliament again, then elected to the Council of State and confirmed as governor of Dover Castle at the end of 1659. But in less than a year, Charles the Second was restored to the throne.

Now, here were the three regicides in Hadley. All they had worked for had fallen apart, or had it? The British monarchy never again had the autocratic power wielded so disastrously by Charles the First. Whalley, Goffe, and Dixwell, to their dying days, never gave up their devotion to their cause. On that cold February day in 1665, I hope they were overjoyed to be together. Wouldn't they have talked and talked? Surely Dixwell described his life in Hanau, and his means of escaping Germany after Barkstead and Okey were caught. Did they shake their heads in disbelief at George Downing's willingness to betray men who had been his friends? Downing stood in stark contrast to John Russell, who, with others among the fifty or so families living in Hadley, kept the secret of the concealed regicides for years.

Whalley and Goffe had plenty of escape stories for Dixwell, too. They had left England on May 12, 1660, the same day the House of Commons issued an order for the arrest of all the signers of the death warrant. It was nearly August by the time they arrived in Boston. Back in London, the trials and executions of regicides would not begin until October.

Perhaps because it took months for news to travel from England to Massachusetts, things initially seemed safe for Whalley and Goffe. Many colonists saw them as heroes. Did they tell Dixwell the story I'd read so long ago in Ezra Stiles's book, that Goffe took the challenge of a fencing master who declared no one could best him? Supposedly Goffe, disguised in rustic clothing, climbed onto a stage erected for the fight. Was it in the middle of the Boston Common? He was armed with a muddy mop and had a cheese wrapped in a napkin for a shield. Not only did he win, but he smeared the man's mouth, then his eyes and at last his entire face, with mud as the crowd roared with laughter. "Hence it is proverbial in some parts of New England, in speaking of a champion at athletic and other exercises, to say that none can beat him but Goffe, Whalley, or the Devil."[4] Maybe they told Dixwell what happened after Charles II learned they were in Boston, and they had to flee. Important men sheltered them, men like John Davenport, founder of New Haven and its first minister. They also had several narrow escapes from the king's commissioners. They had lived in a cave. They had hidden under a bridge while their pursuers cantered loudly overhead. Eventually, it got so dangerous not only for the regicides but for the people concealing them, that the best choice was for them to disappear completely by holing up in the tiny frontier town of Hadley.

Fantastic stories. Who knows, however, what the three exiles actually discussed or how long Dixwell lived upstairs in Reverend John Russell's house? But before I move on to the life John Dixwell created for himself in New Haven, there is a little more material about the major generals worth including. Ezra Stiles, that painstaking researcher, was able to get his hands on letters Goffe wrote to his wife in England, letters written as he tended to his father-in-law after Whalley suffered what was probably a stroke. Goffe is gently affectionate as he describes his companion's suffering. "He is scarce capable of any rationall discourse, his understanding, memory and speech doth so much faile him . . . but patiently bears all things and never complains of any thing." Whalley had not "been able, of a long time, to dresse or undresse himself, nor to feed, or ease nature either way, orderly, without help." Goffe took care of him until he died.[5]

Just as I was swept up in the wonder of hearing Dixwell's voice in his letters to Henry Oxinden, my last day in England at the British Library, I'm so moved by the actual words of a man who'd been a major player in the center of so much violence and was now a nurse. There's a similar sweetness in Goffe's response to his wife's concern that he might be angry with her: "Yourself knoweth that I never yet spake an angry word to you, nay I hope I may say (without taking the name of God in vain) the Lord knoweth I never conceived an angry thought towards you, nor do I now, nor I hope I never shall, and in so saying I do not commend myself, for you never gave me the least cause, neither have you now, and I believe never will."[6]

What a tribute to a marriage sustained across an ocean and years of separation and to the bond between the exiled husband and his father-in-law. Whalley and Goffe cared deeply for the families they never saw again and were devoted to each other.

How different from their lives John Dixwell's had been. He had never had a family of his own. Whalley and Goffe not only had wives and children but had fled England together and were together until Whalley died. John Dixwell had been singularly alone. He was now in his early fifties. Did it occur to him, fugitive from justice as he was, that he might find something other than solitude in New Haven?

29

Becoming James Davids

JOHN DIXWELL spent a quarter century of his life in the New Haven Colony, living there even longer than he had at Broome Park. It was time for me to learn about the place. Compared to Hadley, which was in its infancy when he showed up, New Haven was old for the New World. It had come into existence in 1638 when Theophilus Eaton, a wealthy London merchant, and the Reverend John Davenport arrived with 500 English settlers. Davenport was a powerful and popular Puritan preacher who had emigrated first to Holland then to Boston in his frustration with the situation under Charles the First and his bishops. But Boston's brand of Puritanism wasn't rigid enough for him. In New Haven, he would strive to create a Biblically-inspired, perfect community.

Davenport served as the minister, and Eaton became the governor of the fledgling colony. The two men purchased a ten-mile square of land from the Quinnipiac tribe for twelve each of the following items: coats of English trading cloth, alchemy spoons, hatchets, hoes, porringers, and also two dozen knives, and four cases of French knives and scissors. They agreed to protect the Quinnipiacs from the Pequots (the word means "destroyers").

The Quinnipiacs taught them their ways of hunting, fishing, trapping, and planting. The English gave them diseases that nearly wiped them out. Up in Boston, Increase Mather saw all that death as proof God favored the English: "God ended the Controversy by sending the Smallpox amongst the Indians."[1] In New Haven, when the tribe tried to buy back some of their land because they couldn't grow enough food, the English refused.

Davenport and Eaton laid out the town in nine squares, with a central square known today as the New Haven Green (where Dixwell is buried). They had the purest theocracy in New England, and the most tyrannical. No one but church members could vote, they got rid of trial by jury as it wasn't in the Bible, and they turned away people who didn't meet their standards. They treated Quakers violently.

When the civil wars began back home, Charles was beheaded, and Cromwell took the reins, this series of events served Davenport's agenda. The pastor was so convinced of God's hand guiding the sweeping changes that when news of the restoration arrived, he initially refused to believe it. It speaks to his courage and devotion to a new order that upon Whalley and Goffe's arrival in Boston, he sent word that they were welcome to visit him. He and other men in power helped shelter them when the king's commissioners came searching. What could be a safer community for John Dixwell?

He must have known that out of all the New England colonies, none of which was eager to cooperate with Charles the Second, the most resistant colony of all was New Haven. It was especially slow to cooperate with England's new regime, waiting until August 1661, more than a year after Charles II was crowned, to proclaim him.

It also makes sense that Dixwell ended up living with Benjamin and Joanna Ling. They were among the earliest settlers, arriving around 1640. They were likely part of the network that helped get him secretly and safely to his new home. I think this because Davenport mentions Ling in a letter he wrote during his long, ultimately failed, struggle to keep the New Haven Colony its own, idealistic, separate entity.[2] He lost that battle when the Connecticut Colony's new charter allowed it to absorb New Haven.

The man who labored for months in London negotiating that charter was John Winthrop Jr., son of the Massachusetts Bay Colony's first governor and George Downing's first cousin. Winthrop the younger had become governor of the Connecticut Colony in 1657. Perhaps he intended to make it possible for New Haven to retain its autonomy, but in fact his negotiations were the beginning of the end of that possibility.

Davenport's heartbreakingly polite, puzzled, and grammatically tangled letter to Winthrop suggests that Benjamin Ling was part of the political machinery in New Haven, and therefore in a good position to help my seven greats grandfather survive: "If we misunderstood the things which we wanted means to understand from yourself, who, neither in your letter to me from London, dated May 13, 1662 which I received from Mr. Ling, nor in your next, dated March 7, this year, signified to me any other thing than that New Haven is still a distinct colony, notwithstanding the Connecticut patent?"[3]

Less than two years later, in January of 1665, New Haven voted to surrender to Connecticut, ending Davenport's dream. I'm struck by the date. It's only a month before Dixwell showed up in Hadley, Massachusetts. What if he was already in the New World when New Haven had to submit to Connecticut? Maybe he was even staying with the Lings. Might it be possible that Dixwell thought it better to exit New Haven for Hadley than to risk the changes that would surely come from being part of a Connecticut so much more under the thumb of Charles the Second's rule than Davenport or any fiercely independent person could tolerate?

Perhaps Dixwell came up the Connecticut River to Hadley just as some time later he may have come down it, ready to be a different person in New Haven. Did he stay safely invisible in Hadley until things settled down in New Haven and until his false identity was worked out? I could not find the answer. There is an eight-year gap between William Goffe's February 1665 journal entry noting Dixwell's arrival, and 1673, the first year in which Ezra Stiles found written evidence of the new John Dixwell, which is to say James Davids.

Under his assumed name, and with his legal expertise, he is mentioned in probate records as having settled Mr. Ling's estate. Stiles says

Ling, who had no children, and realizing death was near, asked my many greats grandfather to take care of his wife thereafter. Then Stiles says Ling wouldn't have done so unless he had known Dixwell for long enough to have grown to trust him. Stiles conjectures that Benjamin, Joanna, and John likely lived together for several years before Benjamin died.[4]

At his 1673 death, Ling's estate, now Joanna's property, was valued at 939 pounds, a generous sum for that time and place. Being a widow had some material advantages over being a wife, for Joanna Ling now owned the house. It had two stories and sat until 1756 at the corner of what are now Grove and College Streets.

When I was twenty-eight and encountering John Dixwell for the first time, I was shocked by his marriage to Joanna and her death occurring in the same month. Had he quietly caused her demise? But years later a history professor explained to me that in the seventeenth century, if someone asked you to take care of his wife and you agreed, it meant you would marry her. The professor was emphatic that Dixwell would not have tried to kill Joanna. She was elderly. She had just lost her husband of many decades. She simply died, or perhaps she was already ill when they married and preferred, because she had no children, that her estate go to someone she cared about.

Her death left Dixwell in his best situation since Hanau. Overnight, he became a man of property. After thirteen years of being rootless and on the run, he now owned a house, free and clear, not to mention its contents and several parcels of land. Also, Dixwell wasn't sixty-six, as I believed before my trip to England, but sixty years old when this happened, not so very old. When did it occur to him he might marry a woman young enough to bear children? Had he thought, after his brother Mark died and he became responsible for Elizabeth and her children, that he had too many responsibilities to marry and have his own family? Then, after he signed the death warrant, did he assume no woman would be willing to risk marrying a regicide? Once he fled England, marrying and having children would have seemed an absurd fantasy.

But now he had a house, some property, and presumably, good health. Still, it seems he was in no hurry for companionship. Four years passed between Johanna's death and Dixwell's marriage to Bathsheba Howe. What was he doing all that time? Was his main preoccupation keeping a low profile? Ezra Stiles describes him as quiet and devout: "While here he always conducted himself like a pious and exemplary Christian." Stiles shares the memories of people he interviewed. "One says, Mr. Dixwell was a very pious and religious man, and always fasted on Friday of every week constantly. Another says, 'he had the reputation of a worthy old gentleman, a very pious and holy man, and lived very much by himself and retired.'"[5]

How many knew who he really was, and if they did, what was their opinion of his role in the execution of Charles I? Stiles interviewed people who were full of admiration. One elderly man said the regicides "had done what they did out of conscience."[6]

Of course there were others who, had they known his true identity, would have sought his death for his role in the regicide. One was the royal colonial administrator Edmund Andros, much disliked by Puritans in the New World for his authoritarian ways and loyalty to the king. Around 1686, when he was in New Haven, Andros attended church. There he spotted Dixwell worshiping, became suspicious, and inquired about him. According to Stiles, Dixwell did not attend the afternoon service.

New Haven had only one church for all the years that John Dixwell lived there. A young man named James Pierpont, who came from Boston in 1685 to serve as its minister, became Dixwell's best friend in his last few years of life. In 1701 Pierpont headed up the group of ten ministers who founded what eventually became Yale University.

By chance Dixwell and he were neighbors, both their houses standing within Davenport's nine-square, scripturally-inspired utopia. But Pierpont and Dixwell had more in common than the locations of their homes. It must have helped their friendship that Pierpont, although he had been born in New England and had nothing like Dixwell's seven years in London at Lincoln's Inn to develop his mind, nevertheless had as thorough a formal education as was attainable in the New World. He was a graduate of Roxbury Latin and Harvard College. When he arrived in New Haven he was only twenty-six, decades younger than John Dixwell, but both men loved books. Stiles's description of their relationship had touched me when I read it in the British Museum in 1980:

> Colonel Dixwell carried on no secular business, but employed his time in reading and rural walks into the neighboring fields, groves and woods adjacent to his house. Mr. Pierpont had a large library, from whence as well as from his own collection, he could be supplied with a variety of books. He often spent his evenings at Mr. Pierpont's, and when they were by themselves retired together in his study, they indulged themselves with great familiarity and humour, respect and honor, and free and un-restrained conversation upon all matters, whether of religion or politics.[7]

Stiles notes that Dixwell left his treasured copy of Sir Walter Raleigh's *History of the World* to Pierpont.

"This book is now before me," Stiles writes excitedly, and quotes its in-scription in Pierpont's hand, which says, in Latin, that it was a gift from John Dixwell. But what particularly moves Stiles is that Raleigh, like Dix-well, paid dearly for his political actions. "What Raleigh wrote for the use of the learned world, as well as for his own amusement during a fourteen years' imprisonment, under condemnation for treason, became the enter-tainment of Dixwell, during his twenty-eight years' exile, under the same high accusation and imprisonment."[8]

Stiles has a charming description of Dixwell's and Pierpont's friend-ship. They were so fond of each other's company, he says, that they "had beaten a path in walking across their lots to meet and converse at the fence" to the mystification of Pierpont's wife, who wondered what was so interesting about their elderly neighbor. "To whom he [Pierpont] replied, that he [Dixwell] was a very knowing and learned man; that he under-stood more about religion and other things than any other man in town, and that if she knew the worth and value of that old man, she would not wonder at it."[9]

I love this story, but it doesn't stand up. During the years the men were friends and neighbors, young James Pierpont was still a bachelor. Later, he had a series of three wives. Two survived less than two years. The

202 REGICIDE IN THE FAMILY

third, however, bore him eight children, one of whom, Sarah, married the preacher Jonathan Edwards and had eleven children. Pierpont married his first wife, Abigail Davenport (granddaughter of John Davenport), on October 27, 1691, long after John Dixwell was laid to rest. Poor Abigail was not quite twenty-two when she died on February 3, 1692. But the point is that in the late 1680s, James Pierpont had no wife watching him leaning on the fence, deep in conversation with an aging regicide.

John Dixwell, however, did have a wife, and by 1685, the year of James Pierpont's installation as pastor of New Haven's church, his home contained not only young Bathsheba, but little children. I was surprised when I realized Stiles's description of the conversation between James Pierpont and his not-yet-existing wife was a fabrication, but I treasure the thought of my seven greats grandfather and young Pierpont having such a good time talking about everything under the sun.

30

Enter Bathsheba Howe

PERHAPS JOHN DIXWELL WAS EQUALLY DELIGHTED with what was going on in his house. Even in 1980, as I sat in the reading room of the British Museum with my scalp prickling at the thought that I might be descended from a man who had killed a king, I was touched when I read that he had married a much younger woman in his place of exile and had three children in the final decade of his long life.

Now that I had been to England and seen how privileged a life he led before he had to flee his homeland, I wanted to find whatever I could about the young woman who agreed to become his second wife.

Bathsheba Howe was in the first generation of her family born in the New World. An elegant Howe family website says her father, Jeremiah, was born in London about 1614 (which makes him one year younger than John Dixwell), and came to New England on board a ship named the *Truelove* in 1635. He started out in Lynn, Massachusetts. His father Edward was a farmer and his brother Ephraim, a mariner, was shipwrecked on a desolate island near Nova Scotia where he managed to survive alone for months after the rest of the crew died one by one.[1] The seventeenth-century Howes were tenacious, hard-working people, not landed gentry like the Dixwells, who were knights or baronets or had "esquire" attached to their names. Basil, Mark, and John had all served in Parliament.

The Howe website notes that by 1645 Jeremiah had moved to New Haven, where he was licensed to sell "strong water," i.e., alcohol. He probably ran a tavern. But in a will he made in 1677 (he died in 1690, a year after his son-in-law John Dixwell) he stated that he, like Ephraim, was a mariner, about to set sail for Barbados. Perhaps he drew up a will because it was his first such voyage and he feared he wouldn't survive it.

When I read about "strong water" and Barbados, I immediately thought of the previously mentioned, horrific sugar plantations that were ubiquitous in the West Indies for centuries. It's possible Jeremiah Howe profited indirectly from slavery, at the very least from the brisk commerce that went on between New England and the Caribbean. Had he been poor, then grown comparatively wealthy? Was this part of John Dixwell's attraction to Bathsheba? Though it was uncommon for brides to be given dowries, Howe's dealings in Barbados may have enabled him to provide his daughters with goods for their new households when they married.

Bathsheba, the third of Jeremiah and Elizabeth's eight children, was born in New Haven on May 15, 1648. She and her big sister Elizabeth had six brothers. Twin boys came along when Bathsheba was eight. Might she have spent years taking care of those twins and her other brothers? Maybe their care and her family's need to fund the upbringing of eight kids contributed to her arriving at the age of twenty-nine still unmarried. She was six or seven years past the average age women married in her day, and still living with her parents. In Puritan New England, single people living alone were eyed with suspicion and could be compelled by town officials to live with a family.

What was Bathsheba Howe's life like? I had found a wealth of historical material about her husband and his activities on the world stage, but what could I learn about this woman who had spent most of her days ensuring the survival of children and grandchildren? Without Bathsheba, there would be no Dixwell descendants in the United States, but I suspected I would find almost nothing about her, and that upset me. I've identified with her for years not only because she is my seven greats grandmother, but also because I became a single mother of a little girl and a little boy at almost the same age she did (her third child died young). I wanted to honor her. It had taken me a full year, after getting back from England, to write up all I had learned there about the Dixwells. Perhaps I would find only scraps about Bathsheba.

One day, surfing the net, I learned her tombstone is in Middletown, Connecticut and is still legible. I knew she had moved from New Haven to live with her daughter Mary after Mary's marriage to a Middletown resident, but it was too good to be true that her gravestone was still intact. Could I visit it? I was told by a woman in the town hall that the cemetery is kept locked by a man named Augie DeFrance, the local champion of ancient burial grounds. She gave me his phone number. Augie answered on the second ring and told me to come to the fire station to get the key to the padlock on the graveyard's main gate. Another key!

It felt good to get back on the road after so many months of sitting in my study writing. I parked on Main Street. In the fire station, a fireman showed me where the key hangs. I signed it out then set off in the direction of a diner, supposedly in front of the graveyard. But all I could see nearby were a Catholic church, a parochial school, a railroad, and a pale blue suspension bridge. Confused, I wandered alongside a road turning sharply to dive under an overpass. Then I noticed that the shoulder of the highway sloped up toward a distant spiky iron fence. I began jogging in my excitement, and soon arrived at a big gate with a sign informing me that rubbing gravestones is a Class D Felony.

I pulled the key out of my pocket and turned it in the heavy padlock. The gate creaked as I pushed it open. I stood gazing, just as transported as I had been on the pastures near Broome Park. I was in a secret garden. It was carpeted with rough grass some kind person, perhaps Augie, kept mowed in the summer, but nevertheless the place felt deserted. A big tree was in the process of silently engulfing two tombstones. There were no pots of flowers anywhere.

Slowly I wandered the rows until I found Bathsheba's reddish tombstone topped with a stylized skull framed by angel wings. It was stained blue-green with lichen. I knelt in the damp grass to study it. Some graves were crumbling so badly their inscriptions were illegible, but not this one:

Here lyeth the Body of Mrs Bathshua Dixwell Relict [widow] of Mr John Dixwell Esq Who departed this life December ye 27th 1729 Aged 83 Years

How long had it been since a relative visited her grave? I wished I had brought flowers, or a small stone. Quietly, I told her who I was, and thanked her for bringing her children safely to adulthood. I told her I was descended from her son John, and that I was born in Boston, the city where he learned his trade and opened his silversmith business. I promised her I would tell as much of her story as I could.

It felt like coming out of a dream to stand up and take in the rest of the burial ground. Side by side in the far right corner was direct evidence of Connecticut's slave-holding past in the form of two tombstones: "Sambo Negro Servant to Thomas Hulberd" and "Fillis Wife of Cuff

Bathsheba Dixwell's grave.

Negro." Sambo had died in 1776, "aged about 70 years." Fillis's death date was hidden by thick grass.

There were many stones carved with "Meigs," my mother's maiden name, some with the first name of Return, perhaps the same ancestors Mum had shown me in her family tree book so many years ago, when I'd come back from London to ask if we were related to John Dixwell. I began to feel overwhelmed by all the stories, told and untold, and had to leave.

After hanging the key back on its hook in the fire station, I drove to New Haven and had pizza for lunch, working my way through several slices to strengthen myself for my next stop, the New Haven Museum and Historical Society on Whitney Avenue.

Research librarian, Frances Skelton, remembered my previous visit, when I had marveled at the originals of the letters John Dixwell received during his exile and legal documents he had drafted. They'd been given to the museum in 1889 by my great great grandfather Epes Sargent Dixwell. I wanted to see them again, this time looking for Bathsheba clues.

Frances had a cloud of gray hair pulled up in a bun and a gentle, very soft voice. She wanted me to meet Eugene MacMullan, a conservator, because new Dixwell material had come to light recently. Eugene approached us, holding an extraordinary file folder. It was made of thin animal skin folded in half. Inside were several sheets of paper covered with handwriting as beautiful and tiny and elegant as Epes's on the label of my key. With a pencil, Eugene was carefully transcribing every word he could decipher onto yellow legal paper. The museum had them all along, but they'd been filed in another collection and been overlooked.

Bathsheba was right on the first page: "Here follows a record of several deeds recorded at the desire of Mrs. Bathshua Davids at the allowance of the countie court." It was dated October 10, 1682. She used the surname Davids, of course. The document had been written five years into her marriage. It was an indenture, by means of which John Dixwell was trying to secure Bathsheba's financial future.

This indenture made the tenth of October in the year of our Lord God one thousand six hundred eighty-two, between John Dixwell alias James

Davids of the priory of Folkestone in the countie of Kent Esquire of the one part, and Bathshua Dixwell, his wife, on the other part, Witnesseth, That the said John Dixwell, alias James Davids, for the natural love and affection he beareth to his said wife, Hath given, granted and confirmed unto the said Bathshua Dixwell, his wife, All that his farm lying in the parish of Hougham, in the countie of Kent, with the houses and buildings, and all the lands arable, and pasture and meadows . . .

Amazing. First generation Bathsheba, daughter of a tavern keeper, was being given land in England. But how could this be? As a barrister, Dixwell certainly knew married women couldn't own land. All their possessions, including any money they earned, belonged by law to their husbands. Widows, though, could own property. He must have been thinking ahead for his young wife, making provisions that he hoped would help her and their children after his death. But what was he doing, as a wanted man living under an assumed name, putting his real identity on paper, stamped with his seal? Was it the same seal he had stamped on Charles's death warrant? On the lower left was written, "Sealed, signed and Delivered in the presence of Joseph Allsup, James Clarke and Joseph Allsup, Junior."[2] Then it came to me. Bathsheba or some trusted person had waited until after he died to actually file the papers

Before I left, I walked across the New Haven Green to visit Dixwell's grave behind Center Church. This time, because of what I had learned about New Haven's history, I noticed Theophilus Eaton had a big monument near Dixwell's iron fence. On the back wall of the church behind it was a plaque honoring Edward Whalley and William Goffe. It recounted their story. But as I drove home, my thoughts were with Bathsheba. She was my focus now.

31

What Bathsheba Knew

THE NEW HAVEN BATHSHEBA GREW UP IN was punitive and unforgiving. Under John Davenport's theocratic rule, not even his cofounder's wife was immune. He excommunicated Anne Eaton for questioning his stance on infant baptism. For the rest of her years in the colony, people were required to shun her. Unsurprisingly, she returned to England as soon as Theophilus's death freed her to do so.

The harshness was not confined to adults. New Haven's misbehaving children could, by law, be hanged. Thankfully, there's no evidence any actually were, but over the years many were required to stand in the town center with nooses around their necks.

Bathsheba, born into this rigid, exclusive little world, had no exposure to anything else. To her, fines and floggings for minor infractions were life as usual. Normal, too, were limited schooling opportunities for women. As a child, she may not have known that back in England, women with means could be educated. That's one reason Anne Eaton, and Anne Hutchinson up in the Massachusetts Bay Colony, got in so much trouble. They'd had good educations in the Old World. Both boldly expressed their views in their new communities, became influential and then were severely punished. In New Haven, John Davenport did his best to silence women. Boys were taught various subjects, but girls, the colony decreed, needed only to learn to read so they could study the Bible. Up until her marriage, Bathsheba might have read nothing else.

John Dixwell was much more fortunate. Before he went to Lincoln's Inn, at the age of eighteen, he and his brother Mark probably had tutors for academic subjects, and lessons in music, dance, and fencing. Uncle Basil must have had a private library full of books. On the other side of the Atlantic, Bathsheba most likely learned to: sew and mend; grow, prepare, and preserve food; make beer and bake bread; and keep a household functioning. She wouldn't have learned all of this at home. New Haven parents were wary of spoiling their teenagers, so families provided each other with servants by farming out their adolescent boys and girls. It's likely she lived with another family for several years.

There were small, but better, educational opportunities for girls whose parents had extra money, but the Howes had six boys and two girls to raise. I was hoping Bathsheba and her big sister Elizabeth had gone to a dame school, a small school run in someone's home, but then I found evidence of something better. In the 1650s, New Haven had a school for girls run by "Goodwife Wickham." A seventeenth-century volume of town records makes reference both to that school and to a Howe girl who got in trouble for being too mouthy. It looks as if the girl destined to marry a regicide already questioned authority, or had a sister who did: "How, the daughter of Capt. How, was called before the Court (her mother being p'sent) and told that she is complained of for a prophane swearer; not only as she is a Christian, and by her soule, but by the Holy name of God: with other stubborne miscarriages to her mother" etc.

In short, the Howe girl said the Bible was "not worth the reading," refused to repent, and "said she desired it (the Bible) might be proved."

Her mother deflected the blame onto someone else. "Mrs. Howe said that her daughter had learned some of this ill carriage at Goodwife Wickams, where she went to scoole."[1] The court fined the family ten shillings and sentenced the girl to a public whipping. If the Howes had used the story of Anne Eaton's excommunication and shunning as a cautionary tale, it failed to teach their daughter to keep her mouth shut. I hope she was glad she had spoken her mind.

Another tantalizing item is in the subsequent volume of town records. Both Howe girls were having too much fun. When Elizabeth was eighteen and Bathsheba fifteen, they were caught with boys in a girl's bedroom, but luckily they weren't the ones who really got in trouble. We can assume all the persons named were teenagers, working as servants in other people's homes. Hester Clarke invited Sam Hall into her "chamber" in her master's home one evening "when the moone shined, and he thought John Gold and Elizabeth How was to goe along with him."[2]

Asked who else was involved, Hester "named Elizabeth and Bathshua How" and four young men. These hijinks took place in the home of none other than John Davenport Junior. Both Sam and Hester were apologetic, and were fined, respectively, five and three pounds, heavy fines. Sam was sent to prison. There is no subsequent mention of the Howe daughters. Apparently, they escaped punishment.

The next recorded fact of Bathsheba's life is my seven greats grandparents' marriage, in 1677. Bathsheba, now twenty-nine, must have been living with her parents, helping to run their household. Perhaps some of her brothers still lived there too, though the youngest, at this point, was twenty-one. When did she become aware of John Dixwell?

It's possible her parents kept a watchful and interested eye on "James Davids" in the four years he was single after his brief marriage to Joanna Ling. But what about him led the Howes to think he might make a good husband for Bathsheba? Was it material goods? Mr. Davids might be old, but he had a nice house, and all of the Lings' property. Perhaps the community's only church, where everyone was required to spend hours each Sunday, was the place where "James Davids," Mr. and Mrs. Howe, and Bathsheba first thought about each other. During the endless sermonizing, wouldn't their eyes have surveyed everyone in the sanctuary?

I keep wondering why Dixwell presented himself to Bathsheba and her family as being seventy when he was actually sixty-four. He was already awfully old for her. But perhaps she had thought, until he arrived in her life, she'd missed her chance to marry and have a family. She may have felt she was so old herself, it was no obstacle when her betrothed said he was seventy. He must have told her that because his tombstone says he was "in the 82nd year of his age" when he died in 1689. Why? Did he do it to hide his identity? Could the loss of his father and the scattering of his birth family when he was only three have made him uncertain of his age? Did he deliberately lie?

A possible explanation is in Atul Gawande's *Being Mortal, Medicine and What Matters in the End.* He says that in earlier times living to an old age was unusual, and that the old were treated with much respect. "So much respect accrued to the elderly that people used to pretend to be older than they were, not younger, when giving their age. People have always lied about how old they are. Demographers call the phenomenon 'age heaping' and have contrived complex quantitative contortions to correct for all the lying in censuses. . . . The dignity of old age was something to which everyone aspired."[3]

Bathsheba might have felt honored that such a venerable gentleman wanted to marry her. No man in her immediate family had anything approaching the education of John Dixwell, the knowledge of world affairs, the fluency in Latin, French, and probably Dutch and German. I hope it was an exciting step up for her.

I try to picture the beginning of this marriage between a twenty-nine-year-old first-generation New Havenite and a sixty-four-year-old political radical who'd avoided the long arm of the law for seventeen years. Bathsheba moved into the Lings' house, doubtless still furnished with all their belongings. She may not have lived very far from her parents, and her next-door neighbor would eventually be the well-educated young preacher with a library of books, James Pierpont.

Just down the street were William and Hannah Jones, who would be important characters in Bathsheba's later life. They had every reason to care for the widow of a regicide, for William Jones's father was a regicide. Providentially, William and Hannah had crossed the Atlantic in the summer of 1660 on the same ship as Edward Whalley and William Goffe. A few months after he and Hannah arrived in New England, William

Jones's father John Jones, aged eighty-one, was taken into custody. He would be hanged, drawn and quartered the following October, maintaining an extraordinary calm. "He greeted the sight of the sledge that was to pull him to his death with a joke: 'It is like Elijah's fiery chariot—only it goes through Fleet Street!' He told those who loved him not to mourn" but to keep their thoughts on Jesus Christ, and "met his death with such courage and faith that minor miracles were believed to have occurred that day in his honour."[4] How unbearable for his son, thousands of miles away in New Haven, to learn of his father's fate.

William Jones was a wealthy man and held many high governmental positions. He and Hannah had numerous children, and their house, a sprawling mansion built by his late father-in-law Theophilus Eaton in the shape of the letter E, was an easy walk from the Dixwells. Perhaps the Dixwell children played with the Jones children. They would have loved the house. The Joneses' house, said to be the fanciest in the New Haven Colony, had become available when Anne Eaton seized the opportunity to shake the dreary dust of New Haven off her feet, and returned to England. As luck would have it, she didn't live long enough to see the monarchy restored, for she died in 1659, less than a year before everything fell apart and various regicides began fleeing the country. Charles the Second set sail from the Netherlands for Dover on May 1, 1660. Anne's daughter Hannah and her husband William Jones departed Gravesend aboard the *Prudent Mary* on May 12, bound for Boston. Two men calling themselves Richardson and Stephenson were passengers as well. Their names were aliases. When Charles arrived in Dover on May 25, Whalley and Goffe were safe somewhere in the Atlantic. The *Prudent Mary* sailed into Boston Harbor on the twenty-seventh of July.

By February 1661, the two regicides had to flee Cambridge. The list of some of the people who sheltered them reads like a Who's Who of prominent men—John Winthrop junior, John Davenport, and William Jones. Whalley and Goffe spent two weeks in the Joneses' E-shaped home. Years later, when Dixwell drew up his will, the Joneses agreed to be the guardians of his family after his death. How fortunate for Bathsheba to have such wealthy, courageous, and politically powerful people looking after her.

Recently I found another connection between Bathsheba and the Jones family, a tragic one. The terrible voyage her uncle Ephraim Howe took that ended in his being marooned for months off Nova Scotia on a barren island, had begun in New Haven, in August of 1676, about a year before Bathsheba married John Dixwell. Six men were on Ephraim's boat. Two were his sons, Bathsheba's first cousins. Another was William and Hannah Jones's son Caleb. Everyone but Ephraim died, and it is incredible he did not. There was no fresh water on the island, but a barrel of wine and a cask of gunpowder that floated ashore from the wreck kept him alive. He subsisted on seabirds.[5]

By now, I was as obsessed with digging up information about Bathsheba as I had been about finding all things Dixwell in England. It was marvelous what Ezra Stiles had been able to learn in the eighteenth century. In the nineteenth, another meticulous researcher came along, Franklin Bowditch Dexter. Dexter, who lived from 1842 to 1920 and worked as a librarian and administrator at Yale University, was a history and genealogy buff. He wrote wonderfully about early New Haven. I'd learned of him years before because it was he who'd transcribed and edited the Dixwell Papers that Epes Sargent Dixwell had given to New Haven's historical society.

Two of Dexter's papers are especially helpful for peering into Bathsheba's world. In one, he examines colonial New Englanders' estate inventories to see what kind of libraries they had in their homes. You can learn a lot from estate inventories, which in that era were lists of everything a deceased person owned. Dexter used them to conclude that libraries were nonexistent in the majority of households. "For New England, the fact remains, and can hardly be stated too baldly, that the early settlers and their children lived without the inspiration of literature."[6] The inventories usually listed a Bible or two, and no other books.

This probably describes the Howe family's situation, but not the house Bathsheba moved into upon her marriage. Whatever books Dixwell had, plus the ones the Lings had left when they died, must have amazed her. At first, she may even have had time to peruse them, for twenty months passed before the arrival of Mary, her firstborn.

In the other paper, Dexter provides a wealth of details about domestic life as Bathsheba would have known it. He scrutinizes the account book of Captain Francis Browne. Browne made many voyages on the *Speedwell*, a sloop that plied the waters between New Haven and Boston. Centuries before the canal was dug, the *Speedwell* carried goods all the way around Cape Cod.

Browne's day-book goes from 1707 to 1716. Although Bathsheba was already a widow in this time period, not much had changed since she was a wife. New Haven's streets had no names and its "intercourse with the outside world was maintained by post as well as by water."[7] The community lacked artisans, so people bartered whatever they could grow or produce for Boston's more sophisticated goods.

As Dexter pored over Browne's day-book, he compiled lists of foodstuffs that suggest what Bathsheba grew up eating and may have served her family. New Haven residents sent to Boston wheat, Indian corn, rye, oats, spring butter, pork and bacon, "some peas and beans but no other vegetables," honey and beeswax, bayberry wax, hazel nuts, butternuts and chestnuts, an occasional basket of eggs.[8]

The paper also describes the materials Bathsheba might have used to make her family's clothes. When Captain Browne set sail for Boston, he brought flax and wool in the raw, manufactured tow cloth (a coarse, heavy linen used for clothing), and a great variety of skins. Dexter lists wolf, bear, fox, raccoon, mink, otter, marten, beaver, and wildcat.

From Boston, the people of New Haven got silk handkerchiefs, paper, brass kettles, scissors, and jack knives. They often ordered spoons, buckles, and other items fashioned from silver by Bathsheba's son, now a successful Boston silversmith. "In a large number of accounts, for instance, there is evidence of the most intimate friendly and business connections with John Dixwell, jr., the only son of the New Haven regicide and a leading gold and silversmith."[9] When he was about fourteen or fifteen, young John had moved to Boston for his apprenticeship, as there were no silversmiths in New Haven.

Bostonians had more interesting food and drink than New Havenites, who "imported sugar, molasses, salt and spices and liquors, salad oil, salt mackerel, figs, raisins and currants."[10] They did not yet use coffee or tea, Dexter notes, though it was already the rage in England. Nor did they use forks. One young woman traded four and half pounds of beeswax for a silver pound, with which she was able to purchase a single wine glass.

I was reveling in all the details when I came across a reference to Bathsheba in Dexter's section on "another marked group with claims to distinction . . . honourable women . . . not a few, who made more or less regular purchases from Captain Browne. There were, for instance, Mrs. Dixwell, the venerable relict of the regicide, on the garden of whose home this building stands, and who lies buried in the city Green."[11] Not exactly. Dexter delivered his paper at New Haven's history museum, but Bathsheba is in Middletown.

I could forgive Dexter for being wrong about the location of her grave, but I wish he had included what she purchased. Dexter notes that the day-book had been recently given to Yale. If Yale still owned it, more than a century later, maybe I could see it for myself. I inquired. At first, they thought not, then a librarian got interested and found it off-site.

I drove down on a dreary November day to Yale's beautiful Sterling Memorial library where manuscripts can be studied. Surrounded by elaborately decorated wood paneling, I pored over Captain Browne's day-book. Young John Dixwell was mentioned frequently. Browne wrote, in his wild penmanship, "by money paid to Mr. John Dixwell" or "by Expense with Dixwell." But I turned page after page of the tall, narrow account book without finding any mention of Bathsheba. It required such intense concentration to decipher Browne's hand-ruled entries with their irregular spelling that my back and neck started to ache.

Four hours went by. Then, there she was. In May of 1711, Browne wrote: "Mrs. Dixwell Credit −00-05-00," meaning five shillings. What had she purchased with that small sum of money, which was perhaps a lot for her? By now, I thought to myself, she was living in Middletown with her daughter Mary and however many of Mary's six children had come into the world. My eyes moved from credits across to debits. On the facing page was written: "Mrs. Dixwell. ½ thousand pins."

Pins! No Boston luxuries for Bathsheba. She got 500 pins for four shillings and three pence. This was the only entry I found for her in five hours of searching. I looked up from the account book at the gothic elegance of the reading room, suddenly exhausted. Was this all I would ever uncover of my seven greats grandmother's long widowhood?

It was quite dark when I emerged. All the way home I couldn't stop thinking about those pins. John Dixwell had signed his name to a death warrant for a king. Bathsheba Dixwell had ordered and paid for pins. Yet in the end, her steady work ensured the survival of her children after John Dixwell died. I wouldn't be here, bearing her married name, if it weren't for Bathsheba.

32

Babies Born in the New World

ALMOST EVERYTHING ELSE I was able to learn about Bathsheba was in John Dixwell's writings. His compelling voice, not hers, has come down through the centuries. It captures his delight at becoming, at the age of sixty-six, a father. It carefully constructs an argument for his new family getting money and land in England after his death, and it rails against the Dixwell relatives who ignored him in his hour of need.

I discovered his delight thanks to Franklin Dexter, whose transcriptions of the Dixwell papers brought my attention to a note John Dixwell penned on the day Bathsheba gave birth to their first child. He wrote it on the back of one of the letters he received from his niece Elizabeth: "Endorsement, in the handwriting of Colonel John Dixwell. 'On ye 9th day of June being ye 2d day of ye week my daughter Marie was borne about a quarter of an houre before nine in ye morning being in ye yeare 1679.'"[1]

His actual handwriting? I had to go back to New Haven to lay eyes on the original.

Seeing it brought tears to my eyes. His excitement and possibly his exhaustion are captured in those two blots and a smear. He didn't have to include the moment of her arrival down to the minute, 8:45 a.m., but he did. You might think he would have entered Mary's birth in the family

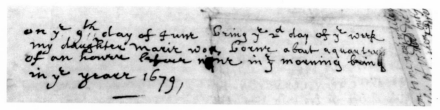

John Dixwell's notation of Mary's birth.

Bible, and perhaps that happened as well, but how lovely that he put it on the back of a letter from his beloved niece Elizabeth, the only Dixwell relative who remained loyal to him. Did he name his baby after his mother, the mother he'd had to leave after his father Edward died and he and Mark were sent to Uncle Basil in Kent?

There's no handwritten record of his son John's arrival twenty-one months later, nor of Elizabeth's sixteen months after that. There must have been joy, but nothing can equal the astonishment of the moment one's first child comes into the world.

I like to imagine Mary getting a lot of attention from her proud papa. Did he teach her to read and write? He may have taken the time to give her more book learning than Bathsheba was ever given, and he owned quite a few books. Wonderfully, there's direct evidence of his interest in Mary's education in an addendum to his will, dated May 7, 1688, less than a year before his death. Little Elizabeth had already died; Mary was almost nine: "I do also hereby signify my mind and will to be, that such of my books as have my daughter's name written upon them, belong to her, and that she shall enjoy them."[2]

John Dixwell wasn't leaving Mary a Bible, the only book John Davenport thought women should need to read, or wouldn't he have said so? He left her literature, and not one book, but "books," inscribed with her name. Best of all, he wanted her to "enjoy" them. He doesn't say, "be instructed by them." I imagine him carefully writing her name in book after book, as the years went by. Then one day she was able to sign them herself. I love this touching evidence that my namesake, the reason I am known as "Dixie," was a man who not only loved literature but thought women should love it too.

How long did John and Bathsheba have their other little daughter? While she was alive, Dixwell created a legal instrument to provide for her and the rest of his new family. It was October of 1682. Mary was three, John almost two, and Elizabeth three months old. His indenture states that if his son John had no children and "no brother yet to be born, then I grant all the houses and lands beforesaid to my two daughters Mary and Elizabeth, and to their heirs forever."[3] Six years later, when Dixwell drew up his last will and testament, Elizabeth's name was missing.

New Haven's Vital Statistics Office, which has records of births and deaths all the way back to the 1640s, has no death record for Elizabeth. Babies died so often, parents didn't necessarily record their passing. She may have lived a few years, but whenever her death occurred, losing her had to have been wrenching. Did it make them decide to have no more children? Nearly seven years elapsed between her birth and the departure of her father, on March 18, 1688, just three days shy of his seventy-sixth birthday, but there were no more babies.

When did John start to fall apart, leaving Bathsheba with the care not only of two young children but an increasingly frail husband? Dixwell died of the "dropsy," an archaic term for congestive heart failure. He had this condition for at least a decade. In 1678 his niece Elizabeth wrote him, "I have sent you cloath for a sut & coat & for shouses for ease for yr feet which you say is apt to swell which if you would wash them with brandy it would doe you good I hope."[4] The poor circulation caused by a weakening heart leads to painful fluid buildup in the feet and lower legs.

I picture Bathsheba sturdily managing as best she could, but her husband had no predictable source of income. The generous sum he'd taken to Germany in 1660 must have been mostly gone, and his inheritance from Joanna Ling was dwindling even as his expenses, with a wife and children, were increasing. He had to rely on handouts from people an ocean away. The letters in the Dixwell Papers at the New Haven Museum reveal that money and parcels occasionally and unpredictably trickled in from England. In December 1676, about a year before his marriage to Bathsheba, his niece Elizabeth sent him "books of intelligence," namely pamphlets containing news of political events, and five guineas. Guineas were gold coins minted for the first time under Charles II, so Dix-well's cash from England would have displayed the profile of the man who sought to punish him.

Five guineas might have kept food on the table for a good while, but probably panicked a man used to considerable wealth. Now, he had to count every penny. His friend Francis Prince, writing him from Amsterdam, managed to get him five pounds in 1679. But in 1681, writing from London, Prince said he was "truely sorry that you have nott reced the five pound" in the same letter that he apologized for Dixwell's promised books not arriving, "that losse that happened to you, by my mans giving your Lattin Books to Coll White, instead a Comp of old papers & Books of his which where worth nothing."[5] Dixwell got White's package of books and papers and his were permanently lost.

No more money arrived from England until 1685, when Elizabeth sent him thirty pounds. In the meantime, things seem to have gotten pretty difficult. He drafted three indentures dated October 10, 20, and 22 of 1682. The urgent tone of the third and longest one makes me wonder if something even harder might have been happening that month. Could baby Elizabeth have been sick or actually dying? What motivated him just then to document everything he'd owned in England and all that he'd done for his brother Mark's family?

A facsimile of the third indenture is sitting on my desk. It's the one my father showed me in 1980, and the handwriting is the same as that in Dix-well's note about Mary's birth. In other words, he wrote it himself. Clearly, he was determined to set the record straight and plead his case: "Whereas my brother, Mark Dixwell, of Broome, in the county of Kent, Esquire, deceased, did by his deed of bargain and sale convey and settle his whole estate upon me for the consideration of thirteen thousand pounds..." That sum would have been a fortune for anyone living in the New Haven Colony—the equivalent of nearly three million dollars today.

Dixwell details what good care he took of it, dividing those thirteen thousand pounds among Mark's five children: "to his two daughters Elizabeth and Bennet, two thousand pounds apiece at the time of marriage, or at the age of eighteen years, and to his second son, Heardson, three thousand pounds, at his age of one and twenty years, and also to his son William, two thousand pounds, at his age of one and twenty years, and likewise to his eldest son, Basil, four thousand pounds, at his age of two and twenty years."

Basil was the firstborn son, so he got the most, but had to wait the longest for it. It's interesting that the girls got just as much as the third son, three years earlier than he did. All this was a far cry from anything John Dixwell's children could hope for in the New Haven Colony.

The indenture goes on to lay out all the ways that John increased land and money for Basil in the course of seventeen years. Now, in October of 1682, John is disillusioned and hurt by Basil's treatment of him:

> And being confident of my nephew's ingenuity and honesty . . . when I settled his father's estate upon him; but most ungratefully and injuriously he refused to allow any thing to me for this considerable sum, nor shew any respect for the care I had of him, by making some provision for me in my afflicted state. And that there was such a sum due to me from Basil, my brother's eldest son, his mother, now the Lady of Oxinden, was so persuaded of it she offered me two thousand pounds for it, and if she be living can testify to the truth of what I say, and to the particulars before mentioned.

Lady of Oxinden! I remembered my last frantic day in London's British Library, where I learned that Mark's widow Elizabeth rejected the advances of her already-married neighbor Henry Oxinden but then married his first cousin, also named Henry Oxinden.

The Oxindens were among the oldest landed gentry in Kent, unlike the nouveau riche Dixwells. Did that alliance play into her eventual abandonment of John Dixwell? How could she, after living with him at Broome Park for eighteen years after she was widowed? I suspect she encouraged her son Basil's cowardly cold-heartedness toward his fugitive uncle. How hard would it have been for someone as rich as he to secretly send money to the man who'd raised him? But as it happens, Basil didn't have that big a window of time in which he might have been compassionate, for he died in 1668, at the age of twenty-eight. It was his son, another Basil, who carried on the cruelty. This Basil lived until 1750. For a few years in the eighteenth century he was kind to John Dixwell's son, the silversmith, but that is a story for a later chapter.

In the indenture, John is angry not with the Basil who is still alive, but with that Basil's dead father and his grandmother (now Lady Elizabeth Oxinden), the people John had lived with for so many years. "Besides, for seventeen years I was at great expense and trouble in managing his estate and therefore in justice there ought to be an allowance for the same: And also for detaining such a sum from me, taking advantage of my condition, and shewing unmercifulness in that they would allow me nothing for my present maintenance . . ." I'm so struck by three things as I study his words. The first is John's conviction, thirty-three years after the regicide, that he had done the right thing. The second is his faith that right will overcome might, when all is said and done. To his dying day he will hold fast to the "good old cause," the idea of a republic, not a monarchy, in his native land. The third is his joy in his new family. The whole indenture is one massive paragraph. Here's the section that moves me the most: "if the Lord had not extraordinarily provided for me, I had perished for want. Now being confident that the Lord will appear for people and the good old cause for which I suffer, and that there will be those in power again that will relieve the injured and oppressed, the Lord having given me opportunity to change my condition, and also given me children, I think I am bound to use the best means I can whereby they may enjoy what is so injuriously kept from me." He goes on to appoint his niece Elizabeth Westrow and her husband Thomas as his attorneys to demand from young Basil 2,500 pounds, plus interest for the last twenty-two years.[6]

This did not come to pass. Nor did any descendants of John Dixwell return to the mother country to live out their lives, as he had hoped they would. Instead, they stayed in the New World, passing John Dixwell's key to Dover Castle from generation to generation until my father handed it over to me.

33

Goods and Chattel

HOW BAD WAS IT for the family as the years went on and little money arrived from England? Ezra Stiles notes Dixwell "carried on no secular business," and indeed, how could he when he had to keep a low profile and was in failing health? By the time he died, the estate he'd inherited from the Lings had shrunk from 939 to 276 pounds. That sounds pretty drastic, but Stiles didn't think so. "By a cursory review of a number of inventories about this time I should judge Mr. Dixwell's estate better than those of half the inhabitants of New-Haven, who were comfortable livers; and consequently that he was not reduced to indigency. I have often been in his house, which was standing till twenty or twenty-five years ago. It was a comfortable, two story, old fashioned house."[1]

I wanted to picture their lives in that house, and Bathsheba's life before she married. The Connecticut State Library in Hartford has original wills and inventories not only for Benjamin Ling and James Davids, but also for Bathsheba's parents, Jeremiah and Elizabeth Howe. Everything was off-site, but the library ordered them for me, and gave me a date to come.

As I drove to Hartford, I thought about how John Dixwell, as a new father, was confronted with advancing age and increasing pain. His present life was in such contrast to his active life in London at the House of Commons, or in the marbled elegance of Broome Park. The man who once was the governor of Dover Castle spent his last years in the rigid society of the New Haven Colony with a wife, small children, failing health, and a shrinking next egg. He was lucky Bathsheba was strong.

In the quiet state archives, I looked at the originals of page after page of seventeenth-century New Haven estate inventories. Most totaled 200 pounds or less, and only a few were valued at a thousand or more pounds. Ezra Stiles was right. Dixwell's holdings, even though they must have seemed alarmingly small to him, were similar to those of many other people.

I found Benjamin Ling's. Although it was the earliest of the ones I'd come to see, recorded on June 6, 1673, it was perfectly legible, in dark black ink. Many pages later, past James Davids's and Jeremiah Howe's, Elizabeth Howe's will from 1690 was almost illegibly pale and had two ink blotches where she had signed her name in awkward outsized letters, as if she didn't know how to write.

The staff let me photograph, without a flash, every inventory I needed. Now I had wonderful raw material, but I struggled with reading and understanding seventeenth-century writing. Help came in the form of a graduate student with a New England Puritan name—Emma Curry-Stodder. I emailed her my images a few at a time, and soon a careful transcription of Benjamin Ling's will and estate inventory appeared in my inbox.

Emma had even gone the extra mile and translated a few incomprehensible terms, such as "white china plate" for "cheny plate," or "wether" which is a castrated sheep. I called to thank her and she explained another odd entry: 194 pounds of "porke, wheate and pease" were in Benjamin Ling's inventory. Did "pounds" mean money or the weight of all that food? Money, she said, and added that it certainly meant a great deal of food! While she worked on the next will and inventory, Ling's made me see how fortunate Dixwell had been to inherit his estate.

Ling gave "to my deare and loving wife Johanna Ling" his house and all his land—a mixture of different types that had been carefully parceled out by Theophilus Eaton and John Davenport as they were creating New Haven in Biblical perfection thirty years earlier. He had orchards, gardens and outbuildings, four acres of land at a place called Beaver Pond, and the privilege of using the town commons for pasturing his animals. He had at least two servants. "I give to my old servant widow Joane twentie shillings . . . I give unto my servant Dorothy Moore forty shillings, to be payd her within a month after she hath served her full time according to her indenture." Now I knew John Dixwell had servants, at least for a while.

Ling gave gifts to others, such as a gold ring to a Mrs. Coster, a book to a friend, and twenty shillings each to two other friends. He gave the largest sum, five pounds, to the son of his cousin Sarah. At the end of his will he made Johanna his sole executrix. He signed and sealed it on March 25, 1673.

He must have died within a few months, for his estate inventory is dated June 6, 1673. It starts with his chest of linen, which, with its sheets, tablecloths and napkins was worth twenty-eight pounds. The Lings were well equipped. They had pillows, featherbed bolsters, rugs, and blankets. They had tables, utensils for the fireplace like andirons, tongs, and a fire shovel; they had bedstead curtains, tables, stools, chairs. They had a gun and a pistol, twelve beehives, numerous kettles, pots and skillets, all kinds of flax, tow, linen and woolen yarn, silver money, and eighty pounds worth of money and wampum. Wampum was (and is) polished, cylindrical Native American beads, often made from quahog clamshells, which at that time were used as currency as well as for decorative purposes.

They had pitchforks, hoes, rakes and shovels, a cow, two ewes, the aforementioned wether, three lambs, and two pigs. They had 809 pounds of iron and three bushels of wheat. To a New Englander like me, who grew up watching my father wielding a beautiful old-fashioned scythe, cutting great swaths of our field with each broad swing of his strong arms, or being told by my grandmother that the round polished brass pans with long wooden handles that hung on the wall had been used by her parents to take the chill out of their beds on cold winter nights, Benjamin Ling's belongings weren't just fascinating, but familiar. I was pleased to note that he had two "warming pans."[2]

What's striking about Dixwell's will is that, unlike Ling, he gives actual money to no one but his daughter Mary, to whom he leaves twenty pounds, which suggests he did not have enough to be generous to anyone beyond his immediate family. He does, however, as I said earlier, give his copy of Raleigh's *History of the World* to his neighbor and minister James Pierpont.

His will shows that he had acquired two additional parcels of land, and he gives everything to Bathsheba to use during her lifetime, and to his son after her death, or to Mary if her brother predeceased her. Wonderfully, Dixwell is specific about objects that may have been with him since he left England nearly thirty years before: "I give to my son John all the rest of my books, and my silver standish I used to write with, and my twesers [tweezers] which is in a red tortoise-shell case, my sword and my gun, all of which I desire may be carefully kept for him."

He doesn't mention his key to Dover Castle, but it must have been Bathsheba's job to keep it safe for her nine-year-old son and give it to him, perhaps when he was fourteen, as he departed for his silversmith apprenticeship in Boston. I hope distant Dixwell cousins, somewhere in America, have his sword, his gun, the silver standish, and that pair of tweezers in a tortoise-shell case.

The end of John Dixwell's will makes it clear he wanted his children to move to England if Bathsheba died prematurely. In the meantime, they were to be looked after by "William Jones and Mrs. Jones . . . unto whom I have committed the care and education of them, that they would receive them into their family and take care of them till my friends have opportunity to send for them, and what charge and expence they shall be at thereby, to be repaid to them."

By "my friends," Dixwell means his niece Elizabeth and her son Thomas Westrowe in England. Even as he described all his holdings in New Haven, he thought riches in England would replace poverty in Connecticut. Either he never grasped, or never accepted, the truth that his English wealth was gone.

When Emma Curry-Stodder's transcription of Dixwell's estate inventory arrived, I put it side by side with Benjamin Ling's for comparison. There are striking differences. In John's the sheep are gone. So are the pigs and the beehives, though there are two cows and a calf. I hope he and his two servants, in the four years before Bathsheba arrived, ate all 194 pounds' worth of "porke, wheate and pease." Did Dixwell, despite his dwindling funds, have expensive tastes? Ling's inventory lists bushels of wheat and malt whereas Dixwell's lists no grain or meat, but fruit, spice, and cordials. On the other hand, Ling's has rum. Dixwell's doesn't.

The beds, bedding, furniture, and kitchenware stayed on and were added to, but Dixwell's damask napkins and silk laces were worth only a few pounds compared to Ling's "chest of linen," valued at twenty-eight pounds, one of the largest items on his inventory aside from all that food, the wampum, and "several parcels of trading goods" valued at seventy-five pounds. Still, Dixwell's inventory is noteworthy for the value of his clothing. Ling's doesn't even mention "wearing apparel," whereas it is the first and most valuable item in the entire list of Dixwell's household goods. His clothes were valued at thirty pounds, five shillings. Nothing else, with the exception of his land, came close to that amount, and most things, even furniture, were valued at less than ten pounds.

There were items I found touching. Unlike Ling's, Dixwell's includes "childbed linen" which I'm guessing was for Bathsheba's labors and deliveries, a trundle bed, "small bedstead," and children's blankets.

I was intrigued by archaic belongings, some with unfamiliar names and obsolete purposes. Both men had hourglasses and various scales, and "stil-yards" which were used for weighing goods. They both had a "close stoole," I assume the same one, which was a commode, namely a wooden box enclosing a seat under which you put a chamber pot. They didn't have to go outside to an outhouse on cold winter nights. Each had many pots and pans, skillets, and other equipment for preparing food, and "smoothing irons" for getting the wrinkles out of napkins, tablecloths, and clothing.

Three items in Dixwell's inventory that aren't in Benjamin Ling's caught my attention: sizzers (scissors), a writing desk, and spectacles.[3] I suspect he used them all the time, writing letters, drafting indentures, and making sure young Mary would get the books with her name written in them.

When Emma finished transcribing Jeremiah and Elizabeth Howe's wills and inventories, I studied them as best I could. Jeremiah's will was short and to the point. He gave everything to his wife, specifying that she have it disposed, after her death, "as she shall see good among my Children." He doesn't actually name a child nor does he give anything to anyone but his wife. Elizabeth's is more than twice as long and names Bathsheba's five surviving brothers, giving land or money to each. She makes no mention of either of her daughters, but perhaps because they were already married, she had no need to provide for them. She does, however, give some of her clothing to "my Grandchild Lydia How that dwells with me." It's likely that Lydia, according to the custom of the time, had been sent to her grandmother's as an indentured servant, to be a teenager under someone else's roof.

Jeremiah's estate was valued, in 1690, at 243 pounds, sixteen shillings. Five years later Elizabeth's was similar: 218 pounds, seven shillings, but it looked as if she'd sold off some land. Jeremiah's had thirty-five but Elizabeth's only twenty-eight acres. I was interested to see that Jeremiah had "seafaring books and Instruments" in his inventory, which he must have used on his voyages to the West Indies. Elizabeth still had them when she died. Bathsheba's parents had a very long marriage, fifty years. Of their eight children, only one, the twin Ebenezer, didn't have a long life. The youngest, John, was in his nineties when he died in 1750.

But where was a second set of eyes to help me get more out of these materials? As it happened, right in New Haven, at Yale's Art Gallery. To learn about later generations of Dixwells, I contacted a curator there, Patricia Kane, because she is an expert on colonial silver. She wrote two Dixwell entries in a massive 1998 book entitled *Colonial Massachusetts Silversmiths and Jewelers,* one on John junior and the other on his son Basil.[4]

She kindly offered to show me some of the many John Dixwell-made silver items in Yale's possession. The day I went, I brought Emma's transcriptions in case there was time for Kane to examine them. I had so many Dixwell items I wanted her to see that I filled a small suitcase with them. She took the time to look at everything. We spent, including lunch, five hours together.

She was brilliant. She knew, instantly, what the wills and inventories revealed about the way the Lings, John and Bathsheba, and the Howes had lived. Benjamin Ling was "really farming," she said. You could tell by all his farm animals and tools, whereas Dixwell, she said, lingering over his inventory and slipping into the present tense, "does not have all the stuff you need to farm. He doesn't have any tools. He does have yarn, a fork and tine," and then she explained that the former was a pitchfork for digging, and the latter, with its thin tines, was for haying. He and Bathsheba may have had a kitchen garden, which they took care of themselves. "Maybe they grew a little flax . . . it wasn't a farming operation, that's for sure, but it *really* is for Ling."

She moved on to Jeremiah Howe. "If he's in the West Indian trade, chances are he'd make substantial means." Howe, like Ling, "is really farming, among other things. He has oxen."[5]

Kane explained that Bathsheba, since her family had means, may have been educated until she was sixteen. This surprised me, and as proof of my theory that she may not have been able to write, I pulled out my photocopy of Bathsheba's shaky signature on her will, but this did not sway Kane. "It's cursive!" she said. Then she asked a smart question. "How old was she when she made her will?"[6]

"In her eighties," I responded.

"She was old and probably sick," Pat said. Of course! Bathsheba's ancient hands may well have trembled as she signed her will. Kane also thought Bathsheba's mother Elizabeth could write, then she looked more closely at the will with its two ink blotches. "But it's a clerk's handwriting . . . the fact that he says 'her mark' almost implies that she couldn't write. It's anomalous."

Pat Kane's expertise gave me more evidence for what I already suspected about John Dixwell's last years. He wasn't overseeing a farming operation. He was too old, and too weak from congestive heart failure. Bathsheba, having grown up in a family that was actively farming, had the youth, the strength, and the know-how to work a kitchen garden to feed her ailing husband and two young children. Perhaps with hired help, and they probably couldn't afford much, Bathsheba did the physical work; John spent hours writing and reading. Did he take his niece Elizabeth's advice and wash his swollen feet with brandy as he sat at his desk?

At the end of those extraordinary five hours, I drove home in a thoughtful mood. Pat Kane had answered so many of my questions that, for the first time in many years, I could feel myself pulling into the finish line on my research into John Dixwell's life. There were only two things I still needed to look into, both in New Haven. One was the letters John Dixwell had received in exile, the ones my great great grandfather had presented to the museum in 1889. I understood so much more now, I wanted to study the originals again.

The other thing I wanted to see, if possible, was the silver snuffbox which Epes had donated along with the papers. He wrote, when he made the gift, that it had "descended as an heirloom in our family, and has always been said to have belonged to the exile."[7]

I had told Pat Kane I'd recently asked to see it, but had been told by a chagrined staff person the museum had lost it. Kane was unperturbed. She knew the museum's collections manager, Mary Christ, who was in the process of making a complete inventory of everything the museum had. Kane gave me Mary Christ's email address and expressed confidence that she would find the box.

Sure enough, Mary Christ answered my email right away with, "I believe I have located the snuff box in question," and an offer to meet with me when I returned to New Haven.

34

Eliza the Loyal and the Good Old Cause

MARY CHRIST, when I visited New Haven again, kindly let me photograph the silver snuffbox. My image looks crooked because only at that angle could I reduce the shine enough to capture details.

It is so magnificent, even if the helmet at the top resembles a duck, perhaps Daffy or Donald, in profile. I was supplied with purple gloves so I could handle the box without leaving fingerprints, and given copies of all the museum's information about it. There was a 1985 letter from a former curator to a man named Brent Lathrop, surely a distant Dixwell cousin, who had written from Ogallala, Nebraska to inquire about the box and the Dixwell papers.[1]

The curator, Robert Egleston, politely suggests the box isn't what my great great grandfather thought it was. "E. S. Dixwell, who donated the box in 1889, felt that the box had been the property of Col. Dixwell, but I do not think that anyone who has really studied the box has been at all confident of the donor's opinion."[2] He says the top and bottom don't match. I looked. Sure enough, the thing is clearly cobbled together. The lid is hammered silver whereas the rest of the box is smooth, rolled silver.

I was so surprised, I texted a few photos to Pat Kane, asking for her opinion. She answered instantly and unequivocally: "The snuff box post

The silver snuffbox.

dates John Dixwell. I would think it was made ca. 1720." Oh well. But then I had an idea. What if the silversmith John Dixwell (1681-1725) made it, modeling it on the seal with the Dixwell coat of arms his father probably left him? Mightn't it have been the same seal the regicide used to stamp the red blob of sealing wax next to his signature on Charles the First's death warrant? During his decades in New Haven, John Dixwell senior often sealed documents with his coat of arms. That seal may have traveled with him when he fled to Germany, then Flanders, then Hadley, and finally New Haven.

Now corroborating evidence was before me, as a librarian placed an original John Dixwell indenture on my table. It was dated 1682 and bore a red blob, stamped with the coat of arms replicated on the silver snuffbox, complete with three fleurs de lis.[3] There it was—the same image I'd copied from the 1841 edition of Burke's *Extinct Baronetcies* into my red notebook in 1980, as I sat enthralled in the Reading Room of the British Museum. Here are both:

Dixwell's coat of arms. My 1980 sketch of the same.

Who else in the New World but the regicide's son would have even known what the Dixwell coat of arms looked like, or had the silver, tools, and expertise to fashion an embellished version of it? If Pat Kane's estimated date of 1720 was accurate, silversmith John Dixwell was thirty-nine years old and at the height of his career. Who else would have cared enough about the fugitive from justice who died under an assumed name to hammer that beautiful lid and inscribe it with not only the family coat of arms but also a helmet? Maybe the helmet was intended to honor his father's militant role in killing a king to usher in the "good old cause" of a republic.

Mary Christ came back to my table, packed up the snuffbox and the purple gloves, and a librarian brought me the originals of the letters John Dixwell received in exile. They are in beautiful condition. Niece Elizabeth's handwriting fairly leaps off the page with its big loops and strong slant to the right.

There was something so bold about her penmanship that I couldn't stop gazing at it. Elizabeth! I knew a lot about her now. She put herself at risk of death by supporting her regicide uncle, from his 1660 flight out of

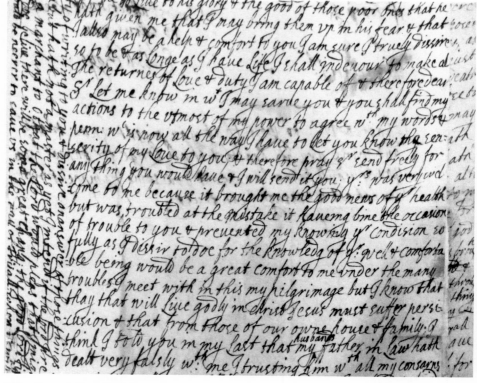

Eliza Boyse's handwriting.

England to his 1689 death in New Haven. For twenty-nine years she took that chance. Her mother, now Elizabeth Dixwell Oxinden because of her second marriage, took a different route. She closed ranks with the royalists. Possibly she did it to protect the wealth of her son Basil, our correspondent's little brother. But he died in his twenties, leaving his son Basil, aged three. I don't know when Elizabeth Oxinden, fiercely protective of her grandson's wealth, dissociated herself completely from her brother-in-law John Dixwell, but that is what she did, even though they'd lived together for more than twenty years and he had helped raise her five children. She must have hated the fact that her daughter Elizabeth, all her life, remained loyal not only to John Dixwell, but also to the "Good Old Cause" of England becoming a republic.

"Deare Sr" young Elizabeth writes her uncle in December of 1676, under the feigned name of Eliza Boyse (I will call her Eliza from now on to distinguish her from her mother). She begins with her distress that her last letter from him was dated February 14, 1675, "& none since and truly I Longe to heare from you."[4] I assume uncle and niece wrote each other from the moment Dixwell's exile began, or as soon thereafter as they were able to devise a safe way to communicate.

I thought about how Eliza was the first baby in the next generation, born while John was still at Lincoln's Inn, her arrival as thrilling to the Dixwell family as Mary's was for John and Bathsheba more than forty years later. He was twenty-three when she came into the world, and barely thirty when his brother Mark was killed at Arundel Castle during the first civil war. From then on, he was legally and no doubt emotionally, her father. She was only eight, the oldest of five children. They all lived together at Broome Park until Eliza's marriage to a man named Edward Chute, who died of smallpox in 1659 (a year before John fled to the Continent), leaving her with two daughters.

By the time she wrote the letter on the table before me, forty-year-old Eliza had remarried, birthed six more children and been widowed again. Despite having a total of eight children and losing two husbands, she managed to maintain friendships with various political radicals, some in Holland, who hated both kings and Cromwell. Her letter announces that she has succeeded in marrying her daughter Eleanor Chute to a man named John Wildman, son of John Wildman, whom the history professor Jason Peacey describes as "the sometime Leveller leader and plotter against the protectorate, who had been imprisoned at the Restoration but who was released in 1667, entered the service of the Duke of Buckingham, and drifted toward active plotting against Charles II and James II."[5]

This marriage was perhaps the nail in the coffin of an already strained relationship between Eliza, her mother, and her mother's stepson, James Oxinden. To add to everyone's difficulties, James was married to Eliza's other daughter by her first marriage, yet another Elizabeth. But to return to Eliza's letter to her sympathetic uncle in New Haven, she hides the identity of her mother and son-in-law by referring to them as "Mrs. Turny and her son." She is furious at them, and they at her: "Mrs. Turny & her son is very discontented with me for it," she writes of the marriage and goes on to describe the money situation with as much resentment and rich detail as John does in his passionate indenture quoted in my earlier chapter.

Her words sizzle off the page as she enumerates her mother's wealth: "tho she have thirteen hundred a year settelled one her son . . . & five hundred a year rent charge for her Joynture & six hundred a year rent charg present maintenance . . ." Eliza isn't just angry; she is well-informed. Soon she arrives at the painful heart of the matter: "I have not had any assistance from any of them in any kind since my deare husbands death."[6] Then things get worse. By the next letter, dated July 25, 1678, her pregnant daughter Eleanor Wildman is already dead. "O pray for me that I may come out of theses ffiery trialls fitted for my masters use; Deare Sr now my hand trembles & my hart growes cold in me to writ this sad & afflicting providence of my god one me of the death of my dear child . . . newly and well marryed wth child & died of the small pox."[7]

John Dixwell, reading this in New Haven, was awaiting the birth of his first child. How I wish I had his response to his niece's terrible loss. In the same letter she explains that she has not delivered missives that John Dixwell had written to her mother, asking Eliza to be the intermediary. "We think it best not to delivere them," she adds after a lengthy description of money coming and going, none of it to her or John Dixwell's advantage, due to the "ungratfull unnaturall wicked world we Live in. I know ther is not one peny to be gotten of any of them, but I shall say noe more not knowing whether this may come to your hand; dear Sr belive me I Longe to hear from you for I am yr most affectionat neece to serve you to my power."[8]

Other letters in the collection paint a picture of the political radicals and nonconformist ministers Eliza and John knew and wrote to each other about. The longest letter is from a man named John Dubois, who wrote Dixwell an "in-depth analysis of European affairs . . . He writes of the secret meetings led by Independent ministers" and of official attempts by those in power in England to "silence dissent, and of the flight of some radicals to the Continent."[9] Dixwell, for the duration of his long life in exile, stayed in touch with those who opposed the status quo.

To return to Eliza, there's a 1680 letter from her assuring her uncle that he wrongly concluded, from a letter he received from a man in Holland, that she was dead. At this point she's forty-four years old. "I am yet in the land of the Living, the Lord help me to Live to his glory and the good of those poor ones he hath given me that I may bring them up in his fear and that I also may be a help and comfort to you."[10] But a year later she isn't well. "I am still in the Land of the Living tho Laboring under many troubles and weekneses of body & mind," and still estranged from her birth family. Her nephew Basil (she does not name him) is at Oxford, "which is all the account I can give. I am a stranger to them all."[11]

By 1685 she is struggling even more with her health, "the reasons I have not writ . . . I have bine so sick that none thought I could have Lived."[12] In this letter, she's still upset with her mother, who had spent the previous winter in London. It sounds as though every one of Elizabeth Oxinden's children has died except her namesake. "I had not seen her in six years till this winter; I could tell you how much she forgets her only child as I am sure you would be troubled at, but I will forbare in hopes the Lord will in mercy bring us together again & and therefore I would not have it trouble you that she should forget you."[13]

The next letter in the Dixwell Papers addresses John Dixwell as "Worthy Sr" and is written by Eliza's son by her second marriage, Thomas Westrowe. He writes from London on September 23, 1689, not knowing that his great uncle John has already died. He begins with a charming apology, the more charming because of the wildly original spelling. "I must confisse I am heily to blame that I have bin soo negectfull in not writing to you before for wch I beage your pardon, of wch I dout not of." With William and Mary in power, the political climate is finally favorable for Dixwell's return. "Finding all things going soo well and our King is bent to ye Onnest parte I have indeverd to gitt your pardone wch I dout not but to obtaine and also an acct of Parlement to backe it. For wch reson

I would desir you and your Famely to macke all the hayest you can pos-sibill to Amsterdam in Hollande where I have frinds that will rescue you and you may bee as safe as wher you are."[14] If Dixwell had lived one more year, he might have had no descendants in New England.

The next letter, the last from family, is dated June 1690 and is signed "Eliza Westrowe," instead of "Eliza Boyse" because John's loyal niece can now, after the Glorious Revolution, use her real name. She doesn't address it to her uncle. She knows he is dead. She writes to the aunt she will never meet, Bathsheba. On the back of this letter (no one used envelopes), she writes "For Madm Davids at Mr James Pierpont in New Haven in New England." She must have felt it would be risky to address her as Madam Dixwell.

By this time, the father-in-law of her deceased daughter Eleanor, John Wildman, has been appointed Postmaster General, despite his radical past and years as a prisoner in the Tower of London after Charles II's 1660 restoration to the throne. I love Eliza's proud delivery instructions: "pray diricke your Letter to Madm Elizab Westrowe then put a cover over it and diricte it to Major Wildman general poastmaster of England."[15] What a help for safe letter delivery in dangerous times to have John Wildman in charge of the mail!

This final family letter is short and touching. Interestingly, it suggests that Bathsheba was able to write, just as Patricia Kane had said, for it was she who informed Eliza of John Dixwell's death. "I have recd yours of the 12 of Septr wch brought me the sad and afflicting newes of the death of my deare frind . . ." Eliza worries that sharing her grief might make Bath-sheba feel worse: "should I say what was in my harte it would perhaps sture those afflictions wch may be a great damage to you, so I think it my duty to modirat, and therefore will tell you that I will doe what I can to serve you and your children that leyes in mye power and if you pleayes to lett me know his mind I shall yous my outmoust indevers to performe it in all respickes."[16]

She encloses ten pounds "as a token of my Love to the Children & you and desir to here from you as sone as you can with an acct of your condis-sion and the eage of you children and what they have bin brought up to."

She explains to Bathsheba that her younger son, to whom Bathsheba had addressed her letter, "the Lorde has taken to him selfe som years" but that she and her son Thomas will do everything they can for Bathsheba and her kids. She ends with this about John Dixwell:

> Wee had not heard from him nor of him in 2 years tell this from you wch brought me the news wch I fered to here, but I shall concloud this with the assurance of all Love and servis to you and yours who am
>
> > Your truely afflicted but
> >
> > very affectionate and ffaith servat
> >
> > ELIZA : WESTROWE[17]

Eliza lived until 1695, outliving her uncle by six years, and also her mother, who died in 1691. She was not quite sixty at her death. There are no more letters from her, or none preserved, but what treasures these are. They provide an especially vivid sense of John Dixwell as a person, and here is why: His relationship with Eliza was the longest and most constant of his life, lasting more than fifty years. She alone among his family in England supported his decision to judge a king and admired and loved him all his life. Like him, she was rejected by the Dixwells, and like him she never wavered in her faith that a different, God-ordained way of being in the world was to be striven toward, no matter the cost.

John Dixwell spent half his life paying for his role in a king's death. I've spent more than half my own life thinking about what he did, and learning enough about his times to move from horrified dismay to pride. My thinking, though, goes on being complicated, not clear-cut, and that is as it should be. Writing this book has brought me a new appreciation for the way looking at small things with great care helps to bring the big picture into focus. Who knew I'd be poring over bills for room and board from 1588, or seventeenth-century estate inventories, or the hand-ruled account book of a ship captain in my quest? It will be difficult to stop chasing the Dixwells.

Mijung and I continue to study together once a week. We just finished Nathaniel Hawthorne's *The Scarlet Letter*, awed by its brilliantly critical look at the world of New England Puritanism, the world where John Dix-well spent the last decades of this life, and the world in which he left the son from whom I'm descended. Hawthorne pokes holes in the hollow pomposity and narrow thinking of the men in power who punished a woman for adultery and adulated the pastor who couldn't admit he'd impregnated her. He reserves the highest respect for Hester Prynne, the single mother who lives according to her beliefs despite being ostracized by her entire community.

Hawthorne brought the same respect to the regicides who stood up to a king and fought for a system of government of, for, and by its citizens. In his short story, "The Gray Champion," one of the three regicides who fled to New England returns as a ghost to once again defy royal tyranny. The setting is Boston in 1686, where the same Edmund Andros who spied Dixwell in church in New Haven is now Governor of New England and much hated for his dictatorial ways. As his redcoats advance in formation against the resistant colonists, they cry out for a champion to rescue them.

"Suddenly, there was seen the figure of an ancient man, who seemed to have emerged from among the people, and was walking by himself along the centre of the street, to confront the armed band." No one recognizes him. He marches in time to the military music being played for Andros' parade, then stops and says one word to the enemy: "Stand!" Andros asks him if he is insane.

"I have staid the march of a King himself, ere now," he replies. "I am here, Sir Governor, because the cry of an oppressed people hath disturbed me in my secret place . . ." His mission, as was John Dixwell's, is the "good old cause." At length, Andros orders his soldiers to retreat. The Gray Champion disappears.

"And who was the Gray Champion?" begins the final paragraph. "Perhaps his name might be found in the records of that stern Court of Justice, which passed a sentence, too mighty for the age, but glorious in all after times, for its humbling lesson to the monarch and its high example to the subject."[18]

Hawthorne's story captures what an extraordinary act the regicide was, and how it grew to mythic proportions in later years, coming to symbolize the imperative to resist autocracy. I am honored to be descended from someone who did such a brave thing, and to have the key that he kept as a reminder of his commitment to defend his country against her enemies, be they within or without.

I'm glad I learned how respected John Dixwell was in New Haven, many years after the regicide. His friends were among the most powerful people in that community. They stood by his widow and children after his death. He had grown up with wealth and privilege in a world where only a few had a voice and those under them voted as a block, following their leaders. He ended his life in relative poverty but in a new world that would give rise, in less than a century, to a bold new government dedicated to individual liberty and modeled to some extent on ideas conceived in the tumultuous decades of the English civil wars and the interregnum. In his last years, Dixwell was still in correspondence with radical friends in Holland. He was true to his convictions to the very end.

A stanza from a poem captures the dire circumstances that led John Dixwell to his fateful choice to condemn a king. It is entitled "The Present Crisis," and was written by James Russell Lowell (1819–1891), the son of a Unitarian minister, who was, among other things, a poet and an abolitionist. In his poem, he was objecting to the Mexican-American War and slavery:

Once to ev'ry man and nation Comes the moment to decide,
In the strife of Truth with Falsehood, for the good or evil side;
Some great cause, God's new Messiah, offering each the bloom or blight,
Parts the goats upon the left hand, and the sheep upon the right,
And the choice goes by forever 'twixt that darkness and that light.

John Dixwell had to choose between the safety of saying nothing and the danger, for the rest of his long life, of signing the death warrant for a king. His decision cost him his career, his home, his lifestyle, and nearly his entire family of origin, but I don't think he regretted it. He died knowing he had held fast to his ideals and would never give up hope. Russell has hope too, for a more just future despite constant disappointments:

> Truth forever on the scaffold, Wrong forever on the throne,—
> Yet that scaffold sways the future, and, behind the dim unknown,
> Standeth God within the shadows, keeping watch above his own.[19]

Afterword–From Generation to Generation

I HAD INTENDED TO WRITE about each Dixwell descendant between John and me. But after spending a couple of years digging up everything I could about John and Bathsheba's lives in New Haven, then writing about my findings, something happened to me as I finished the last chapter.

I felt done.

This surprised me. Then I remembered my writing teacher from years ago who used to ask, about each piece of student writing, "Whose story is it?" Quite often, the writer would be surprised to discover the story belonged to someone other than the character that he or she had intended.

I originally thought this story was about John Dixwell, my father, and me. But I ended up uncovering so much material about John that my father receded into the background. Then, when I went to England and especially when I dived into the letters and indentures, John got so vivid to me my story receded as well. Really, this is John Dixwell's story.

But I'm unwilling to dismiss all the other people who, for the next three hundred years, had his key. I'll tell what I learned of them, not losing sight of whose story this is, for what interests me especially is how each successive person who had charge of the key thought about the man who brought it to New England.

IT'S A GIFT THAT NO ONE EVER LOST IT. Even my father, who seems to have decided never to mention our fugitive-from-justice forebear, managed to pass the key to Dover Castle on to me, though his choice to hand it over in a plastic produce bag is noteworthy. That plastic bag, in which it still lives because I miss my father, is a testimony to Dad's ambivalence. He never showed us the key as we were growing up. He didn't frame it and hang it on the wall. Essentially, he stashed it, as if it were a carrot tucked into the back of a refrigerator.

If I hadn't stumbled on Ezra Stiles's book about the regicides in the reading room of the British Museum in 1980, perhaps John Dixwell's story would have disappeared, at least in our branch of his family. I do think Dad was embarrassed, or even ashamed, to be descended from someone who was such a radical that he signed the death warrant for a king.

I'm the ninth keeper of the key. What did the first one, the John Dixwell who became a noted silversmith in Boston, think of his regicide father? Although Bathsheba immediately changed their surname from Davids to Dixwell, because it was no longer dangerous to own their connection to the regicide once he was dead, it had to have been uncomfortable to bear that name in colonial New England. I hope he was proud, but he also needed to be careful.

He may have grown up feeling torn between what might have been and the reality of his circumstances. His father had been a highly educated man who came from a rich family and wanted his children to return to England, be educated there, and be landed gentry. He was specific about how much they could expect, for in yet another indenture Dixwell wrote that Mary was to be given "one thousand pounds at the day of her marriage . . . then my son John shall have the same."[1] It was a pipe dream. Bathsheba's estate inventory, taken in 1729, totaled fifty-four pounds.

Had Bathsheba managed to fund any education for her son at all? New Haven's first grammar school for boys, the Hopkins School, still exists, so I called the registrar and asked if he had attended. It seemed impossible she'd be able to uncover such ancient history but the next day she told me John, age fourteen, had graduated in 1693, four years after his father's death, the only person in his class.

Within the year, he went to Boston, apprenticed for seven years to a silversmith. I like to think he was full of awe for what his father had stood for, but the evidence suggests he was more focused on getting whatever he could from the British Dixwells. It was half a century before the Revolutionary War so he couldn't have known that his father's radical commitment to establishing a republic would be part of the seedbed of our constitution. What seems to have mattered to him was gaining access to riches in England.

This puzzles me, because he became skilled at his craft and had, by New England standards, a fair share of money and prestige. Silversmiths were in the top echelon of craftspeople, and had high social standing. They were vital to their communities because they functioned as informal bankers. Silver was essentially the currency of the era, a way to keep excess wealth. It went back and forth between being made into coins, or melted down and made into objects like cups and porringers.

Today, Dixwell's silver is found in many places, from Boston's and Cleveland's art museums to the Flynt Center in Historic Deerfield or the Mead Museum at Amherst College. John Dixwell was not only an expert craftsman, but a leading citizen of Boston. He helped form the New North Church and was unanimously elected to be a deacon. And yet, perhaps it grated on him that he had to go into a trade when his father had been a barrister who had served in Parliament, been governor of Dover Castle, and overseen a large estate and elegant manor house. Whatever his attitude, twenty years after his father's death he went to England to declare himself a true and rightful member of the Dixwell family.

No doubt anticipating his relatives might not welcome him with open arms, he brought not only his father's indentures with him but also letters of introduction from Cotton Mather and James Pierpont. It was 1710. He met his first cousin once removed, Baronet Basil Dixwell, son of Eliza's baby brother Basil. This Basil was middle-aged and childless, so the hope was he would ask the silversmith to provide him with an heir.

For this delicate errand, his letters of introduction are masterpieces of diplomacy. Both carefully skirt his father's role in the beheading of a king, even as they praise the regicide's character. Pierpont describes what he and others had thought of the mysterious James Davids: "His accomplishments and accurate gentility shewed him to be no ordinary person. People generally supposed there were great reasons of his reservedness. They made their guess; but could not find him out." The only reference to his role in the regicide and exile is this phrase, "if [he] . . . had not been unhappily necessitated to withdraw."[2]

Mather's letter begins by reminding Basil of how much the original John Dixwell had done for his father: "From remote America there now waits upon you the only son of one who was an uncle and a father to your honorable father."[3] It's amazing that young John got a letter from such a towering figure. Cotton Mather was descended from several famous Puritan preachers: Richard Mather, Increase Mather, and John Cotton. He was a complicated mix: convinced that witches in Salem needed to be rooted out, but also passionate about persuading people to get inoculated against smallpox. Only the latter would eventually prove to be a good idea, but two people who died of the early experiments were the silversmith's first wife, Mary Prout Dixwell, in 1721, and then Dixwell himself in 1725.[4]

Mather is not above using flattery to help young John get whatever he might from Basil. "Sir Basil has too wise and great a soul to let any old, forgotten, dubious, political consideration extinguish his affection for the memory of so excellent an uncle. The temptations of that day, when he was on the stage, were such on both sides, that all generous and compassionate minds easily bury in a just oblivion the differences thereby occasioned."

It strikes me as overblown and obsequious, but the letter is intriguing for the way it shows how colonists, still under the thumb of British rule, were careful with their words. "Impartial posterity will confess there were brave men on both sides; braver than any which espoused either Pompey's cause or Caesar's."

Mather then pulls out all the stops, despite never having met the man he is praising: "Our Dixwell was one of them. *Ours* in regard of his dying with us; and worthy to be *yours* in regard of your kind aspect on his offspring. He had excellencies that render him worthy of esteem, even from enemies. How much more from a kinsman of so polished and sublimed a character, that he perfectly understands how far the ties of nature are strengthened by good quality and superior education."

The difficulty is that the silversmith is an artisan. Mather must convince Basil the baronet that he is worthy of respect: "Do but cast an eye on this his only son. Look upon him, Sir, his personal merit will speak for him. He is one of ingenuity. He has a genius elevated above the common level of the country, where he had his birth and breeding. There is in him, a modest yet sprightly soul; thoughtful and cautious enough too; and a natural good sense agreeable to the flock of which he comes. A little cultivation which the place of his nativity afforded him *not,* would have made him extraordinary."[5]

The visit went well. Basil told John that if he had a son and named him Basil, he would consider him an heir. He gave him a few pounds, too. One year later John named his first son Basil.

Why didn't British Basil make good on his promise? A few years ago, I found the answer in a box of Dixwell papers at the Massachusetts Historical Society. The baronet rejected young Basil because he didn't go to Harvard. That is, he didn't receive the education befitting a gentleman. It did not matter to the baronet that this happened because the silversmith died when the baronet's potential heir Basil was only fourteen, whereupon the young man and his two younger siblings were sent to maternal relatives in New Haven. Uncle John Prout must have known about the title awaiting Basil in England, but he apprenticed him to a silversmith. The baronet had been loving and giving to the first silversmith, but abruptly withdrew his affections and his support when he realized young Basil, like his father, was in the trades.

The contrast between the baronet's treatment of his two American cousins is sharp. I went through a folder of fond letters between John Dixwell and Sir Basil after their long visit in 1710. They share their sorrows and joys. John lost a daughter and writes, "Her name was Elizabeth, she was about 18 months old when she died." The next daughter, also named Elizabeth, had "a very weak constitution," but "my younger child is my son John, born May 16: 1718 a very strong hearty child far exceeding any we had before for bigness at his age."[6] Sir Basil writes of his wife's long ill-ness and then that she "died in my arms, and hath left mee in a very un-happy melancholy condition. She dyed in Ease like a lamb, and life left her without one convulsion, and she is now without doubt in the greatest happiness."[7]

Tragically, the silversmith John Dixwell's wife died as well, and within a few years he was gone too. I wonder if either John Prout or young Basil realized what it would mean to the baronet that Basil did not go to col-lege. The teenager's letters make it clear he did not anticipate that his Brit-ish cousin would be so upset that he was in the trades that the baronet would refuse to receive him at Broome Park if he tried to visit. Writing from the comfort of his manor house, Sir Dixwell calls the young man "headlong and thoughtless" for such a notion and if Basil were to pre-sume "without my approbation to come over, I assure you I never will see you, and shall dispose of any kindness I may otherwise intend you to somebody else who shall be discreet and governable."[8]

Basil's response is abject but persistent: "I must beg your honour's par-don for presuming to trouble you any more, but hoping your Honour is too good to reject the application of orphans, I again humbly desire your protection . . ." He hopes he is not being "troublesome by being too te-dious in repetition of the same."[9]

There are lots more letters, but the one from the baronet to Basil's Uncle Prout has the clearest explanation of the problem of class and money. "Broome, near Canterbury Kent" it says at the top, and in the first sentence gets right to the point. He is "sorry to hear so small an ac-count from you of the substance left by Mr. John Dixwell, for the future subsistence after him of his three children (Basill John and Elizabeth). When he was himself here I thought he gave me a much larger account of his ability and also of his expectations from his wife's relations than what you mention." The baronet also had thought Uncle Prout would do better by Basil's preparation, wishing "you had bred up Basill in the way you at first designed at the College, which might have given him a gen-tleman-like mein, and a foundation for some gentle publick employ there which is possible (if any such there are in that country) might have been applyed and obtained for him, when his age and stature could have made him capable and fit for such, But his being brought up a mechanick prevents that."

The baronet makes a bid for Uncle Prout's sympathy. "I daresay you are not ignorant of my unlucky fate in the world, and the ill management of my predecessors for me in my minority, and the very great misfortunes that attended me on account of Coll Dixwells unhappy share in those times, obliged me to sell part of the estates I ought to have had clear and free from all Incumbrances." He is referring to all those documents I leafed through in the British Museum, on my last day in London, page after page of lands purchased by John Dixwell for his nephew Basil (this Basil's father) that had been seized by the crown at the Restoration. "Attainted of high treason," I read over and over, or "late the possessions of John Dixwell forfeited into his Majestie for the treason of said John Dixwell." How much wealthier this Basil would have been if his great uncle hadn't chosen to judge a king, but how rigid his class consciousness is. He repudiates his one chance at an heir, unable to imagine merit in so much otherness across the Atlantic in the puzzling New World.

To his credit, the baronet adds a kindlier postscript: "Tell me what education has been given to Elizabeth. I desire to know if Basill and John have been fully taught and instructed in all parts of accts and arithmetic, to decimals and Algebra."[10]

Although young Basil never went to England to take over Broome Park and its thousands of acres, he did make it to adulthood. In a painful irony, given his grandfather's efforts to end monarchical rule, he served as a British soldier in the colonial wars, traveling nearly 900 miles northeast to Cape Breton. There, during the Siege of Louisbourg in 1745, he got sick and died at the age of thirty-four. He had no wife or children. British Basil lived to be eighty-five. He never conferred his title but between young Basil's death and his own in 1750, he sent the two remaining Dixwell children, John and Elizabeth, fifty pounds each. When he died, the baronetcy became extinct. I am sad for young Basil's difficult life and early death, but glad the American Dixwells stayed on these shores. The name Basil has the smell of unearned money and privilege. The first John Dixwell had chosen to question all that. How fitting that his key went next to the grandchild bearing his name.

~═──◗

MY FIVE GREATS GRANDFATHER John Dixwell was the baby whom the silversmith had described, in his letter to the baronet, as "a very strong hearty child far exceeding any we had before for bigness at his age." He arrived in 1718, lost his mother when he was three, and his father four years later. Just like his regicide grandfather and great uncle Mark, he and his siblings were packed off to be reared by an uncle, in their case the aforementioned Uncle John Prout in New Haven. And like his brother Basil, he did not get a college education.

He ended up in Boston as an ironmonger, which probably means that he was both a manufacturer and supplier of domestic iron goods. It seems the Dixwells were steadily, though not precipitously, declining in wealth and social status. It didn't help that three consecutive Johns had lost their fathers in childhood. Somehow the key never got lost.

I've found only one account of the third John Dixwell, at the American Antiquarian Society in Worcester. Dying young, he left his pregnant wife Mary and two children, also named John and Mary. His 1749 death notice is in a publication called *The Independent Advertiser*:

> On the 14th Instant died here much lamented, and on the 16th was decently interred (the Gentlemen Cadets, among whom he was an Officer, attending the Funeral) Mr. John Dixwell, aged 31 Years, a considerable Dealer in the Ironmongery Way, a young Gentleman exceedingly beloved and esteemed for his many good qualities by all his acquaintance, he was son of Mr. John Dixwell late of this Place, and grandson to John Dixwell of the Priory of Folkestone in the County of Kent, Esq; who came over into New-England about the year 1660, and settled at New-Haven in Connecticut; he hath left Issue, one Son and a Daughter.[11]

An error and an omission caught my attention. The year the regicide arrived in New England is incorrect. Had the ironmonger lost his father too young to have the story straight? Even more arresting is that there is no mention of the original John Dixwell's role in a king's death. In 1749, exactly a century after Charles's beheading, it was still better not to talk about that. But I also see it as further evidence that the first generations of American Dixwells were more interested in the wealth they wished they could have inherited in England than the radical vision of their forebear.

If Basil had the key and all those letters and indentures first, somehow they got safely to his younger brother, but John died so young I wonder if he had time to get interested in them. Who, then, preserved and passed them on to the next generation, in which only Mary survived? It can only have been her mother, the ironmonger's widow Mary Hunt Dixwell, to whom many bad things happened very fast. She was just thirty-one when she found herself pregnant and alone with two small children. Stiles describes what happened next: "His son John died in three weeks after him, as did his posthumous child."[12] Given those three losses, back to back, I'm impressed that Mary managed to preserve the key and the papers and pass them on to her daughter. She wasn't a direct descendant, but she must have understood how significant they were.

⚷

THERE'S LITTLE DIRECT EVIDENCE OF HER LIFE, but the New Haven Museum has a 1753 letter she wrote to her late husband's relatives in New Haven, asking about Dixwell's land there. As a widow, she was entitled to it. Her handwriting is beautiful and she sounds smart and annoyed. The recipient of her letter has not responded to repeated requests and she carefully writes that she is "persuaded the letters miscarried" as his "known goodness . . . would have prompted you to have taken some notice of me—"[13] Perhaps she got nothing. She may have been struggling to make ends meet. In any event, just a few months later, she married a man named Josias Byles with whom she had six more children.

Her new last name meant the next keeper of the key, her daughter Mary Dixwell, born January 15, 1746, was now the only person in the New World bearing the Dixwell surname. I tracked down a few snippets about her. At the age of twenty-two she tried, just as her mother had, to get some money out of that same Dixwell property in New Haven. In 1768 she wrote a cousin inquiring about land "left me by my Honored Father John Dixwell."[14] Again, I don't know if she got anything.

In 1774, when she was twenty-eight, she married her first cousin Samuel Hunt. Unfortunately, Samuel was a difficult man. After graduating from Harvard in 1765, he became a schoolteacher who was often in trouble with Boston's School Committee. In fact, he flogged his students so severely that the selectmen reprimanded him. Meanwhile Mary was having babies. From 1775 to 1783, the entire span of the Revolutionary War, she had six children. This keeper of the key apparently cared about the regicide, for two sons were named John Dixwell Hunt. Both died young. Remember the highwayman Black Robin and the curse he hurled, just before he was hanged, at the Uncle Basil who built Broome Park? "I will curse the House of Dixwell for one hundred years. And there will be no male heir for a hundred years."

It had been more than a hundred years at this point, but the curse apparently retained some potency in both the old and the new worlds. Cousin Basil Dixwell the baronet died childless in 1750. Now here, too, on the far side of the Atlantic, there were no sons to carry on the Dixwell surname. It hadn't even survived as a middle name—a sad thing for both women. Nevertheless, Mary Hunt Dixwell and her daughter Mary Dixwell Hunt managed to preserve the regicide's legacy. From 1749, the year the ironmonger died, until their deaths more than thirty years later, they are the ones who must have had the key and the papers.

Mary Dixwell Hunt died at the age of thirty-seven on December 4, 1783, a week after delivering her last child. The war that had been fought for the kind of government her great grandfather dreamed of had ended that fall. Had she cared about what he did on the world stage? I think so, and not just because she named those two sons who died young John Dixwell Hunt. In her death notice there is something surprising and brand new: "Mrs. Mary Hunt, wife of Samuel Hunt, A.M. of Boston, departed this life on the 4th ult. She was the only branch of the family of Dixwell, one of the Judges who passed sentence upon King Charles I and who retired to New-England upon the restoration."[15]

I think this is the first time a Dixwell descendant laid claim, publicly and proudly, albeit posthumously, to what her forebear had done, and why not? With the War won, it was a different and exciting world. Note that John Dixwell is not referred to as a regicide, but most respectfully as a judge. At that moment in history the Dixwell name may no longer have existed, but what John Dixwell did had a life of its own and was about to have a second coming. Many citizens of the brand new United States of America could now openly revere the fifty-nine men who, more than a century earlier, had stood up to a tyrannical king.

Down in New Haven, Ezra Stiles, full of admiration verging on idolatry, was hard at work researching the lives of Edward Whalley, William Goffe, and John Dixwell. Because Dixwell was the only regicide to marry and have children in New England, there was a lot more primary material pertaining to him than there was to the other two. And Ezra Stiles, as wonderfully assiduous as he always proves to be, even got information, after Mary Dixwell Hunt's early death, from her husband Samuel Hunt.

Stiles refers twice, in his book, to a man named Jeremy Belknap whom he asked to contact Samuel Hunt. I did a little digging and discovered that Belknap and Hunt overlapped at Harvard. Since at that time there were only about fifty students in each class, they probably knew each other. Belknap loved history. He wrote a massive, three-volume History of New Hampshire, and with nine other men started the Massachusetts Historical Society.

However, it sounds as if Samuel Hunt only let Belknap copy some of Dixwell's papers, for Stiles writes that in 1793 he (Stiles) only had three affidavits, two letters from James Pierpont and one "from the reverend Doctor Cotton Mather, procured for me by the reverend Doctor Belknap, of Boston, from Mr. Samuel Hunt, who married Mary, the last branch of the Dixwell family, in Boston."[16] A few pages later is this, "Some account of the family of Dixwell, taken from sundry papers and fragments now in the possession of Samuel Hunt, by Jeremy Belknap." The account mentions but does not quote the letters I'd seen in New Haven: "Under the assumed name of Davids he corresponded with his niece, Elizabeth Westrow, in London, who assumed the name of Elizabeth Boyse." It then lists the names of all the other correspondents and says of those letters, "They contain chiefly domestic and public news, intermixed with many pious reflections. One of them invites him to Holland, 1689. But it did not arrive till after his death."[17] It must have frustrated Ezra Stiles that he couldn't get copies of every one of those letters.

Clearly, they were precious to the Dixwell family. Nearly a century would pass before Epes Sargent Dixwell, in 1889, gave them to New Haven's historical society. That gift made it possible, another century later, for Jason Peacey to use them as he researched John Dixwell's life, and for Dixie Brown to see John's handwriting announcing the birth of his first baby, scribbled exultantly on the back of a letter from his loyal niece Eliza.

But let's go back to the end of the eighteenth century. Samuel and Mary Hunt's son Samuel, born in 1777, would not only inherit the key and the papers but would also refuse to let the Dixwell surname die. He would give it new life for the next 150 years by going to the Massachusetts Legislature with a petition. On March 16, 1805 just as his regicide ancestor had in the 1660s, he took on a new identity. Dr. Samuel Hunt became Dr. John Dixwell.

My genealogy book says he changed his name because he was a doctor and there was another Dr. Sam Hunt, but I think there was more to it than that. He was the fourth holder of the key to Dover Castle, the letters and indentures, and the silver snuffbox. What if he was excited to be descended from such a radical person?

Dr. Samuel Hunt, a.k.a. John Dixwell (1777–1834)

WHY BE SAMUEL HUNT if you could change your name to John Dixwell? His homeland, thanks to the Revolutionary War, was no longer a British colony. He could be openly proud of his great great grandfather the judge. And what about Stiles's book commemorating Whalley, Goffe, and Dixwell? The newly minted John Dixwell must have had a copy because his father had allowed Stiles to use some of the papers. He probably reveled in Stiles's effusive praise of his ancestor. But there was another reason. He hoped that by changing his name he could prove he was entitled to various estates in England once the property of the regicide. In 1820 he sent a detailed letter to England, asking a man there to inquire into the business.[18] Once again, nothing came of it.

Because Samuel Hunt changed his name, American Dixwells overcame Black Robin's curse and flourished in the nineteenth century. The new John Dixwell had not one but three sons: John James Dixwell (1806–1888), my great great grandfather Epes Sargent Dixwell (1807–1899), and George Basil Dixwell (1814–1885). Epes outlived his brothers, so became the fifth keeper of the key. I'm glad he had the good sense to donate all those papers to the New Haven Museum before he died. And I'm delighted he never said a word about the key.

Before I leave the fourth keeper of the key, I want to describe an artifact I have from the former Samuel Hunt. It is about the size of a bookmark, with glass on either side so you can read the front and the back of a bill charging three dollars for twelve leeches that Dr. John Dixwell applied to Andrew Geyer on October 22, 1834. Two weeks later the doctor, only fifty-six, died. Maybe Epes framed the bill to commemorate his father's last house call. Maybe, too, he loved the look of that famous surname.

Fifth keeper Epes was the least wealthy of the three Dixwell brothers, though he was the only one who got to go to Harvard. He became a schoolteacher, but John and George became merchants. How Baronet Basil would have disapproved. As for me, I was appalled to learn they

Epes Sargent Dixwell (1807–1899)

made a fortune shipping opium from India into China. George was a key player because he was so good at languages. In Shanghai, where he spent many years of his life, he negotiated in both Mandarin and Bengali.[19]

But here's an interesting thing: by now, exactly two hundred years after John Dixwell signed the death warrant for Charles the First, the three Dixwell brothers were immensely proud of what he had done, and wanted to honor him. They used some of that opium money to erect an elegant monument beside the regicide's modest little stone behind the Center Church in New Haven. The four sides of the obelisk include the coat of arms with its three fleurs de lis, and these words:

> Here rest the remains of John DIXWELL, Esq., of the Priory of Kent, in the county of Kent, England, of a family long prominent in Kent and Warwickshire, and himself possessing large estates, and much influence in his country; he espoused the popular cause in the revolution of 1640.

Between 1640 and 1660, he was colonel in the army, an active member of four parliaments, thrice in the council of state, and one of the high court which tried and condemned *King Charles the First*. At the restoration of the monarchy, he was compelled to leave his country; and, after a brief residence in Germany, came to New Haven, and here lived in seclusion, but enjoying the esteem and friendship of its most worthy citizens, till his death, in 1688-9. (west side of monument)

John DIXWELL, a zealous patriot, a sincere Christian, an honest man; he was faithful to duty through good and through evil report; and, having lost fortune, position, and home in the cause of his country, and of human rights, found shelter and sympathy here, among the fathers of New England. His descendants have erected this monument as a tribute of respect to his memory, and as a grateful record of the generous protection extended to him by the early inhabitants of *New Haven*. Erected A.D. 1849 (east side of monument)

The day the monument was installed, November 22, 1849, whoever of the Dixwell brothers was in attendance (and I don't know which one it was), wanted to do more than install a fitting tribute. He wanted his forebear's bones to be examined. The New Haven History Museum has a newspaper clipping describing what happened, written by James F. Babcock, an editor and proprietor of the *New Haven Daily Palladium*. Babcock tactfully explains that because "many people were supposed to entertain a horror" of the regicides, the deed was done early in the morning and that everything was accomplished with permission and great care, but also privately. It sounds as if the editor loved the whole thing, for he waxes poetic, even throwing in a bit of Shakespeare, as he describes what happened. "It was in the early morning while the stars were out and before the dawn had 'dappled the east with spots of gray.' The light used by the diggers was a common lantern."[20]

Ezra Stiles was there in spirit, for they consulted his book's sketch of the grave, measured, and began.

After excavating about two feet, six inches of earth, the outline of the coffin was seen. It was in inky black lines, and apparently only black earth. At my suggestion, the spade was discontinued and a mason's trowel was carefully used, when the forehead of the skeleton was uncovered. There was apparently no decay, or even discoloration, on the top and front of the head. It was a thrilling sight to see thus unveiled, after a rest of nearly two hundred years, the head of a man who had borne such a conspicuous part in the great revolution that had dethroned Charles the First, and placed the renowned Cromwell at the head of the British empire. The lower jaw and ribs of the regicide had become dissolved; but the larger bones of the skeleton, including most of the those of the feet, remained, and were taken up one after another, as wooden moulds are taken away from their clayey bed in an iron foundry. The bones were all placed in a wooden box by the late Edward Herrick, and deposited beneath the monument. Before this was done however, the Hon. Alfred Blackman and myself took the skull, covered by a copy of the New York *Journal of Commerce*, across the Green to the office of Dr. Knight, who took its dimensions by accurate measurement. On our way we met Mayor Skinner, who seemed shocked at our seeming barbarity. He said he had selected that early hour in order to avoid just such barbarity, but had himself been belated. On assuring him that we did not intend to steal the skull, and that our purpose was purely 'scientific,' he let us proceed, though with some misgivings as to the exact propriety of the thing. Mr. Dixwell, however, thanked him for the measurements, and regretted that we had not gone further and taken a cast of the head.

Dr. Knight was practicing phrenology, an overtly racist pseudoscience. Dixwell's measurements, apparently, were alarming. "Now, as to that head: it was very peculiar and well calculated to make a skeptic in the modern phrenological theories a believer in them, for the character of the man was thoroughly indicated in the enormous combative and destructive organs which protruded above and behind his ears. In fact, his head was nearly as round as a bullet, and he was energetic enough to be a prominent leader in the revolution, and destructive enough to cast his vote for the beheading of a king."

Mr. Babcock concludes with this: "I repeat that there was no prejudice expressed anywhere, in my hearing, in regard to this harmless dead man; and it would seem to be hardly creditable to any citizen of New Haven, to harbor abhorrent feelings toward any political or religious opponent who had been driven to the cellars, caves and deserts of New England for a period of years and found safety at last only in the grave which had sheltered him for two hundred years."[21]

I don't know if Epes Sargent Dixwell's skull was as round and "protruded above and behind his ears" as distinctively as his great great great grandfather's, but he was a very bright and well-read man.[22] When he gave all those treasures to the New Haven Museum, he wrote eloquently of the many things he knew about his forebear's life and about the letters and indentures.

> Two hundred years ago an old man of eighty-two years was lying ill in your town of a painful disease which brought his death on the 18th of March, 1689 . . . I am now about the same age as the writer of these papers was when he died, viz. 81+. It is my desire to place them for safety in the hands of some society which will preserve them more carefully than seems probable in the chances of private possession. My family concur in this desire. Where could I place them more properly than in the hands of this Society, thus bringing them back to the place of their origin?[23]

He does not mention that he hasn't included the regicide's key to Dover Castle. I don't know exactly, at this point in my account of the keepers, where the key went in its journey from my great great grandfather to me but I can guess roughly. Epes had five daughters and one son, whom he named, of course, John Dixwell. I assume he gave the key to John, who lived from 1848 to 1931, and died in my hometown of Milton. He became a doctor and took a great interest in helping the poor, from disabled Civil War veterans to retired fishermen in need of housing. He

John Dixwell (1848–1931)

had no children, so once again, the surname Dixwell disappeared in my branch of the family.

A FEW OF MY FINDINGS show that this John Dixwell, like his father, cared intensely about preserving his ancestor's story and reputation. The United States he'd grown up in had survived the trauma of the Civil War and not yet entered the First World War when Dr. John Dixwell received a little package from England. The Massachusetts Historical Society has a fragment of a clay tile from the exterior of Broome Park, sent to my great great Uncle John in 1914 by a friend who wrote from Canterbury, "My Dear Doctor, I visited your ancestral home and found it was built by Sir Basil Dixwell in 1625. . . . It is a grand old place seventy-five rooms or more with 700 acres of land beautiful old trees such as you only find in

England—" A label on the shard says "obtained there from the caretaker by Capt. J. Avery 1914 for Dr. Dixwell Boston Mass U.S.A. The brick face of the Hall there was bright like new/never painted/nor renewed."[24]

Clearly, John had told tales of Broome Park to Captain Avery. I'm certain his father, Epes the schoolteacher, regaled his six children with all that he knew of the regicide's life and deeds in England and then of his reclusive decades in New Haven. What a contrast to my own father's complete silence on the subject even though, when pressed, he knew quite a bit.

All his life, Dr. Dixwell kept the Judge's memory alive. In the late 1920s, he worked hard to get the city of New Haven to maintain the monument, which was getting damaged. "This grave should be protected," he wrote. "Please let me hear from you, as several relatives are quite as anxious as I."[25]

Eventually, his efforts paid off. He got a letter from Mayor Thomas Tully: "You may rest assured that the conditions which you complain of will be taken care of at once and everything possible done to show due respect to the grave of Regicide John Dixwell."[26]

Mary Catherine Dixwell Wigglesworth (1855–1951)

As far as I can see, no one in later generations took much of an interest. Some of that may be because the next two keepers of the key were women who lived in a time when a college education was unthinkable in their families. My great grandmother Mary Catherine Dixwell Wigglesworth, the youngest of Epes's children, probably got the key when her brother John died, for she lived in Milton as well, and outlived him by twenty years. But she, like her own mother, had six children with whom she was passionately involved. I doubt she took much of an interest in the English civil wars fought more than 200 years before her birth.

I have a theory as to why the key went next to my grandmother, Marian Epes Wigglesworth Brown, and then to her son, Thornton Brown, my father. It could simply be that because they all lived in Milton, whatever box contained the key went to each keeper in the subsequent generation more or less by default. My grandmother Marian had only four children, but because the youngest had Down Syndrome, her best efforts went to teaching him much more than any of the experts of the 1920s thought possible. When I consider that her life also spanned two world wars and

Marian Epes Wigglesworth Brown (1884–1973)

Thornton Brown (1913–2000)

the Great Depression, I can see how the beheading of a king in 1649 was not uppermost in her mind.

But she and my father, the keepers of the key closest to me, had their own experiences of the horrors of tyrants—Japan's Emperor Hirohito, Germany's Adolf Hitler, Italy's Benito Mussolini, and Spain's Francisco Franco—when the United States entered World War Two. The democratic ideals Dixwell had devoted his life to supporting were under threat around the globe. My father enlisted as a battalion surgeon in the South Pacific.

My sturdy, softhearted grandmother was determined to reveal none of her fear, pride, or sadness to him on the day he left, in September of 1942. Instead, she tucked into his Marines trunk a letter full of her love (it's also full of the Quaker thee's and thou's she added to her Unitarian sensibilities when she married my grandfather, whose mother was a Friend). She didn't know it, but she was channeling John Dixwell and all he stood for:

Thorntie dear, I am writing this letter now, because if it is all stored up inside me and I want to say it and can't, when the time comes for thee to go, I know that the flood gates will burst and I shall make a fool of myself! So thee'll have to forgive me and just realize that after all, I'm thy mother and I've got to spill over a bit.

Thee'll never know how much I love thee or how proud I am, over everything that thee has accomplished, and the way in which thee has done it—I don't suppose, thee has any idea how people love thee and admire thee. I hear it from all directions—Thee's made a success in everything thee has done since thee was a little boy and always with an absolutely unselfish spirit and thought for others.

And now the next chapter is opening and though it nearly kills me to have thee go, I know, that never before has there been a cause so worth working for—Those who go take an <u>active</u> part in the biggest thing that has ever happened. It is the first step in the remaking of the world. And it is going to be a much better and more just world, I am absolutely convinced. We at home will do our part too, but not as thee will be doing it.

Wherever thee goes dear, and whatever thee does, I will be thinking of thee and loving thee every minute of the day and night.

In after years it will be an open door to thee wherever thee meets other men who have been actively in it. And this time, it will be men in every corner of the Globe.

Thee doesn't need to say anything about this letter. It helped me to write it—I shall know that thee knows what I want to say and couldn't possibly say if I tried to—It's awful to have no control over one's emotions—I am all right until I speak and then my vocal chords go back on me and the rain cometh!!

Lovingly always,
Mother

That letter went all the way to several islands in the South Pacific and made it safely back home. I wonder how often Dad permitted himself to read it. I love that my grandmother, like John Dixwell, believed in the importance of a "cause," which she calls the "remaking of the world." My father shared that belief, which is why, more than twenty years after his death, I go on puzzling as to why he never evinced the least interest in John Dixwell or thought to tell us of the man's existence.

It's true he never talked about much of anything, especially when feelings were involved. He said not a word about his time in the bloody theater of the South Pacific until the last month of his life, when he told me he was frustrated because they did not have the means to airlift the wounded to the nearest field hospital. Mostly, I think, he helped people die in less agony.

Was it the survivor guilt that can accompany the post-traumatic stress disorder he surely had that made him such a quiet workaholic? There was no moment in all the years I knew him when he allowed himself the kind of leisure that I've had to study John Dixwell. And yet, when he was writing letters from the South Pacific to his brand-new fiancée, my mother, he had as much fiery excitement as any of those fifty-nine judges who signed Charles the First's death warrant.

My mother wrote him from Washington, D.C., where she was secretly cracking Japanese codes for the War Department, that she was a little sad and mad that not only had he enlisted, but now he was determined to become a paratrooper so he could float down on battlefields to treat the wounded. His tentmate John Stage wanted to take on the same scary challenge. The letter is dated July 14, 1943:

> Darling, I don't know quite what to say about the Paratroops. I'm sorry to have made you "kind of mad and sad" and I certainly appreciate your broadminded attitude. I really didn't go rushing into them just for my own amusement. I thought about the pros and cons a lot and I tried to see your side too. I finally decided that I should do it on the basis that it was a job that needed to be done and was one that I was well fitted to do in spite of my astigmatic orbs. Though I realize it is very hard on you, who must merely wait and worry, nevertheless this damned business is chiefly waiting and worrying. You'd be doing some of that anyway and if you can stand a little more, I at least will be being useful and therefore much happier. Moreover, there's no reason to worry. Incidentally, Dr. Stage hasn't

confessed to his wife <u>yet</u> I believe. He's scared to still, tho' I guess she's figured it out by now. When at New River she objected to the "troops" but admitted it would probably do no good, thereby making hubby John feel very much the heel.

Yes, the doctors are supposed to be about as tough as the rest. As to the % eliminated it's not so high, chiefly because only the relatively tough volunteer (bragging again). You ought to see me in my new suit. It's a thing of beauty and my, how tough I feel in it!

It made me happy to read his letters. He was a doctor, not a barrister and politician, but he cared intensely about being in the thick of things. Two days later he wrote my mother:

7-16-43. Strangely enough I've been quite busy medically speaking, for the last two days anyway. Yesterday there was a compound fracture of a finger—the result of a little trouble with a tank tread—very reminiscent of my B.C.H. [Boston City Hospital] days. Today there was a slight explosion and I spent an hour or so pulling pieces of wood and metal out of various people's anatomy. No serious casualties, tho' a fellow came very near losing an eye. It was quite exciting to do something, yet it served as a reminder of how difficult it will be to do much in actual combat. Even here with conditions of the best (for the field that is) it seemed pretty crude. This is all very bad for one's surgical habits. I hate to think what I'll do once back in a real hospital again.

The other day I went for a ride in a tank. I can say without hesitation that that is the very bottom. To be cooped up in a smelly little iron box unable to see what's going about you and realizing that a well aimed shell or piece of T.N.T. will end it all in a flash of flame and burning gasoline. No, no. Give me wide open spaces. Just the same they are very nifty machines and knock down trees and go over anything as nice as you please.

Finding and transcribing his war letters made me realize how little I understood what an irresistible young man my mother fell in love with. I'm so glad I have the box of their letters to each other all that horrifying

Sarah Dixwell Brown (1951–)

year. Perhaps one day I will bring the same detailed attention to them I ended up bringing to John Dixwell.

That, in the end is what was transformational for me about my years with John Dixwell. It wasn't getting the key. It was that I had never before brought such sustained attention to so many small and interconnected discoveries. My work brought me the gift of a deeper understanding of the difficult and wondrous times in the life of my seven greats grandfather. During the COVID-19 pandemic the project kept me busy in the midst of the weird isolation and gut fear of living under the most tyrannical president in our nation's history. I wish I could tell John Dixwell how much my study of his times helped me think about my own. But who's to say he doesn't know?

FAMILY TREE

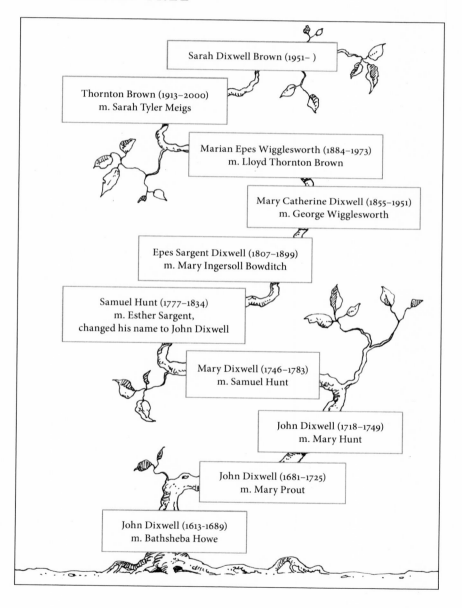

Sarah Dixwell Brown (1951–)

Thornton Brown (1913–2000)
m. Sarah Tyler Meigs

Marian Epes Wigglesworth (1884–1973)
m. Lloyd Thornton Brown

Mary Catherine Dixwell (1855–1951)
m. George Wigglesworth

Epes Sargent Dixwell (1807–1899)
m. Mary Ingersoll Bowditch

Samuel Hunt (1777–1834)
m. Esther Sargent,
changed his name to John Dixwell

Mary Dixwell (1746–1783)
m. Samuel Hunt

John Dixwell (1718–1749)
m. Mary Hunt

John Dixwell (1681–1725)
m. Mary Prout

John Dixwell (1613-1689)
m. Bathsheba Howe

MY BRANCH OF THE
DIXWELL FAMILY GENEALOGY

Henry Herdson (1500–1555) was a skinner and one of the founders of
the Muscovy Company. He was wealthy and an alderman in the City
of London. He had a least a dozen manors, some from Henry VIII.
He owned several manors in County Kent, in particular, Terlingham
and Folkstone, where various Dixwells later lived. Henry had, with
his wife Barbara, twelve children. After Henry died, Barbara married
Richard Champion, who became Lord Mayor of London in 1566.
Barbara died in 1568. The two Herdson children who are important
to the Dixwell family tree are Abigail and John.

Abigail married Charles Dixwell. I do not know when either was born,
but have their death dates. Charles died in 1591, Abigail in 1635. They
had five children:

1. William
2. Edward (circa 1575–1616)
3. Humphrey
4. Basil (1585–1642)
5. Barbara

Abigail's brother John Herdson never married. In 1620 he adopted his
nephew Basil Dixwell.

Edward, second son of Charles and Abigail Dixwell, married Mary
Hawkesworth. They lived in Ponteland, in the far north of England,
where Edward had been appointed vicar. They had six children before Edward died in 1616:

1. Jacobus, born 13 January 1605
2. Anna, born 14 May 1607
3. Marcus, born 18 February 1609
4. Abigail, born 6 March 1611
5. Johannes, born 21 March 1613
6. Carolus, born 20 March 1615

When Edward died, two of his sons, Mark and John, wound up in Kent
with Uncle Basil Dixwell and Great Uncle John Herdson. When John
Herdson died in 1622 he left a hefty inheritance and thousands of
acres of land to Basil. All this went to Mark when Basil died in 1642.

Mark Dixwell married Elizabeth Read. He died in the first civil war, in
1643. She died in 1691. They had five children, but the ones who are
important to my story are the firstborn, Elizabeth (1636–1695) and
the first son, Basil (circa 1640–1668).

Mark's younger brother John became the guardian of Mark's children
and the manager, though not the owner, of the enormous estate after
Mark's death. In 1649 he signed the death warrant for Charles I.

After he fled the country in 1660, he eventually wound up in New
Haven, Connecticut, where he lived under the assumed name of
James Davids until his death in 1689. Back in England, his niece Elizabeth stayed in contact with him until his death. His nephew Basil
cut all ties with him.

In 1673 James Davids (John Dixwell) married Joanna Ling, widow of
Benjamin Ling. She died within the month.

In 1677 he married Bathsheba Howe (15 May 1648–27 December 1729).
Bathsheba was the daughter of Jeremiah Howe (1614–1690) and

Elizabeth (1619–1695). Both were born in England and both died in New Haven. Bathsheba was the fourth of eight children, and was born in New Haven.

John Dixwell and Bathsheba Howe had three children:

1. Mary, born 9 June 1679
2. John, born 6 March 1681, died 2 April 1725
3. Elizabeth, born 14 July 1682, died in infancy

The son John married, in New Haven 1 September 1708, Mary Prout and moved to Boston where he was a silversmith. They had six children:

1. Mary, born 14 December 1709 and died young
2. Basil, born 7 July 1711
3. Elizabeth, born 17 March 1713 who also must have died young
4. Elizabeth, born 12 April 1716
5. John, born 1718 (day unknown), died 1749
6. Mary, born 1 November 1720

The son, John (1718–1749), married Mary Hunt (1718–1781) and they had three children:

1. John (we know only that he is mentioned in his father's will)
2. Mary, born 15 January 1746, died 4 December 1783
3. A child born after his father's death whose name is unknown to me.

Mary Dixwell married Samuel Hunt (born 25 October 1745). They had six children, three of whom they named John Dixwell. Of these three Johns, two died before the age of two, the other at sixteen. There were also Susanna who died at twenty-six of TB, and George.

Their second son, my great great great grandfather Samuel Hunt, was born 6 January 1777.

He married Esther Sargent, born in Gloucester 4 April 1776 to Epes and

Dorcas Sargent. Samuel Hunt and Esther Sargent had three sons after he legally changed his name to John Dixwell in 1805. Their three Dixwell sons are:

1. John James, born 27 June 1806 (died 15 November 1876)
2. Epes Sargent, born 27 December 1807 (died 1 December 1899)
3. George Basil, born 15 December 1814 (died 10 April 1885)

Epes Sargent Dixwell married, 4 June 1839, Mary Ingersoll Bowditch (born in Salem 3 April 1816). They had six children:

1. Fanny Bowditch, born 12 December 1849, died 30 April 1929
2. Esther Sargent, born 19 September 1843, died 20 September 1927
3. Susan Hunt, born 1 June 1845, died 3 February 1924
4. John, born 21 March 1848, died 17 April 1931
5. Arria Sargent, born 1 June 1850, died 6 February 1916
6. Mary Catherine, born 5 June 1855, died 22 January 1951

Mary Catherine Dixwell married George Wigglesworth 20 June 1878. They had six children:

1. Anna Cornelia, born 7 April 1879
2. Norton, born 7 January 1882
3. Marian Epes, born 4 June 1884, died 26 May 1973
4. Ruth, born 19 June 1886
5. Richard, born 25 April 1891
6. Frank, born 7 February 1893

Marian Epes Wigglesworth married Lloyd Thornton Brown (born 20 August 1880, died 13 December 1961) on 14 January 1911. They had four children:

1. Lloyd, born 19 October 1911, died 2004
2. Thornton, born 24 November 1913, died 4 July 2000

3. Ruth, born 22 May 1920, died 10 December 2003
4. Richard, born 22 June 1922, died 18 March 1988

Thornton Brown married, on 28 February 1944, Sarah Tyler Meigs (born 27 April 1917, died 20 July 1998). They had four children:

1. Marian Wigglesworth, born 20 December 1944
2. Edward Meigs, born 22 July 1946
3. Cornelia Wister, born 13 April 1949
4. Sarah Dixwell, born 7 November 1951

ACKNOWLEDGMENTS

I MAY HAVE WRITTEN THIS BOOK, but its production has been a marvelous collaboration. Throughout the decades that I've been obsessed with John Dixwell, kind people read various drafts and helped me with my research. Thanks to Edith Clowes, Eric Fry, Sarah Groves, Nancy Hibbard, Evelyn Hopkins, Stephanie Kraft, Tim Monaghan, Peggy Woods, and Gordon Wyse. Thanks to Patricia E. Kane, curator of American Decorative Arts at Yale University Art Gallery and Amanda Lange, curator at Historic Deerfield. Thanks to John Butman, who served as my agent and helped me put together my proposal before his untimely death in the spring of 2020. Thanks to research librarians Kate Freedman and Melinda McIntosh at the W.E.B. Du Bois library at the University of Massachusetts in Amherst, to the staff at the New Haven Museum, the American Antiquarian Society, the Connecticut State Library, and the Massachusetts Historical Society. Thanks to Steve Strimer for his excitement about my project, and to Greta Sibley, whose excellent skills brought the book from a manuscript to a polished product.

Thanks to Mijung Kim for volunteering to accompany me on my research trip to England, and for being such a kind and resourceful traveling companion.

I am grateful to the many people who made time to meet with me in England and taught me about John Dixwell's era: Eleanor Cracknell at Eton College, Julian Reid at Oxford University's Merton College, Guy Holborn at Lincoln's Inn, Jason Peacey at University College London, Rowena Willard-Wright at Dover Castle, Gillian Matthews at Broome Park, Roger Hailwood at Churchover, Ruth Sheret at Newcastle University's Robinson Library, Lorraine Sencicle of Dover, Josie Marshall, and everyone who helped me at the Woodhorn Museum and Northumberland Archives and the British Library. Sadly, Roger Hailwood died in April, 2020, too soon for me to be able to send him a copy of my book.

Special thanks go to two people in particular. Willis E. Bridegam helped me dive deeper into the politics of seventeenth-century England. As the retired head librarian at Amherst College's Frost Library, he had the expertise to be a research assistant like no other. His generosity with his time, his keen interest in British and American history, and his editorial insights were enormously helpful to me.

As I neared completion of the final draft, my daughter Heidi was equally generous with her time, going through the manuscript with wonderful care and perspicacity. She was a brilliant, gentle, yet tough critic. I especially appreciate the way she held tight to her conviction that the book was important, interesting, and worth all the years that had gone into it. Then she put together the endnotes and bibliography. She was and is a godsend.

Extra special thanks to my son Rob, who listened endlessly to my struggles and ideas, studied my photographs, and gave me courage when my spirits flagged from the sheer magnitude of what I had undertaken. Both my children have been kindness incarnate.

Thanks to my cousins Marcia Dixwell DiMambro, Caroline Dixwell Cabot, and Ann Wigglesworth Clemmitt for the new stories they told me about our family. And thanks to my siblings Marian, Ed, and Nina for their interest and support.

Finally, I thank my tireless writing group, who kept the faith that I could bring this book to fruition as the years went by: Barbara Goldin, Amy Gordon, Jeff Mack, Lauren Mills, and Dennis Nolan. In the most tactful ways, you made me laugh at myself. Then you insisted I keep going. You are the best. I could not have done it without you.

NOTES

Chapter 2: Surprise in the British Museum

1. Ezra Stiles, *A History of Three of the Judges of Charles I. Major-General Whalley, Major-General Goffe, and Colonel Dixwell* (Hartford: Elisha Babcock, 1794).
2. Stiles, *A History.*
3. Stiles, *A History,* 8.
4. Stiles, *A History,* 125.
5. Stiles, *A History,* 128.
6. Stiles, *A History,* 149.

Chapter 3: Was I Named After a King Killer?

1. John Burke, *Burke's Extinct Baronetcies* (London: John Russell Smith, 1841), 161.
2. Burke, *Extinct Baronetcies,* 161.
3. Stiles, *A History,* 150.
4. Stiles, *A History,* 152.

Chapter 5: Why Did John Dixwell Do It?

1. Charles Firth, "John Dixwell," in *Dictionary of National Biography,* eds. Leslie Stephen and Sidney Lee (London, Smith, Elder & Co. 1908), 1035.
2. Firth, "John Dixwell."
3. Firth, "John Dixwell."
4. Firth, "John Dixwell."
5. Firth, "John Dixwell."
6. Firth, "John Dixwell."

Chapter 6: How Charles the First Lost his Head

1. This passage is from the publisher's summary of Cicely Veronica Wedgwood, *A Coffin for King Charles* (New York: Macmillan, 1964). It appears in full on Amazon and other bookseller sites.
2. John Philipps Kenyon, "The Stuarts," in *Great Dynasties* (New York: Windward, 1980), 125-137.
3. Publisher's summary of Wedgwood, *A Coffin*.
4. Ann Hughes, "The Execution of Charles I," *BBC History* (2011), https://www .bbc.co.uk/history/british/civil_war_revolution/charlesi_execution_01.shtml.
5. Hughes, "Execution of Charles I."
6. Cicely Veronica Wedgwood, *A Coffin for King Charles* (New York: Macmillan, 1964), 8.
7. Wedgwood, *A Coffin*, 10.
8. Wedgwood, *A Coffin*, 56.
9. "The Works of King Charles the Martyr, 1687," in Vol. 2 of *Readings in European History: From the Protestant Revolt to the Present Day*, by James Harvey Robinson. Boston: Ginn and Co. 1906), 244.
10. "Works of King Charles," 245.
11. Philip Henry, *Diaries and Letters of Philip Henry, M.A. of Broad Oak, Flintshire, A.D. 1631–1696*, eds. Matthew Henry Lee and Andrew Dickson White (London: Kegan Paul, Trench & Co., 1882), 12.

Chapter 7: Conscience and Consequences

1. Stiles, *A History*, 186.

Chapter 8: Tyrant Number Two: Oliver Cromwell

1. Cicely Veronica Wedgwood, *The Life of Cromwell* (New York: Collier Books, 1966), 91.
2. Wedgwood, *Life of Cromwell*, 99.
3. Wedgwood, *Life of Cromwell*, 109.

Chapter 9: Enter: Mijung Kim

1. Firth, "John Dixwell."
2. Jason Peacey, "John Dixwell," in *Oxford Dictionary of National Biography 2001-2004*, ed. Lawrence Goldman (Oxford: Oxford University Press, 2009), 337–8.

Chapter 10: Jumping Off the Deep End

1. Marge Perry, "Re: Was Regicide John1 Dixwell a son of William Dixwell, or . . . ," Rootsweb.com, discussion forum post, November 30, 2006, thread archived: https://www.slektogdata.no/slektsforum/viewtopic.php?p=175861&si d=38072fdee23bb5f6c2d519179b5b9340#p175861.

2. Roger Hailwood, *Looking Back at Broome Park: The Story of England's Finest Carolean Mansion* (Burton on Trent: Hailwood Enterprises), 2006.

Chapter 12: Finding the Scene of the Crime

1. Death Warrant of King Charles I, January 1649, House of Lords Record Office, London.

Chapter 13: John Dixwell's Family of Origin

1. Hailwood, *Looking Back*, Introduction.
2. Hailwood, *Looking Back*, 11.
3. Hailwood, *Looking Back*, 11.
4. Edmund Ludlow, *Memoirs of Edmund Ludlow, Esq.: With a Collection of Original Papers, Serving to Confirm and Illustrate Many Important Passages Contained in the Memoirs* (Edinburgh, 1751), 329.
5. Ludlow, *Memoirs*, 330.
6. Hailwood, *Looking Back*, 17.

Chapter 14: A Church Full of Dixwells

1. Vol. 21, Pt. 1 of the Parliamentary Papers of the House of Commons and Command, 1672, in *History, Gazetteer, and Directory, of Warwickshire* (Warwickshire: Francis White and Co., 1850).

Chapter 15: Entering Eton College

1. Sir Pelham Grenville Wodehouse, *Something New* (New York: D. Appleton & Company, 1915), 25.
2. "Our History," Eton College, 2014, https://www.etoncollege.com/about-us/our-history/.
3. Sir Henry Churchill Maxwell-Lyte, *A History of Eton College: 1440–1875.* London: MacMillan and Co., 1911.

Chapter 16: On to Oxford University

1. The Quarter Sessions Criminal Records Assizes Sessions for Northumberland 1594–1630, Northumberland Archives, Woodhorn Museum, Ashington.
2. H. M. Wood, *Vicars of Ponteland* (1920), 20.

Chapter 17: A Birth and a Death

1. Madeleine Hope Dodds, "Ecclesiastical History," in Vol. 12 of *A History of Northumberland: The Parishes of Ovingham, Stamfordham and Ponteland* (Newcastle-upon-Tyne: Reid, 1926), 419.
2. Dodds, "Ecclesiastical History," 420.
3. Dodds, "Ecclesiastical History," 420.
4. Dodds, "Ecclesiastical History," 445.

Chapter 18: Learning the Law at Lincoln's Inn

1. Peter Lefevre and Andrew Thrush, "Dixwell, Basil (1585-1642), of Terlingham, Folkestone, Kent; Formerly of Canterbury, Kent; Later of Broome Park, Barham, Kent," *History of Parliament Online* (2010), https://www.historyof parliamentonline.org/volume/1604-1629/member/dixwell-basil-1585-1642.
2. Lefevre and Thrush, "Dixwell."
3. Lefevre and Thrush, "Dixwell."
4. Lefevre and Thrush, "Dixwell."
5. Wilfrid R. Prest, *The Inns of Court under Elizabeth I and the Early Stuarts 1590–1640* (London: Longman, 1972); Wilfrid R. Prest, *The Rise of the Barristers: A Social History of the English Bar 1590–1640* (Oxford: Clarendon Press, 1986).
6. Mary C. D. Wigglesworth, *An Autobiographical Sketch of Epes Sargent Dixwell: Unfinished and Unrevised. Begun for His Children and Found among some Papers Which Came into My Hands after His Death* (Boston: Geo. H. Ellis Co., 1907).
7. Prest, *Rise*, 38.
8. Nicholas Le Poidevin, "Learning the Law," in *A Portrait of Lincoln's Inn*, ed. Angela Holdsworth (London: Third Millennium, 2007), 85.
9. John Donne, "Meditation XVII," in *Devotions upon Emergent Occasions* (Cambridge: The University Press, 1923).

Chapter 19: Lawyers vs the Status Quo

1. Prest, *Rise*, 127.
2. Prest, *Rise*, 106.
3. Prest, *Rise*, 133.
4. Prest, *Rise*, 222.
5. Wallace Notestein, "The Winning of the Initiative by the House of Commons," in Vol. 11 of *Proceedings of the British Academy, Raleigh Lecture on History* (London, 1924).
6. Notestein, "The Winning," 49.
7. Notestein, "The Winning," 50.
8. Notestein, "The Winning," 51.
9. Notestein, "The Winning," 51.
10. Notestein, "The Winning," 53.

Chapter 21: Broome Park: Uncle Basil Dixwell's Big Idea

1. Caroline Dixwell Cabot, "A Concise History of Broome Park." (published privately, 2003).
2. Hailwood, *Looking Back*, 5.
3. Hailwood, *Looking Back*, 5.
4. Hailwood, *Looking Back*, 7.

5. A little about Kitchener: He was a major player in the British Army's imperialist conquests and a colonial administrator. His "scorched earth" policy in the Boer War in South Africa led to military victories for the British at the turn of the twentieth century. The British imprisoned Boer civilians in concentration camps.

Chapter 22: Walking in Green Pastures
1. Charlotte Brontë, *Jane Eyre* (New York: W. W. Norton & Company, 1987).

Chapter 23: The Key Returns to Dover Castle
1. *History of Barham*, compiled by Members of the Barham Women's Institute (Barham, 1959/1966), 18.
2. Tony Arnold, "New Golf and Country Club in Historic Mansion," *East Kent Mercury*, July 16, 1981.

Chapter 24: Face-to-face with Uncle Basil
1 Lefevre and Thrush, "Dixwell."

Chapter 25: Hearing John Dixwell's Voice
1. Sworn Statement by John Okell, Former Servant of John Dixwell, 1665, MS 40717: 1465–1799, Folio 169, Miscellaneous Papers, Western Manuscripts, British Library, London.
2. Survey of the Manor of Buckland (in Faversham Hundred), and of Lands in Hougham and Folkestone, Co. Kent, Formerly Belonging to John Dixwell, and then in the Possession of James, Duke of York, 1661/1662, MS 40717: 1465–1799, Folio 169, Miscellaneous Papers, Western Manuscripts, British Library, London.
3. Dorothy Kempe Gardiner, ed., Vol. 1 of *The Oxinden and Peyton Letters, 1642–1670* (London: Constable & Co Ltd., 1933), xxii.
4. Dorothy Kempe Gardiner, ed., Vol. 2 of *The Oxinden and Peyton Letters, 1607–1642* (London: Sheldon Press, 1937), xxix.
5. Prest, *Rise*, 106.
6. Gardiner, Vol. 1 of *Oxinden Letters*, xxii.
7. Gardiner, Vol. 2 of *Oxinden Letters*, 94.
8. Gardiner, Vol. 2 of *Oxinden Letters*, 110.
9. Gardiner, Vol. 2 of *Oxinden Letters*, 42.
10. Gardiner, Vol. 2 of *Oxinden Letters*, 43.
11. Gardiner, Vol. 2 of *Oxinden Letters*, 81.
12. Gardiner, Vol. 2 of *Oxinden Letters*, 82.
13. Gardiner, Vol. 2 of *Oxinden Letters*, 99.
14. Gardiner, Vol. 2 of *Oxinden Letters*, 100.
15. Gardiner, Vol. 2 of *Oxinden Letters*, 85.
16. Gardiner, Vol. 2 of *Oxinden Letters*, 132.

Chapter 26: Back in the U.S.A.

1. Hailwood, *Looking Back*, 7–8.
2. Jason Peacey, "Dixwell, John (c.1607–89) of Coton, Warwickshire, and Folkestone, Kent," in *The History of Parliament* (Cambridge: Cambridge University Press, forthcoming).
3. Jason Peacey, "'The Good Old Cause for Which I Suffer': The Life of a Regicide in Exile," in *Literatures of Exile in the English Revolution and Its Aftermath, 1640–1690*, ed., Philip Major (Burlington: Ashgate, 2010), 167–180.

Chapter 27: Arriving in the New World, 1665

1. Ludlow, *Memoirs*, 329
2. Ludlow, *Memoirs*, 1250; I am grateful to Vivienne Larminie, at the History of Parliament (a London-based research project), for finding this fragment for me.
3. Dixwell Properties Seized by the Crown, 1661/1662, MS 40717: 1465–1799, Folio 169, Miscellaneous Papers, Western Manuscripts, British Library, London.
4. Personal communication, Katherine Freedman, PhD., 2019.
5. Matthew Jenkinson, *Charles I's Killers in America: The Lives & Afterlives of Edward Whalley & Willam Goffe* (Oxford: Oxford University Press, 2019), 206.

Chapter 28: Hiding in Hadley, Massachusetts

1. Christopher Pagliuco, *The Great Escape of Edward Whalley and William Goffe Smuggled through Connecticut* (Charleston: History Press, 2021), 16.
2. Pagliuco, *Great Escape*, 30–31.
3. A description of Cromwell's districts is in Chapter Eight.
4. Stiles, *A History*, 34.
5. Stiles, *A History*, 118–119.
6. Stiles, *A History*, 124.

Chapter 29: Becoming James Davids in the New Haven Colony

1. "The New England Colonies and the Native Americans," *National Geographic*, June 26, 2020, https://www.nationalgeographic.org/article/new-england-colonies-and-native-americans/.
2. Francis J. Bremer, *Building a New Jerusalem, John Davenport, a Puritan in Three Worlds* (New Haven: Yale University Press, 2012).
3. Bremer, *Building*, 295.
4. Stiles, *A History*, 126.
5. Stiles, *A History*, 127.
6. Stiles, *A History*, 128.
7. Stiles, *A History*, 131.
8. Stiles, *A History*, 132.
9. Stiles, *A History*, 130.

Chapter 30: Enter Bathsheba

1. Archibald Duncan, *The Mariner's Chronicle* (New Haven: G. W. Gorton. 1834).
2. Stiles, *A History*, 138.

Chapter 31: What Bathsheba Knew

1. New Haven Town Records, 1649–1662, Library, New Haven Museum and Historical Society, New Haven, 88.
2. New Haven Town Records, 1662–1684, Library, New Haven Museum and Historical Society, New Haven, 69.
3. Atul Gawande, *Being Mortal, Medicine and What Matters in the End* (New York: Metropolitan Books/Henry Holt and Company, 2014), 18.
4. Charles Spencer, *Killers of the King* (New York: Bloomsbury, 2015), 182–3.
5. Charles Gaylord, *The Book of Shipwrecks: And Narratives of Maritime Discoveries and the Most Popular Voyages, from the Time of Columbus to the Present Day* (Boston: Lilly, Wait, Colman & Holden, 1836), 138.
6. Franklin Bowditch Dexter, "Early Private Libraries in New England," in Vol. 18 of *Proceedings of the American Antiquarian Society* (Worcester: American Antiquarian Society, 1906–1907), 147.
7. Franklin Bowditch Dexter, "The New Haven of Two Hundred Years Ago," in Vol. 8 of New Haven Historical Society Papers (New Haven: New Haven Historical Society, 1914), 349.
8. Dexter, "New Haven," 330.
9. Dexter, "New Haven," 340.
10. Dexter, "New Haven," 342.
11. Dexter, "New Haven," 338–340.

Chapter 32: Babies Born in the New World

1. Franklin B. Dexter, ed., "Dixwell Papers," in Vol. 6 of *Papers of the New Haven Colony Historical Society* (New Haven: New Haven Colony Historical Society, 1900), 347.
2. Stiles, *A History*, 137.
3. Stiles, *A History*, 140.
4. Dexter, "Dixwell Papers," 348.
5. Dexter, "Dixwell Papers," 367.
6. The indenture can also be found in: Stiles, *A History*, 140–143.

Chapter 33: Goods and Chattel

1. Stiles, *A History*, 137.
2. Benjamin Ling's Will and Estate Inventory, 1673, Vol. 1, Pt. 1 of New Haven Probate Record (1647–1687), 157.
3. James Davids's (alias John Dixwell) Will and Estate Inventory, 1688/1689, Vol. 2, Pt. 1 of New Haven Probate Record (1688–1703), 8-9.

4. Patricia E. Kane, ed., *Colonial Massachusetts Silversmiths and Jewelers* (Hanover: Yale University Art Gallery distributed by University Press of New England, 1998).

5. Jeremiah How's Will and Estate Inventory, 1690, Vol. 2, Pt. 1 of New Haven Probate Record (1688–1703), 77–78; Elizabeth How's Will and Estate Inventory, 1695, Vol. 2, Pt. 2 of New Haven Probate Record (1688–1703), 176–177.

6. Bathshua Dixwell's Estate Inventory, 1728/1730, no. 1709; and Will, 1727, Hartford Probate District, Town of Middletown, History and Genealogy Unit, Connecticut State Library, Hartford.

7. Dexter, "Dixwell Papers," 340.

Chapter 34: Eliza the Loyal and the Good Old Cause

1. The silversmith's daughter Elizabeth, b. 12 April 1716, married a Lathrop so yes, a cousin. Maybe the seal is in Ogallala, Nebraska.

2. Robert Egleston to Brent Lathrop, 1985. John Dixwell Papers. MSS-8. Folder J. New Haven Museum Manuscript Collections, New Haven.

3. John Dixwell Indenture, 1682, John Dixwell Papers, MSS-8, Folder G, New Haven Museum Manuscript Collections, New Haven.

4. Eliza Boyse to James Davids, 1676, John Dixwell Papers, MSS-8, Folder C, New Haven Museum Manuscript Collections, New Haven; henceforward, all material from the letters will be quoted from the published Dexter, "Dixwell Papers," as cited below.

5. Peacey, "A Regicide in Exile," 174.
6. Dexter, "Dixwell Papers," 342.
7. Dexter, "Dixwell Papers," 344.
8. Dexter, "Dixwell Papers," 346.
9. Peacey, "A Regicide in Exile," 174.
10. Dexter, "Dixwell Papers," 350.
11. Dexter, "Dixwell Papers," 354.
12. Dexter, "Dixwell Papers," 354.
13. Dexter, "Dixwell Papers," 355.
14. Dexter, "Dixwell Papers," 356.
15. Dexter, "Dixwell Papers," 357.
16. Dexter, "Dixwell Papers," 357.
17. Dexter, "Dixwell Papers," 357.
18. Nathaniel Hawthorne, *Twice-Told Tales* (Boston: American Stationers Co., 1837).
19. James Russell Lowell, "The Present Crisis," in *Poems* (Cambridge/Boston: George Nichols, B.B. Mussey, 1848).

Afterword: From Generation to Generation

1. Stiles, *A History*, 145.
2. Stiles, *A History*, 160.

3. Stiles, *A History*, 161.

4. Stiles says, on page 152, "Inoculation for the small pox was introduced at Boston for the first time in 1721, the same year that, through the recommendation of Lady Montague it was first introduced into England from Constantinople. It is a tradition in the family of Prout here, that Mrs. Dixwell was in the first experiment, and died in inoculation." John then married Martha Remington Bowes but she died within the year. In 1723 he married Abigail Walker Bridgham, who after his death became administrator of his estate, valued at 952 pounds. He did well. Who knows if these things can be compared, but when Bathsheba died four years later, her estate totaled 54 pounds. Pat Kane, page 377, says "Dixwell died from a smallpox inoculation on 2 April 1725 and was buried in the Copp's Hill Burying Ground." Finally, in Volume XV of *The New England Historical and Genealogical Register*, page 204, there's an entry from an eighteenth century diarist with the delightful name of Jeremiah Bumstead. Here's his entry for 21 April 1725: "Mr. Dixwell, Elder of ye New North Church, dyed of a feaver, which much seazed his head—lay about a week—aged 44 years; & buryed on ye 23 day." Stiles, *A History*; Patricia E Kane, "John Dixwell, 1680/81-1725," in *Colonial Massachusetts Silversmiths and Jewelers*, ed. Patricia E. Kane (Hanover: Yale University Art Galler and University Press of New England, 1998); Diary of Jeremiah Bumstead, 21 April 1725, in Vol. 15 of *The New England Historical and Genealogical Register* (Boston: The New England Historic and Genealogical Society, 1861).

5. Stiles, *A History*, 162.

6. John Dixwell (Silversmith) to Basil Dixwell, ca. 1719, Wigglesworth Family Papers (1682–1966), Massachusetts Historical Society, Boston.

7. Sir Basil Dixwell to John Dixwell (silversmith), 8 February 1718/1719, Wigglesworth Family Papers (1682–1966), Massachusetts Historical Society, Boston.

8. Sir Basil Dixwell to Young Basil Dixwell, 21 August 1733, Wigglesworth Family Papers (1682–1966), Massachusetts Historical Society, Boston.

9. Young Basil Dixwell to Sir Basil Dixwell, 1733, Wigglesworth Family Papers (1682–1966), Massachusetts Historical Society, Boston.

10. Sir Basil Dixwell to John Prout, ca. 1731, Wigglesworth Family Papers (1682–1966), Massachusetts Historical Society, Boston.

11. Death Notice for the third John Dixwell, *The Independent Advertiser* (1749).

12. Stiles, *A History*, 167.

13. Mary Hunt Dixwell to Prout Family, 1753, John Dixwell Papers, MSS-8, New Haven Museum, New Haven.

14. Mary Dixwell to a Prout Cousin, 1768, John Dixwell Papers, MSS-8, New Haven Museum, New Haven.

15. Death Notice for Mary Hunt, *Salem Gazette*, January 1, 1784.

16. Stiles, *A History*, 153.

17. Stiles, *A History*, 164.
18. John J. Dixwell to James A. Dickson, 31 May 1820, Wigglesworth Family Papers (1820–1821), Massachusetts Historical Society, Boston.
19. For a full account of the opium story, including the son George had with his Chinese wife, see Thomas Layton, *The Voyage of the Frolic* (Stanford: Stanford University Press, 1997). George's brothers Epes and John refused to acknowledge the child, Teen Seng. A fuller account of their unkind behavior is in Layton's book *The Other Dixwells* (Germantown: Society for Historical Archeology, 2021).
20. James F. Babcock, Article, *The New Haven Daily Palladium*, November 1849, quoting William Shakespeare, Act 5 Scene 3 of *Much Ado About Nothing*.
21. Babcock, Article.
22. Epes Sargent Dixwell was also, I was angered and saddened to learn, racist. When his brother George (great grandfather of my cousin Marcia Dixwell DiMambro) had a child with an upper-class, educated Chinese wife, Epes refused to acknowledge the child and worked hard to erase any evidence of his existence, although the child, Charles Sargent, lived in the Boston area. Even in 1990, the big genealogy book of the Chase-Wigglesworth family makes no mention of George having been married or having a son.
23. Dexter, "Dixwell Papers," 337–8.
24. Roof Tile from Broome Hall, Canterbury, England [artifact], Architecture 02.019, Massachusetts Historical Society, Boston.
25. Dr. John Dixwell to City of New Haven, 25 November 1928, John Dixwell Papers. MSS-8, Folder K, New Haven Museum, New Haven.
26. Mayor Thomas Tully to Dr. John Dixwell, 27 November 1928, John Dixwell Papers, MSS-8, Folder K, New Haven Museum, New Haven.

BIBLIOGRAPHY

Arnold, Tony. "New Golf and Country Club in Historic Mansion." *East Kent Mercury*, July 16, 1981.

Babcock, James F. Article. *The New Haven Daily Palladium*, November 1849.

Bathshua Dixwell's Estate Inventory, 1728/1730, no. 1709; and Will, 1727. Hartford Probate District, Town of Middletown. History and Genealogy Unit. Connecticut State Library, Hartford.

Benjamin Ling's Will and Estate Inventory, 1673. Vol. 1, Pt. 1 of New Haven Probate Record, 1647–1687.

Bremer, Francis J. *Building a New Jerusalem, John Davenport, a Puritan in Three Worlds*. New Haven: Yale University Press, 2012.

Brontë, Charlotte. *Jane Eyre*. New York: W. W. Norton & Company, 1987.

Burke, John. *Burke's Extinct Baronetcies*. London: John Russell Smith, 1841.

Cabot, Caroline Dixwell. "A Concise History of Broome Park." Published privately, 2003.

Diary of Jeremiah Bumstead, 21 April 1725. In Vol. 15 of *The New England Historical and Genealogical* Register, 204. Boston: The New England Historic and Genealogical Society, 1861.

Death notice for the third John Dixwell. *The Independent Advertiser*, 1749.

Death Notice for Mary Hunt. *Salem Gazette*, January 1, 1784.

Death Warrant of King Charles I, January 1649. House of Lords Record Office, London.

Dexter, Franklin B., editor. "Dixwell Papers." In Vol. 6 of *Papers of the New Haven Colony Historical Society*, 337–374. New Haven: New Haven Colony Historical Society, 1900.

Dexter, Franklin Bowditch. "Early Private Libraries in New England." In Vol. 18 of *Proceedings of the American Antiquarian Society*, 135-147. Worcester: American Antiquarian Society, 1906–1907.

Dexter, Franklin Bowditch. "The New Haven of Two Hundred Years Ago." In Vol. 8 of *New Haven Historical Society Papers*, 329-350. New Haven: New Haven Historical Society, 1914.

Dodds, Madeleine Hope. "Ecclesiastical History." In Vol. 12 of *A History of Northumberland: The Parishes of Ovingham, Stamfordham and Ponteland*, 407-447. Newcastle-upon-Tyne: Reid, 1926.

Donne, John. "Meditation XVII." In *Devotions upon Emergent Occasions*. Cambridge: The University Press, 1923.

Duncan, Archibald. *The Mariner's Chronicle*. New Haven: G. W. Gorton. 1834.

Elizabeth How's Will and Estate Inventory, 1695. Vol. 2, Pt. 2 of New Haven Probate Record, 1688-1703.

Firth, Charles. "John Dixwell." In *Dictionary of National Biography*, edited by Leslie Stephen and Sidney Lee, 1035. London: Smith, Elder & Co. 1908.

Freedman, Katherine. Personal communication. 2019.

Gardiner, Dorothy Kempe, editor. Vol. 1 of *The Oxinden and Peyton Letters, 1607-1642*. London: Constable & Co Ltd., 1933.

Gardiner, Dorothy Kempe, editor. Vol. 2 of *The Oxinden and Peyton Letters, 1642-1670*. London: Sheldon Press, 1937.

Gawande, Atul. *Being Mortal, Medicine and What Matters in the End*. New York: Metropolitan Books/Henry Holt and Company, 2014.

Gaylord, Charles. *The Book of Shipwrecks: And Narratives of Maritime Discoveries and the Most Popular Voyages, from the Time of Columbus to the Present Day*. Boston: Lilly, Wait, Colman & Holden, 1836.

Hailwood, Roger. *Looking Back at Broome Park: The Story of England's Finest Carolean Mansion*. Burton on Trent: Hailwood Enterprises, 2006.

Hawthorne, Nathaniel. *Twice-Told Tales*. Boston: American Stationers Co., 1837.

Henry, Philip. Letter in *Diaries and Letters of Philip Henry, M.A. of Broad Oak, Flintshire, A.D. 1631-1696*. Edited by Matthew Henry Lee and Andrew Dickson White. London: Kegan Paul, Trench & Co., 1882.

History of Barham. Compiled by Members of the Barham Women's Institute. Barham, 1959/1966.

Hughes, Ann. "The Execution of Charles I." *BBC History*. 2011. https://www.bbc.co.uk/history/british/civil_war_revolution/charlesi_execution_01.shtml.

James Davids's (alias John Dixwell) Will and Estate Inventory, 1688/1689. Vol. 2, Pt. 1 of New Haven Probate Record, 1688-1703.

Jenkinson, Matthew. *Charles I's Killers in America: The Lives & Afterlives of Edward Whalley & Willam Goffe*. Oxford: Oxford University Press, 2019.

Jeremiah How's Will and Estate Inventory, 1690. Vol. 2, Pt. 1 of New Haven Probate Record, 1688-1703.

John Dixwell Papers. MSS-8. Folders C, G, J, and K. New Haven Museum Manuscript Collections, New Haven.

Kane, Patricia E., editor. *Colonial Massachusetts Silversmiths and Jewelers*. Hanover: Yale University Art Gallery distributed by University Press of New England, 1998.

Kane, Patricia E. "John Dixwell, 1680/81–1725." In *Colonial Massachusetts Silversmiths and Jewelers*, edited by Patricia E. Kane, 375–382. Hanover: Yale University Art Gallery and University Press of New England, 1998.

Kenyon, John Philipps. "The Stuarts." In *Great Dynasties*, 125–137. New York: Windward, 1980.

Layton, Thomas. *The Other Dixwells*. Germantown: Society for Historical Archeology, 2021.

Layton, Thomas. *The Voyage of the Frolic*. Stanford: Stanford University Press, 1997.

Lefevre, Peter, and Andrew Thrush. "Dixwell, Basil (1585-1642), of Terlingham, Folkestone, Kent; Formerly of Canterbury, Kent; Later of Broome Park, Barham, Kent." *History of Parliament Online*, 2010. https://www.historyofparliamentonline.org /volume/1604-1629/member/dixwell-basil-1585-1642.

Lowell, James Russell. "The Present Crisis." In *Poems*. Cambridge/Boston: George Nichols, B.B. Mussey, 1848.

Ludlow, Edmund. *Memoirs of Edmund Ludlow, Esq.: With a Collection of Original Papers, Serving to Confirm and Illustrate Many Important Passages Contained in the Memoirs*. Edinburgh, 1751.

Maxwell-Lyte, Sir Henry Churchill. *A History of Eton College: 1440–1875*. London: MacMillan and Co., 1911.

MS 40717: 1465–1799. Folio 169. Miscellaneous Papers. Western Manuscripts. British Library, London.

"The New England Colonies and the Native Americans." *National Geographic*. June 26, 2020. https://www.nationalgeographic.org/article/new-england-colonies-and-native -americans/.

New Haven Town Records, 1649–1662. Library. New Haven Museum and Historical Society, New Haven.

New Haven Town Records, 1662–1684. Library. New Haven Museum and Historical Society, New Haven.

Notestein, Wallace. "The Winning of the Initiative by the House of Commons." In Vol. 11 of *Proceedings of the British Academy, Raleigh Lecture on History*, 125–175. London, 1924.

"Our History." Eton College, 2014. https://www.etoncollege.com/about-us/our-history/.

Pagliuco, Christopher. *The Great Escape of Edward Whalley and William Goffe Smuggled through Connecticut*. Charleston: History Press, 2021.

Peacey, Jason. "'The Good Old Cause for Which I Suffer': The Life of a Regicide in Exile." In *Literatures of Exile in the English Revolution and Its Aftermath, 1640-1690*, edited by Philip Major, 167–180. Burlington: Ashgate, 2010.

Peacey, Jason. "Dixwell, John (c.1607–89) of Coton, Warwickshire, and Folkestone, Kent." In *The History of Parliament*. Cambridge: Cambridge University Press, forthcoming.

Peacey, Jason. "John Dixwell." In *Oxford Dictionary of National Biography 2001–2004*, edited by Lawrence Goldman, 337-338. Oxford: Oxford University Press, 2009.

Perry, Marge. "Re: Was Regicide John1 Dixwell a son of William Dixwell, or . . . ," Rootsweb.com. Discussion forum post, November 30, 2006. Thread archived: https://www

.slektogdata.no/slektsforum/viewtopic.php?p=175861&sid=38072fdee23bb5f6c2d5191
79b5b9340#p175861.

Poidevin, Nicholas Le. "Learning the Law." In *A Portrait of Lincoln's Inn*, edited by Angela Holdsworth, 85–92. London: Third Millennium, 2007.

Prest, Wilfrid R. *The Inns of Court under Elizabeth I and the Early Stuarts 1590–1640.* London: Longman, 1972.

Prest, Wilfrid R. *The Rise of the Barristers: A Social History of the English Bar 1590–1640.* Oxford: Clarendon Press, 1986.

The Quarter Sessions Criminal Records Assizes Sessions for Northumberland 1594–1630. Northumberland Archives. Woodhorn Museum, Ashington.

Roof Tile from Broome Hall, Canterbury, England [artifact]. Architecture 02.019. Massachusetts Historical Society, Boston.

Spencer, Charles. *Killers of the King.* New York: Bloomsbury, 2015.

Stiles, Ezra. *A History of Three of the Judges of Charles I. Major-General Whalley, Major-General Goffe, and Colonel Dixwell.* Hartford: Elisha Babcock, 1794.

Vol. 21, Pt. 1 of the Parliamentary Papers of the House of Commons and Command, 1672. In *History, Gazetteer, and Directory, of Warwickshire.* Warwickshire: Francis White and Co., 1850.

Wedgwood, Cicely Veronica. *The Life of Cromwell.* New York: Collier Books, 1966.

Wedgwood, Cicely Veronica. *A Coffin for King Charles.* New York: Macmillan, 1964.

Welles, Lemuel A. *The History of the Regicides in New England.* New Haven: Yale University Press, 1935.

Wigglesworth Family Papers (1682-1966). Massachusetts Historical Society, Boston.

Wigglesworth, Mary C. D. *An Autobiographical Sketch of Epes Sargent Dixwell: Unfinished and Unrevised. Begun for His Children and Found among Some Papers Which Came into My Hands after His Death.* Boston: Geo. H. Ellis Co., 1907.

Wodehouse, Sir Pelham Grenville. *Something New.* New York: D. Appleton & Company, 1915.

Wood, H. M. *Vicars of Ponteland*, 1920.

"The Works of King Charles the Martyr, 1687." In Vol. 2 of *Readings in European History: From the Protestant Revolt to the Present Day*, by James Harvey Robinson, 210–250. Boston: Ginn and Co., 1906.

ABOUT THE AUTHOR

SARAH DIXWELL BROWN taught writing at Stanford University, Santa Clara University, Mount Holyoke College and the Commonwealth Honors College at the University of Massachusetts, Amherst. She has published numerous personal essays in national and local publications. This is her first book. It was prompted by her receiving a family heirloom, a key to Dover Castle that once belonged to her direct ancestor, John Dixwell, a regicide of Charles I who escaped to New England in the 1660s. She lives in Western Massachusetts.

The interior of *Regicide in the Family* was designed in Minion and Caslon Antique types by Greta Sibley, cover by Dennis Nolan. The text paper is Cougar Natural, cover stock twelve-point Kromecote, with Royal Sundance Fiber end papers.

Printed and bound by Collective Copies of Amherst, Massachusetts on a Xerox Versant Digital Press and a Duplo binder.